THE POET

Related Titles from Potomac Books

A Tale of Three Cities: The 1962 Baseball Season in New York, Los Angeles, and San Francisco, by Steven Travers

Keepers of the Game, by Dennis D'Agostino

Pull Up a Chair, by Curt Smith

Also by Steven Travers

One Night, Two Teams: Alabama vs. USC and the Game That Changed a Nation

A's Essential: Everything You Need to Know to Be A Real Fan!

Trojans Essential: Everything You Need to Know to Be A Real Fan!

Dodgers Essential: Everything You Need to Know to Be A Real Fan!

Angels Essential: Everything You Need to Know to Be A Real Fan!

Diamondbacks Essential: Everything You Need to Know to Be a Real Fan!

The USC Trojans: College Football's All-Time Greatest Dynasty

The Good, the Bad & the Ugly Los Angeles Lakers

The Good, the Bad & the Ugly Oakland Raiders

The Good, the Bad & the Ugly San Francisco 49ers

Barry Bonds: Baseball's Superman

Pigskin Warriors: 140 Years of College Football's Greatest Games, Players and Traditions

The 1969 Miracle Mets

Dodgers Baseball Yesterday & Today

What it Means to be a Trojan: Southern Cal's Greatest Players Talk about Trojans Football

The Last Icon: Tom Seaver and His Times

What Is Truth? The Powers That Were, the Powers that Are

Vietnam, Longhorns & Duke Wayne's Trojan Wars

THE POET

The Life and *Los Angeles Times* of Jim Murray

STEVEN TRAVERS

Foreword by Linda McCoy-Murray

Potomac Books
Washington, D.C.

Library of Congress Cataloging-in-Publication Data
Travers, Steven, 1959–
    The poet : the life and Los Angeles Times of Jim Murray / Steven Travers.
      pages cm
    Includes bibliographical references and index.
    ISBN 978-1-59797-854-5 (hardcover : alk. paper)
    ISBN 978-1-59797-855-2 (electronic)
    1. Murray, Jim, 1919-1998. 2. Sportswriters—United States—Biography. I. Title.
    GV742.42.M87 T73 2013
    070.4'49796092—dc23
    [B]

                                                                    2012044715

Printed in the United States of America on acid-free paper that meets the American National Standards Institute Z39-48 Standard.

Potomac Books
22841 Quicksilver Drive
Dulles, Virginia 20166

First Edition

10 9 8 7 6 5 4 3 2 1

CONTENTS

FOREWORD

While many recall Pulitzer Prize–winner Jim Murray's innate ability to capture the hearts and minds of those who read his journalistic prose for the nearly four decades that he was the premier sports columnist for the *Los Angeles Times*, a new generation of writers and readers who were unaware of his talent, joy, and influence on the sporting scene is coming along.

Since 2000 the University of Southern California's Annenberg School for Communication and Journalism has produced five $5,000 scholarship winners, known as Murray Scholars, through the annual journalism essay competition sponsored by the Jim Murray Memorial Foundation (JMMF). A Murray Scholar shows by academic excellence, with emphasis in writing, qualities that promise to perpetuate the Jim Murray spirit of journalistic integrity and creativity.

This biography of Jim Murray is a welcome addition to the JMMF scholarship program. Jim was not merely a sportswriter, he was literate, historical, and unique. Many have tried to emulate him, to no avail.

Jim's charming Irish wit is captured in Steve Travers's book for all generations to enjoy. This is not merely a story about Jim Murray of Hartford, Connecticut, and Los Angeles, California, but a history of publisher Otis Chandler and the *Los Angeles Times*. It is the story of a city's growth and a changing America.

Get ready to laugh and cry. Jim had that effect on his readers.

Linda McCoy-Murray
January 1, 2013
Pasadena, California

ACKNOWLEDGMENTS

I have many inspirations, but two were writers at the *Los Angeles Times*. The first is the great Jim Murray, whom I never personally knew, although, just like all those who read him most every day, I felt I did. The other was his associate, Jeff Prugh, whom I did know as a dear friend and mentor.

I hope this book is worthy of both their memories. I want to thank them, as well as Elizabeth Demers, Elizabeth Norris, Sam Dorrance, Amanda Irle, the good folks at Potomac Books; Los Angeles city councilman Tom LaBonge; Bruce Jenkins; Scott Ostler; Bill Dwyre; Steve Bisheff; Jim's widow, Linda McCoy-Murray; and Bill McCoy of the Jim Murray Memorial Foundation.

More information about the Jim Murray Memorial Foundation can be found below.

The Jim Murray Memorial Foundation
P.O. Box 995
La Quinta, CA 92247–0995
info@jimmurrayfoundation.org
www.jimmurrayfoundation.org

1

A Depression Kid

Great discoveries were afoot. In the first decade of Jim Murray's life, America's defining traits—the pursuit of leisure and a better life—were symbolized by the dawning of a "golden age" of sports led by Babe Ruth, the Notre Dame Fighting Irish, and the building of arenas with grandiose monikers such as the Coliseum and the Rose Bowl.

Murray grew up as America grew up. Like so many Easterners, he sensed that the future was in California. He arrived as a postwar baby boom was under way. The Los Angeles he found in 1944 was provincial, but ascending. It became an electoral juggernaut, the city and state of the future. National political trends were formulated no longer in the back rooms of Tammany Hall, but in the broad expanses of the Golden State, propelled by populist anticommunism and the power of political fund-raising.

Murray was born on December 29, 1919, in Hartford, Connecticut, and was an impressionable kid, not quite ten, when the Great Depression hit in October 1929. Much of what makes America great emanates from lessons learned during the 1930s. Much of what detracts from American greatness comes from lessons of the Great Depression now forgotten. Jim Murray was a product of that era. It dominated his sense of self, his writing, and his career. It was a rude awakening for Murray and his country after the hubris of the 1920s. Flush after victory in Europe, the Roaring Twenties had been a time of great prosperity.

Murray had grown up in Connecticut, the burgeoning bedroom community of the new Rome, New York City. The East Coast was where the action was: Wall Street, Yankee Stadium, the Yale Bowl. The American lifestyle had been embodied by a new kind of man, well dressed and coiffed, daily riding the high-speed trains into Manhattan, where he mastered business, manipulated markets in his favor, and then returned to country leisure in towns with biblical names like New Canaan. In 1929 all this came crashing down.

Murray was of Irish Catholic stock. He was not a blue blood of East Coast aristocracy who lived in a tony suburb and came from an old English bloodline. The blue bloods worshiped, not at Catholic mass, but in Episcopalian splendor with the Bushes of Greenwich, scions of the Brown Brothers Harriman Wall Street dynasty. The Irish were still looked down upon, but times were changing. While the Bushes were reputed to be related to the royal families of England and Holland, the Murrays had come to America from the humble Irish county of Sligo in the 1870s.

The Irish, like the Germans, fought well in the Great War. Prior to World War I, there were still loyalty questions, but these and other ethnic classes acquitted themselves with honor. Men such as Joseph P. Kennedy saw politics as the road to new power and respect in America. In 1928 a Catholic, Al Smith, received the Democratic nomination for president. He did not win the election, but his victory at the convention signaled a tremendous change from the old order of things. Still, the class distinction of Irish Catholicism on the East Coast shadowed the life of Jim Murray from his birth until his move to the wilds of Los Angeles.

But being Irish meant being literate. Writing was in Jim Murray's blood. The angst of Irish poets—W. B. Yeats, James Joyce, Oscar Wilde, Samuel Beckett, Jonathan Swift, George Bernard Shaw—influenced a young Irishman long before the days of television and the Internet. If Manhattan was the home of commerce, the New England countryside was the twentieth-century home of American letters. Indeed, Connecticut was the breeding grounds of wordsmiths. Mark Twain wrote *A Connecticut Yankee in King Arthur's Court* in Hartford, long before Jim's birth.

Jim Murray's Uncle Mike bought a home on Pequot Avenue, a "lovely old place with cupolas hanging off it and elm trees all over the yard," wrote Murray in his autobiography. It was filled with papers. "What's this?" Uncle Mike inquired of the real estate agent. He had determined the previous owner was "a slob." Uncle Mike instructed the agent to burn all the papers. They had belonged to the playwright Eugene O'Neill, author of the classic *Long Day's Journey into Night*.

Jim's father was a druggist, the same profession held by Clyde Morrison, the father of a great American Murray later admired. Clyde Morrison's son became John Wayne. Murray's father lost his business and divorced Jim's mother. According to lore, Mr. Murray was arrested for selling "bootleg" whiskey without a "prescription." During Prohibition, one of the ways to buy liquor was by prescription from the pharmacy, hence the term "medicine" for alcohol. "Dad simply paid off the wrong people," recalled Murray.

Irish stereotype or no, Mr. Murray was a drunk. Jim discovered this when he went to boxing matches with him. His father constantly went to the "water cooler." Each time he returned, his eyes were redder, his gait less steady, his speech more slurred. The "water cooler" was filled with bathtub gin. These experiences at the boxing ring helped young Murray realize that Prohibition "prohibited" nothing. They also infused his image of the fight game for the rest of his life.

After his parents were divorced and it became clear his father could not take care of him, Jim was sent to live with his grandparents. If life with father was unhappy, life with his grandparents and numerous uncles was glorious. The house was filled with banter, betting, and enthusiasm for sports. It was the training ground of a young columnist. Jim found his relatives funny and irreverent. His earliest recollection was of Jack Dempsey's boxing matches. Jim thought the heroes of the New York sporting scene were gods. Later, when he met Dempsey and Carl Hubbell, he practically genuflected in their presence.

Sports dominated Murray's life from the beginning. His father, uncles, and grandfather took him to baseball games and boxing matches. He listened to Ted Husing and Graham McNamee's broadcasts on a crystal set radio. He claimed to have learned math by computing earned-run and batting averages. His arithmetic teachers were not the nuns at his parochial school but the daily league standings by which he learned to determine how many games St. Louis trailed the Giants out of first place. It took Murray forever to learn the Apostles' Creed, but compound fractions came easily by virtue of their use in sports statistics.

Murray experienced two bouts of chronic illness in his youth. When he was only three or four, he had what he in his autobiography called "Saint Vitus' Dance," an autoimmune disorder. Later he had a more serious run-in with rheumatic fever. One year before his birth, a flu epidemic had spread in part by soldiers returning from the war killed 50 million people. Childhood diseases were rampant in the 1920s, and more deadly than today.

Pleurisy and pneumonia complicated his recovery from rheumatic fever. The Catholic Church administered last rites as the young boy hovered between life and death. Unable to leave his bed, he amused himself by reading. Adolf Hitler's *Mein Kampf* was an international bestseller of the mid-1920s. Journalist John Gunther recognized that the German was a political figure to be reckoned with. Murray claimed to know all about Hitler before most Germans did. He read about the long military tradition of the German people and developed a lifelong fascination with "the Hun." He would later pepper his writings with militaristic descriptions of football teams "on the march." He developed romantic notions of Ireland, which under Michael Collins had recently gained independence. Murray corresponded with Irish prime minister Eamon De Valera.

He read all the great sports and adventure stories for young men: Jack Armstrong, Frank Merriwell, *The Rover Boys*, Lester Chadwick's *Baseball Joe* series, Zane Grey, and others. Murray liked to write. His first recognized work was a fifty-word essay on his handpicked American Legion all-star team. For winning the contest, he received a razor. He was ten.

Murray never had a desire to play professional sports. When he recovered from the fever, he played baseball in school, and even made the freshman team at Trinity College, but his real dream was to be a fight promoter.

"Don't think—you can only hurt the ball club" was a common refrain of managers. Murray said his vivid imagination would have been his undoing as an athlete. He knew he would always think about the importance of the game. His mind would fill with the statistics on the odds against success and thus prevent him from achieving it. Dodgers announcer Rick Monday often recalled that his teammate Rollie Fingers was so "dumb he didn't know any better" than to throw a "yak slider" on three-two, striking a man out with the bases loaded. Murray knew all too well the dangers of overthinking most any endeavor.

Plus, Murray enjoyed being a spectator. He roped off a ring with clothesline and organized boxing matches between neighborhood boys. He occasionally participated if a substitute was needed, until a kid named John McMahon pulverized him. Some of Murray's earliest sense of sympathy for the man in the arena came from that eternal bout, which lasted two minutes before the bell rang. All the while his nose was bleeding, his lip was cut, his knees felt like they were made of rubber, and he was "trying not to cry."

This experience helped Murray form an aversion to psychiatry. He believed you had to get back up and keep swinging. Football coaches call these difficult moments time to "suck it up." Sports taught Murray these lessons. Told later in life he had "issues" stemming from being "dumped" on his grandparents at an early age by his parents, Murray said as far as he was concerned he was loved, even "spoiled." He learned to adapt, which he said all children are capable of out of necessity. Told he lived on the "wrong side of the tracks," he said he felt like one of the "luckiest guys in the world" living next to railroad tracks. Years after his youth, in a column about the 1970 USC-Alabama football game, Murray's description of a train whistle in the dark night gave a sense of far-away seduction to his writings. When he moved to fancier digs in West Hartford, he found his life far less exciting than it had been by the tracks or the lumberyard.

Murray was highly disciplined from an early age. In his autobiography he wrote on the theme of "psychobabble." He was told he toed the line because his situation was precarious. If he slipped up, he would be shipped off to a reformatory or some such unwanted destination. Murray rejected that theory. He was organized, intelligent, and boring by nature but surrounded by opinionated Irishmen. He became observant and a great listener. He saw the whole picture.

Murray formed a conservative point of view this way. He listened to the Irish constantly complain of "slumlords" but rejected the notion they were rich folks extorting money from the poor in a zero-sum world of haves and have-nots. Accompanying his grandfather to repair the houses he rented out, young Murray observed that the tenants often damaged the property during drunken rages and fights. He realized that substandard dwellings were most often the fault of the tenant, not the slumlord. Murray always saw empty bottles stacked to the ceiling. It was the slumlord who repaired the damages, not the other way around. Tenants often did not pay rent.

"Jim took great pride in property," said his widow, Linda McCoy-Murray. "It was something you have pride in and take care of, whether it be houses, the family cars. People would go into those apartments his grandfather owned during the Great Depression and they'd pull the toilets away from the wall. There'd be holes in the wall. Jim just hated people on the dole, the welfare state. If you didn't own something you took no pride."

But on October 29, 1929, the tables began to turn. On that infamous Black Tuesday, the stock market crashed and the Great Depression began. Jim

Murray was not yet ten years old. He had been fed the false notion that all was well. Despite coming from a broken home and living next to the railroad tracks, he was convinced "the poor" were somebody else. The following decade hit him like a ton of bricks. The Great Depression shaped Murray's outlook on life forever.

The lessons of those years were not lost on young Jim Murray. The Depression showed him that "you never trust the system again," as he wrote in the second line of his 1993 autobiography. He went on a payroll as soon as he could, and he never went off one until the day he died.

The Depression made Murray into a "good soldier" willing to "swallow guff" because he knew what unemployment did to marriages and families. He stated that in 1939, had somebody offered him a contract paying him $32.50 a week for the rest of his life, he would have signed the paper without hesitation. People who said money was not important "always had plenty of it," he noted. Murray was a "terrible businessman" who never argued over a contract.

After Black Tuesday, Murray's father and two sisters moved into Jim's grandparents' crowded tenement. Four families shared a one-bathroom dwelling. Murray's mother lost her job and had to move in with her family, but without her daughters. The irrepressible Murray managed to make "lemons out of lemonade." Calling this period his "Broadway phase," he began writing plays and pressing his sisters into chorus girl duty. He called one of his creations the *Nevertheless Show*.

His grandfather's house was "standing-room-only," the "roster" consisting of Murray, his two sisters, his divorced father, his grandparents, two cousins, and two uncles. Jim roomed with his Uncle Frank, who owned a diner and dance hall. They stayed together in a "made-over attic." Frank smoked fat cigars and told ribald tales. He loved the fight game. Jim's Uncle Ed was a gambler, perhaps the original "Fast Eddie," who cheated at dice. He was so bored by work that "he couldn't even stand to watch people work," wrote Rick Reilly in a 1986 *Sports Illustrated* profile. These slick-talking characters became refrains in a Runyonesque world that Jim Murray mined over and over again for decades.

Eddie occasionally brushed with the law, usually for minor vices. He was one of those fellows who believed working stiffs were fools. A James Cagney look-alike with a sixth-grade education, Eddie was the black sheep of the Murray household. He fought with his brothers, scandalized his sisters, and loved to drink. Young Jim loved him. Over time, as Jim grew older, he quarreled with Eddie. As Jim became a teenager, he asked Uncle Ed to teach him the intricacies of gambling and dice tossing. His uncle refused, pointing to the schoolbooks in Jim's hands. "You'll make more money with them than you'll ever make with a pool cue," he said.

As Jim was working his way through college, he once saw Ed at an illegal gambling house called the Greek American Club. Ed admonished his nephew, saying these sorts of places were for lowlifes, not smart kids like him. Eventually, young Jim came to realize that while Ed spent his life looking for "marks," in the end he himself was the "ultimate mark."

When World War II hit, the factories around Hartford brimmed with activity. Ed increased his gambling operations, but the authorities began to crack down on those trying to swindle soldiers and government workers. He moved his operation to Florida but was in over his head dealing with the mob. Eventually he returned to Hartford but one night ran into trouble when he wrapped his car around a streetcar pole. When the cops investigated, they were directed to Jim, but he was uninvolved in the accident. Everybody in the neighborhood just clammed up. In the end there was not enough evidence to charge Ed or anybody else. It was the "code" of the streets not to rat out others, even if a crime were committed.

One day Ed decided it was time for young Jim to lose his virginity. He took him to a brothel in New York where a gum-chewing hooker named Rosa showed him the promised land. Ed taught Jim that most fights were fixed. Between Ed and his parochial school education, Jim came to understand the nature of man, or what Bible scholars call original sin. Some of the "words to live by" Ed taught his nephew included the following:

"Never bet on a dead horse or a live woman."

"Never take money from an amateur—unless he insists."

"Never play a house game, whether it is a race track, a roulette wheel, or just a tired guy cutting a pot."

"Never play cards with a man with dark glasses or his own deck."

"Never make change for a guy on a train."

"Never play a man who's better than you."

"Never buck a slot machine—they don't make them for you."

"Never play a guy named 'Lucky'—at anything."

"Take your time chalking your cue—they'll wait."

During those Depression-era days, round-trip train fare to New York City was two dollars. Murray stayed at the YMCA for twenty-five cents and ate T-bones that cost half a dollar. A box seat at Yankee Stadium cost $1.65. All this was "big money" in those days. Murray's first Major League game was a doubleheader between the Yankees and Philadelphia Athletics on Labor Day in 1934. Connie Mack's dynasty was gone; Mickey Cochrane, Lefty Grove, Jimmy Dykes, and other stalwarts had been traded to meet payroll. Only Jimmie Foxx remained an Athletic.

With rain threatening, Ruth hit what Murray estimated to be about his seven hundredth career home run. The crowd was modest. There were cheers as Ruth trotted around the bases, and that was it. Murray and his companion, Alvar "Red" Craft, looked at each other. It was anticlimatic. After hearing for years and years about the mighty Babe, Murray expected great fireworks. The experience stuck with Murray throughout his career. "It was, looking back on it, my first lesson that the event itself had to be dramatized," he wrote. "We were there, in a sense, because we had been lured there by years of purple prose. The home run itself was hardly a cataclysmic event. But Grantland Rice made you think it was."

After Ruth's shot, the rain came down hard. This horrified Murray. If the game were rained out before it was made official after five innings, the home run would not count. The teams played the entire doubleheader in a downpour because they refused to lose the gate receipts to refunds. Murray's early experiences with big league stadiums were wet ones. A year later he ventured to the Polo Grounds, but the scheduled doubleheader was rained out.

He turned his attention to the Red Sox. Owner Tom Yawkey was unable to match the Yankees' payroll. The egalitarian Murray was struck by this reality. He began viewing the Yankees as a hegemonic sports empire. His sense of fairness was insulted. Years later he wrote a piece for *Life* magazine called "I Hate the Yankees," finding fault with their riches and power. In this essay, he wrote the immortal line, "Rooting for the Yankees is like rooting for U.S. Steel." That statement became one of the most famous in baseball history, only it was credited to Red Smith, perhaps the leading sports columnist in the nation at the time. Of the discrepancy Murray simply stated, "Journalism is, at best, an imprecise science."

Murray's youthful ventures to big league stadiums were few and far between. They cost money he did not have. He returned to Hartford and followed minor league ball, which helped him understand how hard it is to make it big. Many fine prospects passed through, but only one, Sebastian Sisti, ever played in the Major Leagues. He hit an undistinguished .244 lifetime.

In 1938, when Murray was eighteen years old, his father took him to the World Series between the Yankees and the Chicago Cubs. According to Murray, even the Yankee Stadium crowd booed the home team as they relentlessly destroyed Dizzy Dean and the Cubs in four straight lopsided games. Murray's "hatred" of the Yankees and all they stood for was here to stay. He was a Depression-era kid who rooted for the underdog.

Murray learned a lesson in the cross-pollination of ethnicities, rivalries, and friendship when he befriended an Italian kid named Joey Patrissi. Patrissi was a Sicilian who threw left-handed. He was convinced the best players were southpaws. Murray was an Irish righty, firm in his conviction that right-handers were superior. Joe DiMaggio was an Italian right-handed slugger who broke orthodoxy. Ted Williams was a part-Irish lefty. These two ballplayers helped disabuse Murray and Patrissi of their natural prejudices.

Murray's relationship with Patrissi helped form his political and professional choices. Sports, he discovered, could be discussed with great passion and conviction but with little real rancor. Religion, politics, and race were a whole different story. This was one of the reasons Murray gravitated to sportswriting. When he covered Hollywood in the late 1940s and early 1950s, he once interviewed famed director George Stevens. Stevens was unreceptive to Murray's questions until the discussion turned to baseball; he happily named his all-time favorite players. Only when Jackie Robinson entered the game did the nature of sports fandom and reporting begin to change. In the 1960s, when the issues mattered, Murray was willing to transition from a neutral fan to a partisan.

Long before Strat-O-Matic or fantasy baseball, Murray created a baseball board game using a standard deck of cards. He tinkered with the cards until they resembled real-life averages and probabilities. As he grew older, he discovered his statistics, while not as offensively exciting as he wanted, often were accurate. He never lost his childlike fascination with games. "I suppose I never grew up," he wrote in 1993. "That's all right with me. That's the nice thing about sports. You can be Peter Pan."

When it was time for college, Murray didn't leave Hartford. Trinity College was a mere extension of his childhood, which, despite the Depression and brushes with more than a few unsavory characters, was remarkably innocent. Trinity was a Catholic institution absent the sort of rowdiness or sexual hijinks of a more worldly institution. Murray gravitated to reporting in Connecticut as a campus correspondent for the *Hartford Times* while in college. He graduated from Trinity in 1943 and was a police and federal beat reporter with the *New Haven Register* from 1943 to 1944.

At the time, Jim Murray read books featuring European history. He wanted to be a war correspondent covering the front lines in Europe or the Pacific, but the rheumatic fever in his youth had made him 4-F. He was very disappointed. Since he could not see Europe, he endeavored to move far away. "I wanted to be as far away as I could when the casualties started coming in," he said. "I didn't want any mothers leaning out the window and saying, 'Here's my son with a sleeve where his arm used to be. What's the Murray boy doing walking around like that?'"

Murray would soon discover the world.

2

"Beyond the Darkness, the West"

"I think Jim Murray saw California the way many outsiders do," recalled his longtime friend, Los Angeles City Councilman Tom LaBonge. "Those of us who grow up here take it for granted. Others see this image, and they come out here, and they find it. The Rose Bowl, 90 degrees on New Year's Day, snow-capped peaks in the distance. It's like a Frank Capra movie, Shangri-La."

Indeed, this image had been painted for millions long before Jim Murray made the trek west. The *Los Angeles Times* printed a midwinter edition going back to the nineteenth century, distributed nationally, filled with glorious images of January sunbathers, low-hanging fruit, and all other inducements—always appealing in that while exotic, it was not that exotic. In L.A. the people looked just like the midwesterners and southerners they had left behind. The promotions were tinged with subtle racism; they referred to the Southland as the "white spot," white Anglo-Saxon Protestant, Christian, All-American. San Francisco, in contrast, was rough-hewn and union-heavy with grubby dockworkers and socialists, its Barbary Coast bars and brothels a distinctly unholy environment.

Who built Los Angeles? Above and beyond all other "city fathers" and visionaries was the Chandler family and their *Los Angeles Times*. The patriarch of the family was Gen. Harrison Gray Otis, a Civil War soldier who rose to the rank of general and who strongly supported American expansionism via the Spanish-American War. His daughter married Harry Chandler, who succeeded his father-in-law as publisher of the newspaper. When it is said that the Otis-Chandler family built or shaped L.A. in its image, it is not an exaggeration. More than the moviemakers, the railroad men, the engineers, or the aerospace executives, General Otis, the Chandlers, and their newspaper built the town by dint of pure vision.

"No single family has dominated any major region of the country as the Chandlers have dominated Southern California," historian David Halberstam said in *Inventing L.A.: The Chandlers and Their Times*, a 2009 PBS documentary. "They did not so much foster the growth of Los Angeles as invent it." They created a brilliant marketing and advertising campaign, the image of an Eden in the West targeted mostly at midwestern farmers, whom they enticed with boundless cheap land for the taking. They could abandon the frozen tundra of Wisconsin, Iowa, Nebraska for the year-round sun of California.

The beneficiaries of this jingoism included Los Angeles, California; the *L.A. Times*; and the Chandler family. It was a new world—their world, a kingdom at the end of a boundless expanse described by Jack Kerouac in *On the Road* as, "Beyond the darkness, the west." In the Robert Towne–Roman Polanski classic film of L.A. noir, *Chinatown*, Jake Gittes (Jack Nicholson) asks Noah Cross (John Huston) what he was ultimately buying with all his money. "The future, Mr. Gittes! The future," Cross responds.

3

Noir and Marriage

"Los Angeles was a wildly exciting place" in 1944, when Jim Murray first went to work there as a reporter for the *Los Angeles Examiner*, the writer recalled. "I fell in love with Los Angeles then, an affair of the heart that I doubt I will ever outgrow and it was the *Examiner* that brought us together."

Much of Murray's charm over the years would be his unrequited love for Los Angeles. He would not be provincial. He would write about everybody and everything, no matter the geographical basis of the subject. But he took sides, and L.A. was the winner. He did not reminisce that the East Coast or, by approximation, New York was better, as many transplants did. "Those were gory, glory days for Murray," wrote Rick Reilly.

"There was seldom a dull moment," Murray recalled. "And if there were, the front page of the *Examiner* never admitted it."

When he first started at the *Examiner*, he specialized in murders. He wrote, "We slept with our socks on, like firemen waiting for that next alarm." Once he covered a story about a little girl who was run over by a truck and lost a leg. Murray took the eight dollars he had left from his thirty-eight-dollar paycheck and bought the girl an armful of toys.

The big paper in town was the *L.A. Times*. Secondary papers like the *Examiner* had to sensationalize the news in order to compete. Murray's boss was Jim Richardson, a "one-eyed, iron-lunged, prototypical Hearst city editor," he wrote. Richardson was a "tyrant," but he recognized Murray's talent right away. He made Murray the youngest rewrite man in the Hearst chain.

Murray and Richardson were able to score a scoop for their paper by identifying murder victim Elizabeth Short's body via a new technology called wirephotoing, which later developed into fingerprinting. The FBI had a lab in Washington and was able to determine who she was based in large measure because of Murray's legwork covering the story.

Once the body had been identified, Richardson instructed a reporter named Wain Sutton to telephone Short's mother in Massachusetts. "Don't tell her what happened," Richardson said. "Tell her that her daughter's just won a beauty contest at Camp Roberts. Then get all the information on her." The mother gaily provided details of her daughter's life to Sutton. When Sutton had all the particulars, he put his hand over the phone and stared at Richardson. "Now what do I do?" he asked.

"Now tell her," Richardson "purred," according to the description Murray gave.

"You miserable son of a bitch," Sutton remarked. Richardson smiled.

It was the Black Dahlia murder case, a tremendous scoop and one of the single most lurid tales ever told. Richardson was "such an unholy combination of Attila the Hun and a literary light," wrote Murray, that another rewrite man named Hank Sutherland had dubbed him "Half-Oaf, Half-Elf."

In 1947 John Reece, a City Hall reporter, was "inspired" by Richardson to write a poem, called "The Rewrite Man," which described a style of over-the-top journalism that might be called "yellow." It was certainly sensationalist:

It served the bastard right, of course,
As philosophers will note,
For being a rewrite man at all
When he could have cut his throat.

This poem became an urban legend of sorts. Before the Internet allowed such things to be (or not be) sourced more easily, it was passed around news-rooms from coast to coast. Murray said Reece wrote it on a slow news day when Richardson handed Murray a note about a routine Skid Row suicide. Murray wrote a straight obituary. Richardson handed it back to him requesting more "oomph." Murray made several stabs at it, all to Richardson's dissatisfaction. Finally Murray wrote, "John Jefferson, 51, tired of it all, stepped off a chair into eternity." Richardson looked at it and realized he had "driven me too far." He dropped the story in the wastebasket and told Murray to get a cup of coffee. There was a pathos to Murray's writing that did not lend itself to the sort of scandal sheet style of Jim Richardson and his ilk. Richardson realized then and there that Murray's talents would lead him beyond this "ink-stained wretch" style of reporting, to greater things. Certainly Murray's compassion for humanity would shine brightly in his long career as a columnist.

"In many ways, those were my happiest journalistic years," Murray wrote. Despite Richardson's dark side, Murray had fun at the *Examiner*, a Hearst paper that the "*literati* looked down their noses at." Murray said, the "world was in flames" from the paper's perspective. "We told it all in dripping red headlines." He saw the dark side of the City of Angels. It was good preparation for his Hollywood writing, which came a few years later.

Murray covered a Las Vegas scandal in which an Air Force officer named Cliff Henderson jilted his wife in favor of a chorus girl. His wife shot him dead. During his stay in Vegas, Murray was a guest of Benjamin "Bugsy" Siegel's at the Flamingo Hotel. Murray was stunned how handsome the famous gangster was. One look at the Flamingo and he knew, no matter how rocky its early days, it would be a smash hit. It was.

While Siegel is known as the father of Las Vegas, his town was Los Angeles. Murray saw Siegel hanging out at swank Hollywood nightspots with the Countess Dorothy Di Frasso and other film sirens. He took himself "too seriously," according to Murray. The *Examiner* insisted on calling him Bugsy, a term he hated. When Siegel protested the nickname, Jim Richardson began referring to him in print as Benjamin (Don't Call Me Bugsy) Siegel.

Siegel was murdered a year after the Henderson scandal at the Beverly Hills home of his mistress, Virginia Hill. "Cost overruns," mused Murray. The mob thought he was skimming from the top.

■ ■ ■

In 1945 a young lady named Gerry Brown arrived in Los Angeles from Ann Arbor, Michigan. She was a fabulous pianist who had been featured in a radio show in her hometown. She hoped to make it in Hollywood as a musician. She was unable to bring her piano with her, so she regularly went to a place called the 575 Club, located at 575 South Fairfax Avenue near Hollywood. She asked the owner, Cy Miller, if he would mind her playing on certain evenings.

Gerry was a pretty, dark-haired girl with olive skin and large, luminous eyes. She had a quick smile, a great personality, and a lovely, expressive face. After Miller heard her play, he offered a salary, but she did not want to be tied down to a schedule. She played for free. Gerry quickly developed a following at the 575 Club.

Jim Murray was a regular at the club. The young reporter, recently arrived in town from Hartford, Connecticut, himself, was looking for a "drink and a pickup." Gerry rebuffed him. Cheerful repartee was as far as it went, but he was a regular and they were friendly.

One night Murray went on a double date with a friend, Ed Laurent, and "two dental hygienists." They headed out to the Paris Inn. At some point Murray found a phone and called the 575 Club to check on the action. Cy Miller told him, "I've got Gerry Brown here expecting you. I've convinced her you were crazy about her but I can't keep her much longer. She's skeptical. If you can get over here in the next five minutes, she said she'd like to meet you."

To the chagrin of the two dental hygienists, Murray "never flew out of a nightclub so fast in my life." So did Laurent, apparently unimpressed with their dates and preferring Murray's company, wherever it led them.

"I'm coming, too," Laurent said.

"Why?" Murray asked.

"Because those two girls were mad enough to kill one of us, and it wasn't going to be you. I have just left the two maddest dental hygienists in captivity back at the table," he said.

Driving an eleven-year-old Pierce Arrow, Murray hit 6th Street, ran three stop lights, broke the speed limit by twenty miles an hour, and arrived at the 575 Club just as Gerry was leaving. The rest is history. Theirs "was a 38-year date," wrote Rick Reilly. "The Murrays appeared to be happiest at the piano, with Gerry playing . . . and Jim belting out maudlin Irish songs."

"If the phone rang at two in the morning, you knew who it was," said Tom McEwen of the *Tampa Tribune*. "It was the Murrays saying, 'All right, what do you want to hear?' And you'd say, 'Well, whatever you feel like.' And Murray would break into 'Galway Bay.'"

They had four children, three boys (Ted, Tony, Ricky) and a girl (Pammy). Murray made only $38.50 a week when they were married but was always employed, respected in his profession, and "upwardly mobile." He negotiated a raise to $50 when the Associated Press tried to hire him away from the *Examiner*.

Murray called Gerry "the most beautiful person I have ever known in my life," but it was her soul that Murray found most attractive. She was a truth-teller, his moral compass. After working for Jim Richardson, he needed someone like that. To him, marrying her was a "privilege."

Murray felt lucky to find love and marriage. Jimmy Cannon once said he could not marry because he was wedded to his column and living in a mid-Manhattan hotel. That could have happened to Murray. But the first fifteen years of his marriage to Gerry were "right out of *Ladies Home Journal*," Murray wrote. Gerry had a position with a doctor. They were a team.

"Looking back, it was the best of times, probably the happiest of my life," Murray wrote in his memoir, but he added that memory is always colored by the prism of nostalgia. The tiny, sun-washed apartment they lived in initially was too small, and when they moved to the affluent confines of Malibu and Brentwood, he remembered "only the sunshine."

4

Show Biz Is Not a Business

In 1948 *Time* magazine hired Murray, out of forty candidates interviewed, to be its Los Angeles correspondent. For Murray, leaving his job as a rewrite man was not an easy decision. He flatly admitted that he loved working for the *L.A. Examiner*, but he moved to the stodgier, literate *Time* for the money. He signed on for seven thousand dollars a year plus fringe benefits.

"*Time* didn't linger at what happened," Murray wrote. "They wanted to know why it happened." They did not care about "hibiscus murders" but concerned themselves with the "globally significant."

Time and *Life* magazines were at the heart of the huge media corporation run by Henry Luce. Luce was a global thinker, as was his wife, the respected journalist and former member of Congress, Clare Boothe Luce. Everybody wanted to write for them. America was at the center of everything, the impetus of power, diplomacy, and intrigue. If the Chandler family saw themselves as "shapers" of the American West, Luce and his ambitious wife saw themselves as molders of what Luce himself had called the American Century. To work for Henry Luce was to be at the pinnacle of one's profession.

"Murray longed to be a foreign correspondent—'and wear a trench coat and carry a Luger' but when *Time* called with $7,000 a year, he took it," wrote Rick Reilly. "Over the years he worked on a dozen cover stories on such subjects as Mario Lanza, the Duke, Betty Hutton and Marlon Brando."

Murray was assigned coverage of the comings and goings of the Hollywood film industry. Instead of writing for Hollywood, he wrote about Hollywood. In some ways it was apropos. He had always preferred to be a spectator. He liked watching and writing about sports more than actually playing the games. Now he was commenting on movies and movie stars, not subjecting himself to the whim of directors, actors' egos, shooting schedules, and the fickle opinion of the ticket-buying public. This fit his desires perfectly. He was not paid as well as a top screenwriter penning blockbusters, but he received a check every first and fifteenth of the month. The screenwriter, in contrast, might go months or more in between gigs.

As the cinema correspondent for *Time*, Murray had considerable power. His opinion of an actor's performance, or the viability of a film, helped make or break its nationwide box office potential. Murray loved it. He described himself as "movie-struck." Directors were constantly at his office, promoting themselves.

Henry Luce had decided that three or four times a year, his magazine cover should be graced by a movie figure, preferably a beautiful woman. It was the age of military heroes and politicians wielding power unseen since the days of Caesar Augustus. *Time*'s covers most often featured beribboned images of Dwight Eisenhower or Douglas MacArthur mixed with statesmen such as Harry Truman and George C. Marshall. Often photographed from below, they appeared more like monuments than flesh-and-blood people. Hollywood stars would give *Time* a more human touch.

Murray was tasked with picking out the "next big thing" in show biz. To be selected for a *Time* cover story was tantamount to instant success and credibility. It was a long, long way from Uncle Ed and his gambling habits. Murray found himself mingling with, and courted by, the likes of Cary Grant and Marilyn Monroe. He had aisle seats for the Academy Awards and invites to the hot premieres. "It was pretty hard to keep your feet on the ground in that rarefied atmosphere and I'm not sure I did," he wrote.

Murray's marching orders were to find sex goddesses for the cover. This was difficult. Leading men such as William Holden, Kirk Douglas, Marlon Brando, and Paul Newman dominated the era. The top-of-the-line actresses were talents but not "cheesecake" material: Bette Davis, Kate Hepburn. He managed to find a few, among them Ava Gardner and Rosemary Clooney, but it was a struggle.

In his search for a sex symbol with enough star quality to justify a *Time* cover, Murray came across Marilyn Monroe. Norma Jeane Mortenson grew up in the San Fernando Valley and attended Hollywood High School. Married to and divorced from an L.A. cop, she became the mistress of a shadowy bon vivant named Joe Schenck, a big wig in the movies. He kept beautiful women around to decorate his pool parties. Murray attended one of these soirees in the company of sportswriter Vincent X. Flaherty. Norma Jeane was wearing a tight white bathing suit, "five-feet six inches of whipped cream, a sweet little girl smile," wrote Murray of his first reaction.

She may have thought Murray could help make her a star. In his autobiography, Murray tells the tale without many specifics but with a few hints at possible romance. Murray pitched his boss on a story about her in *Time*. This led to a larger, bigger photo spread in *Life*. In preparing for the interview, Murray dug around. He discovered that Monroe's background was dismal. She had been virtually abandoned, her mother institutionalized. She was shuffled between foster homes. If she sought love in the beds of powerful men, it was not entirely a matter of immoral behavior. She had severe issues from childhood.

Murray picked her up at a hotel on Olympic Boulevard. He waited while she prepared herself in front of the mirror. He "dated" her enough times to develop a routine. He would tell her dinner was for 7 p.m. but make reservations at the restaurant for 8:30. He brought magazines to read while she changed her mind about her hair or her dress. With luck they made the restaurant by 8:45. His first date with her was at an old mob-owned restaurant on Sunset Boulevard, Alan Dale.

His dinner date, really a business meal, an interview with the sex symbol, was "not exactly an AP news flash," wrote Reilly. "Murray was *Time* magazine's Hollywood reporter from 1950 to 1953, and you could throw a bucket of birdseed in any direction at Chasens and not hit anybody who didn't know him. He has played poker with John Wayne ('he was lousy'), kibitzed with Jack Benny (who gave him an inscribed, solid-gold money clip) and golfed with Bing Crosby (later, Crosby sent him clippings and column ideas)."

One night when he was with Monroe, Murray noticed out of the corner of his eye a "famous former athlete" enter the restaurant via a side door. He was escorted to a private dining area by the owner, where a screen was placed around his table. Monroe started looking around.

"What's wrong?" Murray asked. Then Monroe leaned over.

"Do you mind if you don't take me home but I go home with a friend of mine?" she asked.

"Only if you introduce me to Joe DiMaggio first," he replied.

"OK." She waved to a man across the room who sheepishly made his way to the table.

"Jim, I would like you to meet Joe DiMaggio."

Murray noted early on the difference between Hollywood celebrity and sports celebrity. The movie stars and studios courted publicity. It was the lifeblood of their business. Athletes did not. Certainly athletes like DiMaggio and Ted Williams did not need anybody to tout them. Their fame was secure. The 1954 marriage between DiMaggio and Monroe, which lasted about a year, was symbolic of the difference.

Monroe flaunted herself, craving attention. DiMaggio was private. Monroe entertained the troops in Korea. Upon her return she exclaimed, "Joe, Joe, you never heard such cheering."

"Yes, I have," deadpanned her husband.

Murray was one of the first to recognize the screen presence of John "Duke" Wayne. Wayne grew up Marion Morrison in Glendale. He played football for Howard Jones at the University of Southern California. After injuring his shoulder in a bodysurfing accident at Newport Beach, Morrison lost his scholarship. He took up acting at Fox Studios.

Morrison arranged for USC football players to be extras in Hollywood screen epics; they were cast as Napoleon's Grand Armée or Roman legions in biblical epics. He changed his name to John Wayne and became a big star but was not considered an actor of depth such as Henry Fonda or Humphrey Bogart. But Murray's job was to keep tabs on box office records. He knew that Wayne was the most popular actor in the world. The elites of Hollywood and New York favored more stylized artists, but in the "sticks," which was pretty much everywhere else, the Duke was number one. Murray began lobbying for big John Wayne coverage, but his New York bosses did not know who he was. "Nobody in Rye or Mamaroneck or Old Greenwich ever went to one," he wrote of Wayne's movies. "It was a hard sell. The editors wanted to put Kate Hepburn or Clare Bloome on the cover, somebody they wouldn't have to apologize for at the Harvard Club."

Finally, *Time* gave Wayne his due for *The Quiet Man*. Murray loved him, a man's man who lived in a man's world of poker, cronies, and Baja pigeon shooting. Wayne's size and football background added to the image, but Murray discovered an intellectual under his muscles. Wayne never said "ain't" until a movie script made him say it. He was an A student, a high school valedictorian who made excellent marks at USC. Wayne was deeply patriotic and, like another conservative actor, Ronald Reagan, enmeshed in politics.

"Lots of fellows don't put in the care and effort that you do," Wayne wrote to Murray in a letter dated February 28, 1952.

Wayne's most famed director, John Ford, had a real "sadistic" streak, according to Murray. Ford bullied Murray during an interview, but when the writer threatened to walk away, the director laughed, admiring Murray's willingness to stand up for himself.

Murray found Humphrey Bogart to be the opposite of John Wayne. With the Duke, what you saw was what you got. In contrast, Bogart resented his own Park Avenue childhood. The son of a doctor, he pretended he was a "dead end kid." "He was about as tough as a ballroom dancer," wrote Murray.

Murray also frequently interacted with another well-known actor of the era, Marlon Brando. "You'd go knock on Brando's door," Murray said, "and you'd knock and you'd knock for an hour and he'd never answer it. But as soon as you walked away, he'd fling it open and cackle like a rooster." In a letter to Murray, Brando wrote, "Most of all I think it was your lack of preconception and your insistent openness of mind that made it the most pleasant experience with the press to date." Apparently, Jim Murray took the time to understand the inscrutable Brando, and perhaps the actor saw the genius of the writer as well.

Murray believed that most of the movie crowd was sports mad and many studio moguls' inveterate gamblers, which made sense. "Hollywood was the biggest gamble of them all," he wrote.

"When the Dodgers came west," he recalled, "Dodger Stadium had more stars on the club level than the back lot at MGM."

When Lucille Ball and Desi Arnaz were questioned by Congress over their possible Communist affiliation, Arnaz thoroughly destroyed any whiff of Red sympathy by testifying that when he was a youth in Cuba, the Communists came to confiscate his family's property. He hated them, and as a Christian, he despised their atheism. Murray wrote about and supported the couple, whose TV program, *I Love Lucy*, revolutionized the genre. In 1952 the writer received a Christmas card from them in which they wrote "may every day of the new year abound in life's treasures."

After he wrote a flattering piece about Rosemary Clooney, the singer sent him a letter. "A hundred thousand roses couldn't have been sweeter than *Time* magazine was to me this week," she wrote on February 19, 1953.

5

Murray, Nixon, and Checkers

Murray's friends always referred to him as a literate man, an educated fellow, a guy who knew about history and politics. Part of this came from his natural desire to read about these subjects, starting at a young age and lasting all his life. But his years at *Time* added to his frame of reference for current events.

Hollywood coverage naturally bled into politics during the McCarthy era with its blacklist. Many members of the entertainment industry were caught up in the HUAC hearings, whether they liked it or not. But Murray often had assignments beyond the film industry, sometimes straying into politics or other arenas.

As a Christian, Murray was impressed by the phenomenon of the Reverend Billy Graham. In 1949 the evangelist, touring the nation with his popular tent revivals, was all the rage. Murray wrote a fair story about the preacher, and Luce fell in love with Graham, making him a recurring theme in his magazines over many years. Murray received all of twenty dollars for doing the Lord's work.

In 1952 Murray had a break from the movie scene. He was assigned a political story. "He always said he was a Democrat until he made his first $40,000, then he became a Republican," said his widow, Linda McCoy-Murray, laughing. "Yes, he was a 'Los Angeles Republican' of the era, in sync with the politics of Otis Chandler and the *Times*."

Jim Murray was assigned to witness vice presidential candidate Richard Nixon's debut. Since Nixon was a West Coast guy, *Time* wanted somebody with West Coast sensibilities to cover him. Murray contacted a writer named Ernie Brashear, who did a two-part series on Nixon for *The Nation*. He wanted some background and trusted Brashear as a colleague. Brashear told Murray he wanted out of the third part of the series. "I have asked [*Nation* editor] Frieda Kirchway to take my name off of it," he told Murray. "They say some things about Nixon I didn't find to be true and I don't want my name on fabricated news."

Brashear told Murray that the *Los Angeles Daily News*, the *New York Post*, and *Frontier* magazine were planning a big smear piece on Nixon. At the time Murray was accompanying the candidate on a whistle-stop train tour for his *Time* story. Murray had had "a bourbon or two" the night Brashear delivered the news, and he warned Nixon's people, Bill Rogers and Jim Bassett, of the pending scandal story. They were already prepared for it. "It's going to backfire," they told Murray.

The scandal was the infamous 1952 "slush fund." Supposedly, a group of Pasadena Rotarians maintained a fund to keep Nixon "in style." Richard Nixon was a poor man. He came from nothing. Now he was almost a heartbeat from the presidency, since victory for his running mate, Dwight D. Eisenhower, seemed a sure thing.

In fact, Rogers and Bassett underestimated the scandal. The *Washington Post* and the *New York Times* urged Eisenhower to drop Nixon. Murray understood the media and the public well from his years of analyzing their film tastes. Apparently a supporter of Nixon, Murray pleaded with Rogers (later the U.S. attorney general and secretary of state) to "meet the contretemps head on." The Nixon people continued to think it would blow over. It never did.

Murray was along for the ride while Nixon made stops in front of heckling crowds. The candidate tried to convince the crowds how poor he really was, but it did not work. The train was scheduled to go all the way to Seattle, but at two o'clock in the morning, at the Benson Hotel in Portland, Nixon came downstairs. He told the assembled press (probably dragged from their beds or the bar) that he was flying back to Los Angeles to address the issue on national television.

Eisenhower waffled on whether to stick with Nixon. He was famous for making last-second decisions, as with his D-day orders, after every scrap of information became available. Nixon was frustrated.

The Nixon campaign and press contingent were scheduled to fly from Portland to L.A. on a Monday morning. The candidate's speech was scheduled for the next day at 5:00 p.m. *Time* went to press on Monday night. If *Time* waited until Friday, Nixon's speech would be a week old by the time it hit the streets. A taciturn national affairs editor named Max Weeks phoned Murray. He was "a very forbidding character, one of the lions of the company," Murray recalled. Weeks was beside himself. The slush fund was the biggest story of the year, and the most important national magazine in the country had assigned a green West Coast movie reviewer to cover it. Weeks's orders were explicit: find out whether the candidate was taking himself off the ticket—before the candidate announced whether he was taking himself off the ticket.

"How am I supposed to find that out?" Murray screamed at Weeks.

"Just do it." It could have very well meant Murray's job.

On the rail journey back to L.A., Murray was miserable. Nixon was boxed off from the press, in lockdown. Bill Rogers, TV producer Ted Rogers, and Nixon's wife, Patricia, all protected the candidate from nosy reporters. Murray figured that the candidate would eventually have to use the restroom. He planted himself outside the door. Sure enough, Nixon came by.

Nixon liked Murray. He may have sensed that the writer was a supporter and at the least a fair man who would not print lies as *The Nation* had done.

"Dick," Murray pleaded of the thirty-nine-year-old junior senator, "the magazine wants me to find out what you're going to do tomorrow night." He explained the deadline dilemma. Nixon gave him due consideration and then told him to check with Jim Bassett. Bassett later came to Murray's seat and knelt next to him. "What would you do if your family had obligations, debts to pay, but you never took any bribes and struggled along, if your wife and your mother wore cloth coats, and you had a big mortgage?" Bassett did not tell Murray whether Nixon was planning to fight for the ticket or step down. At first Murray wondered why he was getting this story from the campaign aide, but then it dawned on him. Bassett was "giving me the speech"—the same speech Nixon gave during the train stops. He was telling the story of the "fighting Quaker," an image the young legislator had cultivated since returning from naval service at Bougainville in the South Pacific.

On arriving in Los Angeles, Murray found a phone to call *Time* and assure his editors that Nixon was staying on the ticket. The press contingent was at the Ambassador Hotel that evening. Murray repaired to the Press Club for some libations. Bill Best of United Press International found him there. Best told him that UPI was coming out with a rocket, announcing Nixon's resignation from the ticket. Murray knew that at this moment millions of copies of *Time* were rolling off the presses with the opposite announcement. He realized that he was the "Fred Merkle of journalism." As a New York Giants rookie, Merkle had failed to touch second base after a supposed game-winning hit, costing his team the 1908 pennant. The play earned a nickname, Merkle's Boner, that would forever live in infamy.

Murray called Bill Rogers and explained his predicament. Rogers went to talk with Nixon. Four minutes passed, during which Murray envisioned a career as a cab driver or a short-order cook. Rogers returned and said, "The candidate says, quote, 'Murray's got the story, what's he worried about?'"

It turned out UPI's source was a baggage handler who told them the Nixon campaign luggage had not been checked on the train. The theory was that the campaign, if there was still a campaign, would continue as a whistle-stop. But the campaign managers were planning to fly to Montana after Nixon's speech.

The Checkers speech is one of the most famous in history. With Patricia Nixon, wearing a "respectable Republican cloth coat," sitting by his side, Nixon provided embarrassing details of his personal finances and debts. He was not wealthy by any means. To conclude, the candidate explained that his supporters had given him one thing, a cocker spaniel named Checkers. His small daughters, Julie and Tricia, "love the dog." Nixon said that no matter what, he was not going to give it back. It was a brilliant rhetorical move that pulled at America's heartstrings.

In the speech's aftermath, Bill Rogers credited Murray with understanding the gravity of the accusations against Nixon before anybody else did. "We should have listened to him," he stated.

Murray indeed was a Nixon man. In 1960 he flew home from a Hawaiian vacation just to vote for him, even though "I loved John Kennedy." He felt he owed Nixon for the scoop; Murray had correctly called the Checkers speech when so many others had gotten it wrong. It was an enormous step forward in his career.

6

Sports Illustrated

In 1953 Murray took a train to New York to help launch *Sports Illustrated*. Luce put Sidney L. James in charge of the project. James immediately identified Murray as enthusiastic about the new magazine. He was in on the ground floor. At first he and James created mock-ups used to attract Madison Avenue advertising dollars. During Christmas Luce sent Murray a letter thanking him for his hard work and assuring him the magazine was set for publication on schedule.

Murray came up with an idea for a celebrity-style publication too. "If I may say so immodestly, *People* magazine today is exactly what I suggested in the early '50s," Murray wrote in 1993, adding that its later (unattributed to him) success was well known.

The launching of *Sports Illustrated* in August 1954, its initial edition with Milwaukee Braves slugger Eddie Mathews on the cover, turned sports from a regional (with the exception of New York) sideshow into a worldwide phenomenon with big money implications. The magazine had the effect of globalizing sports after radio nationalized it in the 1920s. This combined with television and Major League Baseball's westward expansion created a national stage in which sports stars, promoted by the media and a fan base with tremendous disposable income, combined to create one of the great industries of the century.

Until the 1950s New York had dominated sports media. But in the late 1950s a seismic shift occurred. *Sports Illustrated* did not cater to a New York audience. It was popular in the provinces. Americans began reading sports tales from all over the country. Then the Dodgers and Giants moved west. Now baseball was truly a national pastime.

Frank Gifford recalled,

When *Sports Illustrated* came along it was a big thing. It was the first major publication that focused totally on sports. Now you have all sorts of magazines, two or three for each sport, but *Sports Illustrated* was a big break-through.

Sports Illustrated, and the nationalization of our sport [football], that changed everything. Then they started televising the games nationally and that all changed. This had the effect of making the league a power-house, and not just in New York. It did not have to rely on New York for ratings and interest.

Jim Murray's West symbolized this new world. Its burgeoning population, political significance, sunny weather, geographical beauty, and role as the epi-center of American pop culture were given further approval by the imprimatur of Hollywood glamour. Murray rode the crest. No longer was New York the center of the world. L.A. wasn't yet either, but it was getting there. When the Dodgers moved to L.A. in 1958, everything changed. Los Angeles became a big league town.

Nobody in the media was better suited to describe what all this change meant than Jim Murray. Like the Dodgers franchise, he was from the East Coast, but by the mid-1950s he was comfortably situated in the City of Angels. He could appreciate and give voice to the movement west. His style was almost patrician in tone. He was well read and understood the impact of history. In the 1940s and 1950s, many writers referred to America as a new Rome. Our old enemies—Germany, Japan, or anybody who stood in our way—became modern-day Carthaginians or Gauls.

Perhaps staff member Robert Boyle described the effect of *Sports Illustrated* best: "Sport permeates any number of levels of contemporary society, and it touches up and even deeply influences such disparate elements as status, race relations, business life, automotive design, clothing styles, the concept of the hero, language, and ethical values," he wrote. "For better or worse, it gives form and substance to much in American life."

In 1967 the editors at *Sports Illustrated* said sport itself had been shaped in part by the "vast disarray of war" but was "beginning to set the pace it would maintain for some years to come, perhaps up to that magic milestone, the year 2000, and even beyond."

In 1993 Jim Murray wrote, "I'm proud of what we did, and they did, at *Sports Illustrated*. It played its role in the explosion of sports. So did I."

7

The *Times*, They Are a-Changin'

Murray worked at *Sports Illustrated* from 1953 to 1961. Well-paid but not rich, he became highly respected as a national sportswriter. In 1961 the *Los Angeles Times* hired Murray away from *SI*, a move that had an enormous effect not just on the sportswriting world, but ultimately on the city of Los Angeles itself.

When the Dodgers moved to L.A., the city figured it was the cutting edge town of the future. By 1961 Los Angeles was on the move. The Dodgers regularly filled the cavernous Coliseum, a football stadium, with huge crowds. They were the 1959 World Champions, the darlings of Hollywood, and they had begun building a brand new stadium of their own.

Enter the *Los Angeles Times*. The *Times* had existed since the nineteenth century, but in 1960 it was taken over by Otis Chandler, a young Stanford graduate who had inherited the family business. Chandler, like his family and their newspaper, was a Republican, but like the "times," he was himself a-changing. The *Times* had always reflected the politics of its city. Chandler intuitively understood this dynamic as it evolved over the years.

Otis Chandler was at least a fourth-generation Los Angeleno, the son of Norman Chandler, grandson of Harry Chandler, and great-grandson of Harrison Gray Otis, his namesake. At first, the public dismissed him as a blond playboy, too pretty and concerned only with girls, parties, and sports in a city that, by the 1950s, offered every sensual delight. He did not need to work hard. He did not need to make tough decisions. His life was mapped out. He could live off the "fat of the land" as long as he chose, eschewing controversy. But that was not his nature.

Chandler's background was modern. He respected the legacy of his family, but he wanted to make his own mark. Growing up a rich kid in Southern California, he was an indifferent student, a great athlete, and an avid outdoorsman who learned how to hunt, fish, track, and live off the land. Chandler's love of the outdoors grew to legendary proportions. Over the years, he engaged in wild safaris, big game hunts, and other adventures in some of the most inhospitable, dangerous conditions on earth. He thwarted death at the hands of polar bears, crashed race cars, and survived other hazards, although he sometimes required weeks of hospital care. A profiler once wrote, "If Otis Chandler had not existed, Ernest Hemingway would have created him." He was a larger-than-life figure with an insatiable thirst for adventure. He was also a health nut who never drank or smoked, an original Californian.

Chandler's parents wanted him to go to Stanford University, but his grades were not up to snuff. To improve him academically, they sent him to the prestigious Andover Academy in Massachusetts. The Chandler name carried no weight at Andover, where presidents, Supreme Court justices, and Eastern elites sent their sons. Chandler was a tanned, blond kid, a beach-boy stereotype, and this made him the butt of jokes. To make his life a little more miserable, the dormitory paired him with the black son of a Chicago janitor, a scholarship student. Luckily, Otis enjoyed and sought out the company of people from different backgrounds. His roommate was an excellent student who handled himself with aplomb and engendered grudging admiration from other students. The two hit it off famously.

Chandler became a track star, which made him a big man on campus. He managed to get his grades up too and headed off to Stanford in 1946. A surf aficionado, he regularly hit the waves at nearby Santa Cruz. A world-class shot-putter, he was considered a strong candidate for a spot on the U.S. team for the 1952 Helsinki Olympics but just missed out. He was a fraternity man, a good enough student, and the apple of the eye of every beautiful young girl down on "the Farm," as Stanford's rural campus is called. His nocturnal activities were well known.

During summer vacations while attending college, Chandler had worked in the *Times*'s offices to learn the business. At first he seemed disinclined to follow in his family's footsteps. After graduation he served in the U.S. Air Force. Chandler was advised to settle down. He married Marilyn "Missy" Brant, an attractive fellow Stanford student. She was from the right social order, her family part of old Pasadena–San Marino money. They started a large family.

Chandler went through a rigorous training program at the newspaper, working as a cub reporter. He learned his trade from the ground up. He was not the rock-ribbed, unquestioning Republican his father and particularly his grandfather had been. They had not simply boosted the land and water deals that built the region but invested in and profited from them. The family wealth and power emanated from these and many other deals that crossed the lines of journalism, politics, and business. Chandler turned away from these precepts, but only so far. He knew where his bread was buttered.

The paper backed Richard Nixon's political career, Howard Hughes's business expansion, Joseph McCarthy's Communist investigations, corporate expansion, freeway building, and sports stadiums, while paying little heed to environmentalists concerned about the smog settling over the L.A. Basin. The dirt was thought to be the price of doing business.

Otis Chandler was troubled by all this. His natural inclinations were hardly radical. He was a businessman and by no means rejected the profit motive, but he was also a Christian and a humanitarian at heart. His relationship with his black roommate at prep school and with black teammates and competitors in the sports world opened his eyes to racial injustice. He noticed the city's growing black population, many of whom had come to L.A. during the war to work in the shipyards and other war industries. He was not oblivious to the plight of Mexican Americans, who in the 1950s and 1960s were an ignored underclass in the city. As late as the early 1960s, the *Los Angeles Times* had not yet hired a black reporter. The *Times* covered Hollywood, the aerospace industry, and sports; black South-Central and Latino East L.A. were given short shrift, and residents' objections to the ram-rodding through of the plans to build Dodger Stadium in this "blighted" area were ignored.

The *L.A. Times* was unquestionably the king of newspapers in Southern California. It was a major moneymaker. It boosted business ventures that unashamedly brought in more profits to the company and the Chandler family. But the paper had a bad reputation. The East Coast intelligentsia looked down their noses at it. In various polls conducted in the late 1950s, the *Times* was vilified; some went so far as to call it the worst or second-worst newspaper in the nation. The *Times* was considered jingoistic, blatantly Republican, and provincial.

Otis Chandler's ascension to the publishing suites separated him from his younger siblings. He was the anointed one. Otis was not as partisan as his predecessors (although political editor Kyle Palmer, a Republican kingmaker, was still around). Nixon was the newspaper's obvious choice in 1960. He rode to power in large measure because of the paper's strong backing of his policies in the 1940s and 1950s, when he was elected to Congress, the U.S. Senate, and the vice presidency. Nixon's anticommunism was not just the papers', it was the regions'. Few places were as ruggedly individualistic and rabidly opposed to the Soviet Union to the point of strong John Birch Society influence as Southern California in the early 1960s. While John F. Kennedy cut a striking figure, Nixon was popular in the state. He would take California handily, although the Democrat had his share of support.

Still, despite its backing of Nixon, in 1960, under Otis Chandler, the *L.A. Times* toned down its partisanship considerably. This was a first, albeit important, step in improving the paper's reputation. Chandler made several calculations. The Republicans were popular, but Los Angeles was by no means a one-party town as it had been in the 1920s. Members of the growing Latino population deserved to have somebody speak for them. So did the black population, which simmered with discontent. The city leaders had failed to notice overt racism within the Los Angeles Police Department, which was papered over with the myth that such things did not happen *here*. This sort of social discord occurred in the South and in Eastern cities where ethnic enclaves nursed decades-old animosities toward each other. Not so in Los Angeles. The terrible Watts riots in 1965 proved this theory false.

Chandler decided he would not simply remove the partisan sting from the paper, but he would also upgrade its coverage. This meant creating bureaus in all the major world capitals. He would no longer have to rely on the *New York Times* and the London *Times*, the so-called papers of record, to provide international stories. They would have a *Los Angeles Times* team on the spot. Chandler wanted to create a world-class newspaper for a new, world-class city.

Chandler, editor Nick Williams, and the *L.A. Times* staff set forth to completely change the nature of the paper, and with it, the city they covered. By 1962 the obvious difference they effected was demonstrated when Richard Nixon lost to incumbent Democrat governor Edmund "Pat" Brown. Nixon was stunned that the *Times's* once-fawning coverage had turned on him. In truth, Otis Chandler's paper covered the election straight down the middle. It was still a Republican paper, which endorsed Nixon in 1962 and continued to support Republicans right up to the Reagan era, although not nearly as vociferously as before.

Under Otis Chandler, the paper took an active role in Latino politics, even printing editorials by a writer named Ruben Salazar that could have been considered radical. The editors were caught off guard by the Watts riots but endeavored to understand them with a series of in-depth analyses.

Chandler was as much a businessman as a newspaperman. From the journalistic standpoint, he advocated fair reporting and opinion. His affinity for the Right was never so obvious as to spark outright claims of bias. Perhaps his greatest contribution was giving his writers and editors incredible journalistic freedom with little concern for cost. His newspaper printed long, detailed, analytical pieces of the type normally found in a weekly or even monthly magazine like the *New Yorker* or *The Economist*. Many argued that fast-paced Los Angelenos were too rushed to read long essays spread across a thick daily packed with enormous volumes of information, and a Sunday paper that reached as many as four hundred pages.

Chandler routinely green-lighted stories that required reporters to travel to the four corners of the world, always in first-class style. Articles about the environment, exotic animals, and tiny subcultures were prominently featured without the slightest watering down of content or length. For writers, it was heaven.

He created new sections. He hired writers away from his competitors. His paper was called the "velvet coffin" because working there was so great that nobody could be compelled to leave. It was the best place for writers to practice their craft, to develop their chops.

Slowly, year by year in the 1960s, the *Los Angeles Times* changed, molded by the vision of Otis Chandler. It improved, largely in an effort to stay competitive with the *New York Times*, which had recently expanded into the West. A reporter named Dick Bergholz ruffled Richard Nixon's feathers during his 1962 campaign for governor. Many of the reporters manning the paper's Washington bureau were Easterners, poached for higher salaries from establishment papers. Many were Jewish. A battle of sorts emerged between the newcomers and the still mostly conservative Chandler-type WASPs. It symbolized the divide of the turbulent 1960s; some reporters and even editors grew their hair long, hippie-style, while others found the new trends repellent.

8

Decade of Change

Jim Murray's first column for the *Los Angeles Times* appeared on February 12, 1961. Titled "In This Corner, With the Pen, Is the New Guy," it began, "I have been urged by my friends—all of whom mean well—to begin writing in this space without introducing myself, as if I have been standing here all the while only you haven't noticed. But I don't think I'll do that. I think I'll start off by telling you a little about myself and what I believe in. That way, we can start to fight right away."

From there Murray presented a potpourri of sports items and his opinion on each. He told readers he was taking sides, that he was not playing it down the middle, that he was unabashedly partisan. He spoke of historical sports figures (John McGraw, Frank Chance), drew from history (Bears quarterback Billy Wade gave up ground faster than "Mussolini at the end of a war"), and mentioned as many things that were outside of Los Angeles as were within Los Angeles. He was telling L.A. that he was not provincial because L.A. was not provincial. He was a hit.

"I used to read Red Smith," said Frank Gifford. "He was terrific. They weren't cutthroat back then. They were all established and there were not as many of them. They were not as competitive. I'd have to put Murray right there."

Shortly after Kennedy's inauguration in January 1961, Dodgers owner Walter O'Malley and a few others approached Richard Nixon about becoming commissioner of baseball. He reluctantly declined. The job went to Ford C. Frick, who, that same year, put an asterisk on Roger Maris's sixty-first home run.

Nixon returned to California. He joined a fancy downtown law firm on Wilshire Boulevard and made real money for the first time. He moved into a mansion atop Beverly Hills, but that year a terrible fire threatened his home while burning down those of his prominent movie star neighbors. He was shocked when Chandler's *Times* had the temerity to question his house loan.

Nixon spent two years practicing law in L.A. while writing his memoir, *Six Crises*. In 1962 he made a failed run for governor, which resulted in his move to New York to work on Wall Street—the "fast track" as he called it.

A study of *Times* headlines during this period, compared with those from just a few years before the ascension of Otis Chandler, reflected a much greater emphasis on national and international affairs. By the 1960s the paper featured major coverage of the globe rather than elections in the Southland, Disneyland, and other local issues.

Jim Murray hit the ground running. After his first column, he wrote three columns about Hall of Fame baseball stars. His August 23 column, "Drysdale's Double Life," was one of the best things that could have happened to Dodgers pitcher Don Drysdale, who was considered a loudmouth and a complainer because he attributed his mediocre statistics to the Coliseum's hitter-friendly dimensions. Murray's column depicted him as a fierce competitor who seemed to enjoy plunking the likes of Frank Robinson with beanballs but who was a true gentleman off the field. Murray called him "Dr. Drysdale" and "Mr. Hyde." The piece had the effect of personalizing Big D to the Dodgers' fans.

Eight days later Murray wrote a column about Drysdale's friend and pitching partner, Sandy Koufax. Drysdale had painted a glorious picture of Los Angeles to the young Brooklynite when the team moved west. Koufax seemed to relax away from the pressures of family and friends and the expectations of him in his hometown. In 1961 he came into his own. Murray's column included an amazing statistic: the previous year, Koufax averaged 155 pitches per start. Murray wrote that the intellectual Koufax preferred Felix Mendelssohn and Ludwig von Beethoven to rock 'n' roll. He correctly predicted that the new Dodger Stadium would have a tremendously positive effect on Koufax's career.

On October 8 Murray wrote "Yogi Berra, the Legend." Berra, the Hall of Fame Yankee catcher, was now toiling in left field while Elston Howard handled the plate. The 1961 Yanks were one of the greatest teams in history and were taking on the overmatched Cincinnati Reds in the World Series. When the Series shifted to quaint Crosley Field, Murray predicted that Berra would be challenged by Crosley's odd outfield configurations. "The outfield in this place is so steep in places the players should have oxygen and a Sherpa guide to scale it," he wrote. "It has produced more pratfalls than Mack Sennett in his heyday." He added that watching Berra negotiate it would be funnier than watching "Jackie Gleason and Elsa Maxwell trying to cha-cha." Murray's "prediction" that Yogi would have trouble negotiating Crosley Field's warning track never materialized. His team was dominant in a five-game Series triumph.

By year's end Murray's fame was spreading. Groucho Marx wrote him a letter stating that he had hated waking up in the morning until moving to Los Angeles. "Now I leap out of my wife's bed and rush for your column," wrote the comic. "This is quite a tribute to your literary prowess, for my wife happens to be a very beautiful woman."

■ ■ ■

The year 1962 stands out in American history. Like 1927, 1962 was a year of culture and sports. It was a distinctly Los Angeles and California year in many respects. It stands out as a year of unique nostalgia in the American psyche. As depicted in the 1970s film *American Graffiti*, 1962 was the last year of innocence before Kennedy's assassination in 1963, the turmoil of the Vietnam War, and the civil rights movement.

In October Kennedy ordered a blockade of Cuba after nuclear weapons were discovered there. Ultimately the "other fellow just blinked," as Secretary of State Dean Rusk put it. But the Cuban missile crisis forced the United States to agree not to invade Cuba or try to kill Fidel Castro, its goals in the first two years of the JFK administration.

The Cuban missile crisis was JFK's finest hour, and it allowed the Democrats to buck historical trends in the 1962 midterm elections. This included the California gubernatorial race between incumbent democrat Pat Brown and Richard Nixon. One of the most contentious campaigns in history, it marked the first fissure in Southland voting trends and the editorial stance of the *Los Angeles Times*.

Greater Los Angeles was Nixon country. Nixon all but took his hometown for granted, although he did not sweep the old precincts as he expected to. Orange County held, but L.A. swung toward Brown, who was wildly popular in his native Northern California.

It was a key moment of decision for Otis Chandler. The moderately conservative Republican was a Nixon man but did not allow that to color his newspaper's coverage. Nixon felt betrayed. Seeing the powerful *Times* critical of Nixon, other media felt free to open up and target the former vice president.

The Cuban missile crisis swung the electorate toward JFK and by implication his party. In a close election, Nixon lost. In his "last press conference" at the Beverly Hilton Hotel, he lashed out at the press and tacitly "retired" from politics. "You don't have Nixon to kick around anymore," he said.

If 1961 was an "L.A. year," then 1962 may have been its greatest, not just for L.A. sports, but for the entire state of California. It was a key year in the mighty Los Angeles–San Francisco rivalry. The two cities had battled each other in sports, politics, and culture at least since the Owens Valley Aqueduct had been completed in 1913 and certainly since USC emerged as a collegiate football power in 1926.

When the University of California–Los Angeles (UCLA) took its place as USC's key rival beginning in the late 1930s, a sense of jealousy pervaded Northern California schools. By the early 1960s the L.A. schools dominated the University of California–Berkeley (Cal) and Stanford. Professionally, the San Francisco 49ers had great players, but the Los Angeles Rams had better teams. L.A. had pro basketball. San Francisco did not. The Dodgers came out west with a greater reputation than the Giants and, after four years on the West Coast, were still the more prestigious organization.

By 1962 San Francisco was facing a major crisis of identity. San Franciscans thought of themselves as having the more elegant, sophisticated city, but everything important seemed to be happening in L.A. San Francisco had Herb Caen and literature, but Los Angeles had Howard Hughes and Jim Murray. San Francisco had beatniks. L.A. had movie stars and the Sunset Strip.

But of all the comparisons in the "who is better?" argument between the two cities, perhaps the quality of the newspapers was the greatest disparity. Chandler had effectively accomplished his task by 1962. The *L.A. Times* may not yet have won a poll on the best paper in the world—the East Coast bias was still too prevalent—but in truth it was a vastly better paper than the *Washington Post* and was able to compete on par with the *New York Times*. The latter was dry. It lived by old journalistic standards and refused to acquiesce to increasing reader demand for greater color and excitement. Chandler did not publish a scandal tabloid or a wild-headline Hearst-style paper, but he did understand the value of vivid photographs, human interest stories, and colorful prose, which was by then identified as the "West Coast style." Jim Murray epitomized this type of writing.

San Francisco was burdened by a real rag of a paper, the *San Francisco Chronicle*. The *Chronicle* had several capable sportswriters, but it was riddled with errors. Its three star writers were talented, but they were also controversial. Herb Caen was uniquely loved in the Bay Area, but he seemed to feel San Francisco was the only place worth living. Naturally San Franciscans fell for this, but Caen's hatred of L.A. bordered on the obsessive. Charles McCabe and Art Hoppe were both wildly left wing. McCabe openly stated that France was a greater nation than America. By the end of the 1960s Hoppe wrote in his column that he had finally come around to openly rooting for the North Vietnamese.

The other San Francisco paper, the *Examiner*, had higher production value, but it was an afternoon daily with less power and influence. It was certainly not in the same league with the *Times*.

San Franciscans and Los Angelenos had endless barroom disputes. L.A. fans argued the Dodgers over the Giants, USC and UCLA over Cal and Stanford, the beaches over the bay, the babes over the beatniks; none of these fazed the hardcore San Franciscan. But L.A. had a few aces up its sleeve when it came to bragging rights. It had Vin Scully. Even Giants fans were resigned to admitting Scully's greatness as a broadcaster. It had the *Los Angeles Times*. Nobody could argue the superiority of the *Chronicle*. Herb Caen was a notorious gossip. He did not care if what he wrote ruined somebody's life. Murray never had that mean edge to him. In the entire history of journalism, Caen was the single most provincial writer who ever lived. Murray was the least.

Murray took exception to the claptrap from "Baghdad by the Bay," which was Caen's moniker for the City, as they called it, in those pre–Saddam Hussein days. In 1962 he wrote that San Francisco was a "no host bar" and criticized the Giants for allowing their groundskeeper to turn the base paths at Candlestick Park into a "peat moss" pit so as to slow down L.A. speedster Maury Wills.

Murray mentioned Caen when he pointed out that *Sports Illustrated* put the knock on "Frisco," the most hated of all names out-of-towners give to the City, in an article titled "Akron of the West." Joe David Brown wrote that it was "not a big league town . . . Full of drunks . . . A citadel of intolerance . . . Vulgar and cheap." Finally, in perhaps the unkindest cut of all, he wrote that the City was "not the lovely lady I had imagined but a vulgar old broad." San Francisco "leads the nation in suicides, mental disease, alcoholism." Murray did not necessarily agree with Brown's assessment, but he did not entirely disagree. One of Murray's keenest observations came when he wrote that subconsciously San Francisco does not "want to win."

L.A. went for victory, with all its ugly, jarring connotations, as fervently as Howard Hughes tried to land contracts to build rocket boosters. San Francisco embellished the stereotypical British tenet that "no gentleman ever plays a game too well." When the City got the best player in baseball, Willie Mays, they rejected him at first. His great talent was almost too vulgar a display of excellence.

Charles McCabe wrote of this strange neurosis, stating that San Franciscans rejected ultimate victory as too jarring. Murray said that San Francisco has an "insurance against victory better than any Lloyd's can give him." In 1962 it certainly appeared that he was right. The Giants won one of the all-time most difficult pennant races ever fought, defeating the Dodgers to capture the National League crown. But they and the City seemed happy to settle for that. Everybody appeared perfectly OK with merely making a good showing in an epic seven-game loss to the New York Yankees, a team and a city with no problem handling ultimate victory, in the World Series. Given a chance at redemption in 1963, the Dodgers dispatched the mighty Yankees in four straight in the Fall Classic. The Giants settled for "bridesmaid" status throughout the decade, not ascending the mountaintop until 2010.

Murray, the East Coast native, seemed to recognize California's north-south dynamic as well as anybody. He loved San Francisco—its ambience, its views, its architecture. He had chances to move up the ladder in the writing game and, in so doing, to live in Boston, New York, D.C., Europe—the salons of international power and politics. He consciously chose to stay in L.A. because he loved the city, its dirty air, congested traffic, cultural plasticity, and all. He was L.A., and L.A. was Murray. He instinctively defended it and refused to concede that its rival was superior. He also realized that Los Angeles was by the 1960s one of those salons of international power and politics, whether it set out to be or not. It was already a given by 1962.

By 1975 L.A. had passed Chicago and possibly even New York as the American and, by extension, global metropolis. It produced two Republican presidents, Nixon and Ronald Reagan, who were reelected in landslides. It was the home of political movements that shook the world.

Murray was a man of social pathos but not of radicalism. He was unimpressed with the protest movements of the 1960s. Steve Bisheff, a longtime Los Angeles sportswriter, said that Murray "was liberal, and I'm liberal," but he was talking about Murray's stance on integration in the 1960s. Jim Murray was keenly aware that Democrats ran the Jim Crow South, and he had no respect for their tactics there. Watergate changed him, as it did many, but mainly he felt betrayed by Richard Nixon, not the party. In the 1960s and beyond, San Francisco identified Los Angeles as conservative. This dynamic played itself out in sports as well, especially in the Northern California attitude toward USC and in the Candlestick Park fans' boorish treatment of the Dodgers. Murray identified with L.A.

But Murray never lost his admiration for greatness no matter where it was found. He found it in Willie Mays. As the classic 1962 campaign was heating up, he wrote a laudatory column about Mays on May 23. After reading it, as with so many of Murray's columns, one is almost ashamed to be writing about Jim Murray. Nobody can capture him, or even come close. The temptation is to reproduce two hundred or three hundred pages of Murray's quotes, columns, and observations, rather than to critique or paraphrase. So it is with the Mays piece, an astonishing bit of existential writing in which Murray describes Mays as would a doctor or a policeman, breaking him down to his essence: "iron, calcium, antimony and whatever baser metal a human being is composed of." It is the sort of approach no other writer—not Grantland Rice, Jimmy Cannon, Ring Lardner, Red Smith, Jimmy Breslin, or even Hunter S. Thompson—would take. His brilliance is beyond ability, existing in the sheer originality of thought.

The Dodgers-Giants 1962 death struggle captured Murray's imagination throughout the summer. In a piece on L.A.'s catcher, Murray wrote, "On road trips, if John Roseboro isn't at a movie, he's at a laundry. He has more wardrobe changes than Loretta Young."

The Giants were notorious for slumping in June, what the press coined their annual "June swoon." Murray wrote, "A business executive is standing in his office looking down over the city and is chatting to his secretary. Suddenly, a falling figure shoots past the window. 'Oh oh,' says the man, glancing at his chronometer. 'It must be June. There go the Giants.'"

The Candlestick Park groundskeepers watered their base paths in an effort to slow down Maury Wills. Of this Murray observed, "One more squirt and the Red Cross would have declared a disaster area and begun to evacuate the Dodgers by rowboat. . . . An aircraft carrier would've run aground."

After Los Angeles blew a 4-2 ninth-inning lead in game three of the play-offs at Dodger Stadium—a combination of wild pitching, errors, bad scouting, and terrible managing—Murray focused on beleaguered Dodgers manager Walter Alston, who lived in small-town Ohio each off-season. "Down in the dugout, manager Walt Alston was poring over the stagecoach schedules to Darrtown," he wrote. With a week to go, Los Angeles had blown a four-game lead, capped by defeat in the three-game play-off, reminiscent of their collapse in 1951. Murray's line: "Wanted, one nearly new 1962 National League pennant, slightly soiled with tear stain in center. Last seen blowing toward San Francisco. . . . Warning: if you return pennant to Dodgers direct, be sure to tape it to their hands."

The sense of nostalgia for all things 1962 was greatly enhanced by that year's magical "Sunset Strip summer" of the Los Angeles Angels, owned by Gene Autry. A second-year expansion team, they rented Dodger Stadium. The Dodgers were the pride of the city; they had set the all-time Major League attendance record and hosted every big name in the entertainment industry. At Dodger Stadium, the Angels played before friends and family.

Autry's club featured a playboy southpaw named Bo Belinsky. In one of the few scoops of the era that evaded Murray, Bud "the Steamer" Furillo of the *Los Angeles Herald-Examiner* broke the story in March. Bo was a career minor leaguer of little reputation, but he held out for all of fifteen hundred dollars that spring. Asked what he was doing to pass the time, Bo told Bud he was "laying a lot of broads and playing high-stakes pool matches" up and down the East Coast. The rest was history. Bo finally signed, came to L.A., and made a well-publicized swath through the starlet population of Hollywood that put Errol Flynn to shame. An arrest at 5 a.m. courtesy of the Los Angeles Police Department and daily gossip columns courtesy of Walter Winchell stoked the fires.

It was rumored that Dodgers owner Walter O'Malley kept the *L.A. Times* and its sportswriters "happy." Undoubtedly, they published the bulk of the team's publicity and feature stories. The Belinsky act, at least in the beginning, may have been too tabloid for the high-class *Times*, but it surely sold the *Herald-Examiner* and the scandal rags. When Bo pitched a no-hitter, nobody could ignore him. His team was in first place on July 4 and finished a creditable third behind New York and Minnesota.

Furillo was Murray's rival and a comparable talent, albeit a much different personality. His style more suited the underdog *Los Angeles Herald-Examiner*. Furillo was more provincial, an "L.A. homer" whose love for the USC Trojans and for the Dodgers, especially, could have crossed journalistic boundaries. His enthusiasm and genuine likeability were so great he could get away with it. Furillo became sports editor, a job Murray never held. Many leading L.A. sportswriters credit him with their development, including Doug Krikorian and Steve Bisheff. He was a beloved figure. He announced USC's football games replayed on Sunday local television in the 1970s and was a regular on KABC radio's *Dodger Talk* with another legend, Stu Nahan, in the 1980s.

"I don't think they were rivals," recalled Furillo's son Andy, working in 2010 for the *Sacramento Bee*.

> I only heard my dad say good things about Murray. One thing about Murray that always stood out with me, he worked hard. I remember going to games early and watching him and Mel Durslag working the dugouts and the area behind the batting cages. They'd talk to everybody, take notes. Then they'd go write their columns after the game, in their own voices, stacked with authority and information based on great reporting. Something you don't see much in columnists these days.

While Andy Furillo disputed the notion that his father and Murray were "rivals," Bud's ex-wife, Cherie Kerr, insisted they were. She recalled,

> Bud would call Melvin Durslag every day, he was jealous of Murray. Not jealous as in he did not like him. Jealous that Murray worked for the bigger paper and was considered so above it all, such a figure of high esteem. So Bud called Durslag among other daily phone calls around town, often trying to gather intelligence on Jim Murray. Whatever Murray was writing about determined what Bud's approach was. He wanted to upstage Murray, not be scooped by him. Murray represented a high level of professionalism. To Bud, attaining that level of respect was something you did in the pursuit of excellence.

"I think he liked Mel Durslag," said Linda McCoy-Murray of her husband. "They got along fine. There were professional rivalries in L.A. Bud Furillo and Durslag certainly tailored their message based on what Jim was writing, and Jim paid attention, but it was all friendly."

Murray wrote a column about Bob Cousy of the Boston Celtics that was a paean to his own East Coast roots. He admired the old-school methods of Cousy, a truly skilled player aging in a game that was becoming more high-flying and acrobatic every year.

He wrote three hard-hitting pieces about boxers, old and new. Sonny Liston was the new champion. His emergence seemed to signal the end of boxing as Murray knew it. The "sweet science" was always an East Coast specialty—Madison Square Garden on a Friday night. Run by the Mafia. Liston may or may not have been the last of the mob-controlled fighters, but the sport was moving with television and other demographics into a larger-scale circus, beyond the mob's immediate reach. Murray also wrote about the anti-Liston, Joe Louis, "the most honest athlete in the history of any sport." Light-heavy-weight champion Archie Moore was the "the Rembrandt of boxing." This was the sort of specialty phrase millions associated with Murray.

■ ■ ■

By 1963 Murray was an institution. It was the golden age of Los Angeles sports. He was its royal chronicler and court jester. Among his 1963 columns was "Elgin Has Elegance," in which he stated straight out that Lakers superstar Elgin Baylor was probably the best basketball player in the world. Quite a statement, as many all-time greats were at the height of their powers in 1963: Bill Russell, Bob Cousy, Wilt Chamberlain, and Jerry West. Murray portrayed Baylor as a "motor mouth," constantly kidding and joking. He was also "the only born Republican I know who campaigned for Kennedy," said teammate "Hot Rod" Hundley.

Murray's October 2 column on Henry Aaron was a classic in which his opening paragraph compared the Braves' superstar to Spencer Tracy acting, Jan Peerce singing, Rudolph Nureyev dancing, or the sun setting on "an open body of water." It was the kind of prose nobody had heard before, and it was an important column for Aaron. He was the 1957 National League Most Valuable Player on a World Championship team playing before record-breaking crowds, but somehow Willie Mays, Mickey Mantle, Roberto Clemente, Frank Robinson, and Ernie Banks among position players had a greater place in the pantheon. Murray pointed out that, all things considered, Aaron need not take a backseat to any of them.

■ ■ ■

The year 1964 was a dividing line in American history. Between civil rights and Vietnam, it represented the beginning of the greatest period of change within the shortest period of time in history. In David Halberstam's book *October 1964*, he used the World Series between the Yankees and St. Louis Cardinals as metaphors for that change. The Cardinals were like the Democrats, a winning coalition of whites, blacks, and Latinos. The Yankees were the old-school GOP, country club Republicans, white, corporate, at the end of their string.

The *Times* gave Barry Goldwater and Lyndon Johnson each a fair hearing. Each wrote a series of articles. Goldwater's "Where I Stand" came in the late summer and was followed by Johnson's "My Hope for America" on September 28.

Orange County stepped forward to the national stage in 1964. Republican Goldwater was an underfunded underdog running against billionaire New York governor Nelson Rockefeller in the primaries, but the Right went for the Arizona senator. Ultimately, Orange County gave Goldwater California, and convention delegates gave him the Republican nomination at the Cow Palace in San Francisco. Angels owner Gene Autry decided Orange County was the future. He built a stadium there and moved his team to Anaheim.

Otis Chandler's paper gave Goldwater relatively favorable coverage. The Orange County market was big and growing. The *Santa Ana Register* was openly conservative, and the *Times* was determined to maintain its dominance. Goldwater, Nixon, and Ronald Reagan would all be identified with "Orange County Republican politics," with local and national implications over the next decades. Liberals chided Orange County as John Birch land, the "Orange Curtain," a place of intolerant, racist extremists of the Christian Right. Chandler personally had begun to lean toward the Democrats (although he continued to be a Republican all his life), or at least gave them the benefit of the doubt, but the editorial board and the Chandler family made it clear that the *L.A. Times* was still a Republican paper. It officially endorsed Goldwater, although it was not a strong endorsement.

■ ■ ■

In April 1965 Mayor Sam Yorty was reelected. In August the Watts riots destroyed the idyllic calm of a city trying to promote its race-neutral Beach Boys image. The *Times*, in a front-page August 13 story written by Jack McCurdy and Art Berman, held nothing back in describing the rioters as "mobs." In an eerie headline portending a dark future, that same front page also featured the story, "Second U.S. Jet Downed by Missile Near Hanoi." Below that was the story of a tiny hamlet called Duc Co, which was besieged by the Viet Cong.

"In 1961 I was a big-time sports fan growing up in Culver City," recalled sportscaster and Los Angeles native Fred Wallin.

> I was a Dodger fan and as a young guy I thought Murray knew his stuff. As I read more and more I realized he was up there and everybody else was a notch below, like Vin Scully, one in a million. Lots of people stole from him, he was the reason the *Times* improved. The *Herald-Examiner* had good writers, but they were more on the beats, but nobody had his eloquence of words.
>
> My brother died of leukemia in 1965. A few weeks later came Sandy Koufax's perfect game, and listening to Scully for a few hours gave me a respite from grieving for my brother. This was the influence of some of these people, like Scully and Jim Murray, on our lives. It was like when they honored Roy Campanella after he was paralyzed. I was there, it was one of those nights you never forget.
>
> When you read Murray, as he was traveling with the Dodgers, it didn't matter if the team was in first place or last, he was so funny and he said things that nobody else came up with. He had such ingenuity.

In a column about Celtics superstar Bill Russell, Murray wrote that Russell rules basketball "the way Russia rules Bulgaria—without seeming to." Against Russell, Oscar Robertson, the "Big O," was "just a zero." Wilt Chamberlain "is just a pituitary freak."

■ ■ ■

The year 1966 brought one of the great lessons of politics. Two years after being left for dead, the Republicans made huge gains in the U.S. Congress and state houses. Richard Nixon, now a Wall Street attorney on a corporate salary with an expense account, traveled the nation, campaigning on behalf of his party, earning huge chits for 1968. The GOP's victory was in large measure a response to the Left. The Vietnam War had taken a turn for the worse. Privately, Secretary of Defense Robert McNamara knew it. Publicly, Gen. William Westmoreland told the nation we were winning.

Running largely on a promise to clean up the antiwar riots at Berkeley, Ronald Reagan "moved into national prominence," according to a November 9 *Times* story by Dick Bergholz. Washington bureau chief Robert Donovan predicted that the 1966 victory portended presidential success in 1968, and listed Reagan, Nelson Rockefeller, George Romney, and Richard Nixon as leading candidates. A *Times* headline screamed, in an article by Lawrence Burd, that the Democrats lost up to forty-five House seats. The paper's national reach was exhibited in an article by a staff writer in Boston, Tom Foley, who wrote of Massachusetts's election of "Negro Republican" Edward Brooke.

Covering an otherwise ordinary Indianapolis 500, Murray penned one of his most famed lines: "Gentlemen, start your coffins." Of the Indy Murray also wrote, "It's not so much a sport as a death watch" held, "fittingly, on Memorial Day. It has long since tied the one-day extermination record set by the German *Luftwaffe* in Poland in 1939, and since tied by the Red Army in Budapest a couple of years ago. They should start the race with 'Taps.'" Perhaps Jim Murray's treatment of the Indy inspired screenwriter John Milius to write in *Apocalypse Now*, "Charging a man with murder around this place was like handing out speeding tickets at the Indy 500." Murray was one of the great satirists of all time.

In October he wrote an article about "Old Man River," the ancient golfer Sam Snead. "To find a comparable accomplishment" to Snead's continued success, he wrote "you would have to imagine General Pershing being in charge in Vietnam, Spencer Tracy playing a college kid."

■ ■ ■

If the sixties started not in 1960 but on November 22, 1963, then its high point (pun intended) was the summer of 1967 at Golden Gate Park in San Francisco. School let out, and seemingly every wayward child from Maine to

Marin County descended on the corner of Haight and Ashbury Streets. It was the Summer of Love. Writers such as Ken Kesey, Hunter S. Thompson, and Tom Wolfe made it the story of a generation. The rock music revolution of England and the beach vibes of California were joined by a new wave of bands, an explosion of artistic expression not seen since the Renaissance. The Doors, the Byrds, Buffalo Springfield, Jefferson Airplane, Jimi Hendrix, Janis Joplin, and dozens of others spoke for a generation.

Campuses exploded in protest against the Vietnam War, now a nightly TV event that featured soldiers returning home in body bags. The music, sex, drugs, and the protests seemed to upend American society. To Jim Murray's generation, it was jarring.

The cultural upheaval did not stop 1967 from being one of the best sports years ever. It was the biggest college football season in the history of Los Angeles. In November at the Coliseum, USC and UCLA met for the national championship. O. J. Simpson, as ballyhooed a football recruit as Lew Alcindor was to basketball, ran sixty-four yards for the winning touchdown in Troy's scintillating 21-20 triumph. "Whew!" Murray wrote.

> I'm glad I didn't go to the opera Saturday afternoon, after all. This was the first time in a long time where the advance ballyhoo didn't live up to the game.
>
> The last time these many cosmic events were settled by one day of battle, they struck off a commemorative stamp and elected the winner President.
>
> On that commemorative stamp, they can put the double image— one of UCLA's Gary Beban and one of USC's Orenthal James Simpson. They can send that Heisman Trophy out with two straws, please.

UCLA quarterback Beban won the Heisman Trophy. The Trojans finished number one when they beat Indiana in the Rose Bowl. It was Coach John McKay's second national title.

Murray's line about the opera was not gratuitous. "Ever since Jim was young he loved the opera," said his widow, Linda McCoy-Murray.

> Yes, he loved listening to Caruso and certainly enjoyed Pavarotti, Placido Domingo, and the great operatic classics. He played *Carmen* on cassette

at a volume that would shatter crystal. While in Barcelona for the 1992 Summer Olympics we went to Barcelona's renowned opera house to hear the three tenors, Placido Domingo, Jose Carreras, and Luciano Pavarotti, who would perform at the Olympics' opening and closing ceremonies. I took a picture of Jim talking with Placido Domingo, a photo he cherished. So no, he was not just pulling this stuff out of a hat when he wrote about it.

Murray wrote a column about former Boston Celtics coach Red Auerbach, who he said had no sense of humor. Auerbach wrote a book called *Basketball for the Player, the Fan, and the Coach*, which the columnist joked was "the most practical advice this side of *How to Rob a Bank*." It featured tidbits on how to grab or pull down pants, cheating on the scorer's and timer's table, and how to manipulate everything in your favor. Murray wrote that Auerbach, who was never home for Christmas during his career, had a strict policy against socializing with the Celtics' wives, including his own. His daughters not only did not believe in Santa Claus, "they were a little suspicious of that fable about Dad." He played the "game of life as if it were sure sudden-death overtime."

On April 27 Murray's column, "Louisville Loudmouth Secedes from the Union," addressed the great athlete of the day: Cassius Clay. The headline and language within the piece began a well-worn path he would return to: the themes of secession and the roles of the Founding Fathers as a guidebook to understanding modern behavior. The column walks a high-wire tightrope. The headline is not favorable to Clay—an unpopular figure after he chose to evade the draft, was stripped of his heavyweight boxing crown, and joined the Nation of Islam.

Murray would seem to have found little in Clay to admire. But the fact is that he had been happily settling in as a cub reporter in the comfortable climes of L.A. in 1944, when Americans were dying at Normandy and Bastogne. Still, Murray unquestionably favored the guys who fought with George Patton over the man who would not fight because "ain't no Viet Cong never called me n———r." Murray's racial compassion was already publicly known, but his column made it clear that no sympathy was due Clay based on race alone. He cited the Gettysburg Address, the battles, and the sacrifices of the men who fought the Civil War to ensure that by 1967 Cassius Clay and others like him were able to speak freely.

"Is it our fault?" he wrote. "Or his? Has he dishonored the dead? Or have we?" He disdained Clay's admonition that blacks "don't own no railroads," perhaps naively pointing out that owning a railroad was a mere creature of capitalism. Murray neglected to draw a conclusion, allowing the reader to draw one for him- or herself. The column was part of a new age of sports journalism in which talents like Jim Murray went well beyond hits, runs, and errors.

"Everybody knew who he wrote about when he made subliminal messages," said Linda McCoy-Murray. "He never went after somebody in a heavy manner, to criticize like writers do today. He would write something, about certain behavior, without naming names, but everybody including that person read it and knew who he was talking about."

■ ■ ■

The events of 1968 made 1962 seem like ancient history. Never had the passage of a mere six years been marked by such a chasm. The promise, the horror, and the sensual excitement of the decade could be wrapped up in one terrible, wonderful year. Most of the love found at Golden Gate Park in 1967 was now screaming bloody murder across the bay at Berkeley in 1968. It was a year of riots, tear gas, hatred, and the assassinations of Martin Luther King Jr. and Robert Kennedy.

Yet, social unrest did not prevent the wonderful world of sports from being wonderful. Murray wrote a column about Los Angeles defensive lineman David "Deacon" Jones, describing how in one game Jones had a bone sticking out of his thumb until "Jack Pardee had to push it back into place."

He also wrote a piece about Detroit Red Wings superstar Gordie Howe, whom he described as "the greatest hockey player who ever lived" and, to Canadians at least, equal to "the 12 Apostles." Murray's columns included much research. His subjects were struck by the fact he might interview them for thirty minutes or an hour, then barely quote them or not quote them at all. Murray went against a time-honored journalistic principle—get quotes—but his own words were better than anybody else's. It was, as Dizzy Dean would say, "not braggin'." It was just a fact.

■ ■ ■

On April 27, 1969, Murray wrote a column called "It's a Bird! A Man! A Car! A Bullet! . . ." Like his 1962 column on Willie Mays, his descriptions of Jerry West were over-the-top, the kind of hyperbolic verbiage that almost no other writer, no matter how talented, could get away with. Almost forty years later, on November 4, 2008, *Times* sports editor Bill Dwyre used Murray's West column as an example of his humbling talent in "Jim Murray: Of Pulitzers and Pretenders":

> This is how it goes now in the life of a sports columnist at the *Los Angeles Times*, an existence also known as: living in the eternal shadow of Jim Murray.
>
> You get some access to former basketball superstar Jerry West. You know there is a column there. You know he is one of those sports names that people always remain interested in. You go, you interview.
>
> West is great, accessible, his normal tortured self, which makes him among the most interesting of subjects to write about. Other sports stars—any normal person—learn to rationalize defeats, setbacks. It is the way of survival. Not West. They still burn in him, even some of his high school games back in the 1950s.
>
> His nickname shouldn't be "Mr. Clutch." It should be "Mr. Glass Half Empty."
>
> You are excited. A writer who can't get excited about a chance to attempt, once again, to capture the essence of such a fascinating character is not a writer at all.

Dwyre went on to describe his satisfaction with the column he wrote after he had been given this opportunity—that is, until he attended a dinner honoring the superstar during which Murray's 1969 column (refusing to write down to his audience, Murray included unattributed references to the Irish stage production *Finian's Rainbow*) was distributed at the tables:

> The first time you see Jerry West, you're tempted to ask him how things are in Gloccamorra. The Lakers didn't draft him, they found him—under a rainbow. . . . There are those who swear Jerry arrives for work everyday by reindeer. He wears the perpetually startled expression of a guy who just heard a dog talk. . . . He has the quickest hands and feet of a guy without a police record. If they put a cap on him sideways and turned him loose on the streets of London, there wouldn't be a wallet in town by nightfall.

"There was more, another 20 inches or so," wrote Dwyre. "It just got better. You ponder getting into another business, maybe dry cleaning or lawn mower repair. You end up taking a deep breath, eating dessert and pondering the definition of immortality."

In his September 2 column on Rocky Marciano, who had been killed in a plane crash two days earlier, Murray made a backhanded swipe at Muhammad Ali (the name Cassius Clay adopted after his conversion to Islam). "There is a new breed of snarling winners today, but Rocky was apologetic," he wrote.

In college football, Texas defeated Arkansas in Fayetteville in a classic battle for number one, attended by President Nixon. Afterward, Murray was slammed into a chain-link fence by a Secret Service man who apparently thought the writer looked suspicious. Murray found himself a foot off the ground, suspended only by his collar, when Nixon walked by. "How ya' doin,' Jim?" Nixon, who well recalled *Time*'s correspondent from the 1952 Checkers campaign, asked him.

"I'd be better," Murray said, "if you could get this monkey to put me down."

Sports in Los Angeles were profoundly different, but they were nothing compared with the seismic cultural shifts in the city and the world between 1960 and 1969. The city of Los Angeles and the state of California, despite taking a few punches here and there, were the cutting edge of the American future. Ronald Reagan was a successful, albeit controversial governor. Goldwater conservatism was on the ascendancy, largely a reaction to social changes the silent majority found horrifying. Long hair, hippies, dirty kids, free love, abortion, drug excess, immorality, anti-Americanism, war protesters, draft dodgers, rejection of Christianity, and a host of other New Age phenomena spurred the right-wing reaction. Out of the new zeitgeist grew violent, radical elements in the form of the Weather Underground, the Symbionese Liberation Army (SLA), the Zebra killers, and in Europe, the Baader-Meinhof Complex. The Republicans played it for all it was worth. The question was whether they could handle the reins of power as the world entered the 1970s.

Los Angeles and California were diverse. In Southern California the counterculture was still somewhat underground. In the Bay Area, Cal, Stanford, and San Francisco State were taken over by radical elements. In Los Angeles, UCLA was increasingly subject to them, but USC was immune. An agitator named "Brother Lennie" tried to organize an antiwar protest, but assistant football coach Marv Goux told him to "get yer ass outta here." Debate followed in the *Los Angeles Times* for a week, but Coach John McKay and President Norman Topping backed Goux.

Despite the Watts riots, images of the smiling Trojan O. J. Simpson and the Olympic-decathlon-champ-turned-sportscaster Rafer Johnson gave people the idea, right or wrong, that in matters of race, L.A. had gotten it right. Real estate prices were going through the roof. The military-industrial complex hummed along the 405 corridor. Orange County was a growing behemoth of wealth and success. Great athletes grew seemingly like oranges all over the Southland. Its nightlife was legendary. L.A. was "the place."

9

The Column

"The trouble with writing a column is, it's like running a railroad," Murray recalled. "You can never step back and take stock of what you've done." A book, a play, a movie, an opera, a ballet, a poem—all allow for reflected glory. The column is like the athletes it covers; it cannot rest on its laurels but must stay on top of its game. The fans are fickle and always ask, "What have you done for me lately?" The column, Murray once wrote, is "around the fish."

Bill Caplan was a boxing promoter and one of Jim's best friends. "It seems I knew him forever," recalled Caplan.

I did promotions since late in 1962. I was freelance, then I was on the payroll for Aileen Eaton at the Olympic Auditorium. George Parnassus was promoting a fight at the new Forum. They had seven sellouts in two years. I worked for Don King and Bob Arum. The point is that every job I got was because of my friendship with Jim Murray. I was able to get a lot of jobs because of Jim's influence.

Let me take it one step further. For whatever reason, he was number one in the West and one of the best in the country. I think he was easily the best columnist around. I could get him to write a column about a fight I was promoting. This really helped me. I was hired because people knew I could get a Jim Murray column.

The only column he ever turned me down was when I asked him to get together with a fighter and he said he couldn't because he was going to be in Augusta for The Masters. I was very lucky to have him as a friend. He always knew I would never bring him a stiff. Boxing is full of colorful characters and he would do a wonderful job crafting stories about those kinds of people.

The column became a consuming passion that took a toll on his marriage, which was kept steady for so many years because his wife was something close to a saint, in Murray's view. It would force him to close his door to his kids, who had been warned by Gerry not to make too much noise. He could not take ancillary opportunities, such as writing a screenplay about Ben Hogan, because the column required all his creative juices.

By the end of the 1960s Jim Murray was the king of sports columnists. He was considered not just the best of his day but, increasingly, the best ever, anywhere. His writing was the keynote of a newspaper that, within that same time frame, rose to a position of prominence and respect in the world. While Watergate created a major chasm between Republicans and the mainstream media, in 1969 the Californian Nixon still felt the *Times* to be the fairest, most balanced of all news outlets. Nixon and his cabinet regularly called on *Times* correspondents, by name and affiliation, giving them excellent access. The *New York Times* and *Washington Post* were already "enemies" of Nixon, in his view.

Unquestionably, Murray benefited from the changes of the 1960s. Los Angeles had gone from a minor league town to the biggest of big league cities. Its stadiums were palaces. Murray was the best of the Los Angeles press corps, but L.A. featured some of the greatest, most colorful scribes ever assembled, including Bud Furillo and Mel Durslag of the *Los Angeles Herald-Examiner*, Loel Schrader of the *Long Beach Press-Telegram*, and his colleagues at the *L.A. Times*: Mal Florence, John Hall, and Allan Malamud. The combination of these wits often mixed with alcohol and the likes of John McKay, who enjoyed pulling a cork, in relaxed settings like Julie's, a USC watering hole, or Ernie's House of Surface, a Crenshaw district sports hangout. These environments produced some real doozies, many of which never made print.

Within four years of starting at the *Times*, Murray had turned his columns into a book, *The Best of Jim Murray* (1965); he compiled a second collection in 1968 (*The Sporting World of Jim Murray*). In *The Best of Jim Murray*, he wrote, "It's not possible to measure what baseball owes to Ring Lardner, what football is in debt to Grantland Rice, or what boxing owes to Dan Parker." By 1970 Murray was greater than any of them.

Casey Stengel was "a white American male with a speech pattern that ranges somewhere between the sound a porpoise makes underwater and an Abyssinian rug merchant." When Stengel and the Mets came to Los Angeles to play the Dodgers, Murray showed his smarts. He rarely quoted his subjects, but for his column on Stengel, he knew that his subject was the ultimate wordmeister.

Murray also wrote about cities. "When he went around the country talking about different cities you laughed because it was something you never forget," said Fred Wallin, one of the hosts of *Dodger Talk* on KABC in the 1980s. "He could get away with it. You'd look forward to trips around this big world with Jim Murray." Murray's words were meant to be funny and lighthearted, but sometimes he engendered enmity. Cincinnati was a particular target. "Now, if you have any sense, you don't want to be in Cincinnati at all . . . ," he wrote. "You'd have to think that when Dan'l Boone was fighting the Indians for this territory he didn't have Cincinnati in mind for it."

The Dodgers built a state-of-the-art spring training facility in Vero Beach, Florida, but Murray was unimpressed—not with the facility but with Vero Beach. "A Letter from Jail" described his opinion of the place. Dodgertown was "a fancy name for Andersonville." This was a further example of his unwillingness to write down to his audience. Murray did not have to explain that Andersonville was the infamous South Carolina Confederate prison camp where Union soldiers languished and died during the Civil War. He did not treat his readers like second graders. Vero Beach, Murray wrote, was not in the United States, but in the Confederate States of America. He did not want to say the water tasted funny, "but you do wonder whose swimming pool they pumped it out of."

San Francisco was a continuing particular target. He took exception not just to the hatred San Franciscans had for L.A., but also to the snooty attitude of the locals. He called it "Akron of the West," borrowing from a *Time* article. It was a "citadel of intolerance" where Willie McCovey heard taunts "that couldn't be used in *Tropic of Cancer*." Los Angeles, in contrast, was integrated, although there were still problems. Some blacks were not allowed to rent in Pasadena, which was, ironically, the hometown of Jackie Robinson, but its schools, sports teams, and neighborhoods were way ahead of the rest of America in the 1960s. There is little if any anecdotal evidence of black or Latino athletes enduring racial fan abuse at the Coliseum, Dodger Stadium, the Forum, or any other L.A. locale.

Murray saw hypocrisy in San Francisco. The City had tried to bar Willie Mays, of all people, from buying a house there. Eventually Mays did buy.

St. Louis Cardinals outfielder Curt Flood, an all-star but no Willie Mays, was a Bay Area native who also tried to buy in San Francisco. He was turned away flat because he was black. No similar stories about John Roseboro, Elgin Baylor, Deacon Jones, or anybody else on L.A. teams existed, at least not publicly, in the 1960s.

Candlestick Park was a joke as soon as it was built in 1960. Murray pointed to it as an example of San Francisco's goofiness and mediocrity. He would not have minded San Francisco being San Francisco had its residents not reserved so much dislike for Los Angeles, a city Murray was perfectly willing to admit had its faults, although he was biased in its favor.

Of Spokane, Washington, he wrote the only trouble with the place was there was nothing to do "after 10 o'clock. In the morning." Of Malibu, where he lived until moving to Brentwood, he said that from his house he could look down the beach and see an "outdoor Eden" in which "all the girls look like Brigitte Bardot." Of surf culture he wrote, "The Pacific Coast Highway is suddenly awash with jalopies, doodle-bugs, station wagons and convertibles speeding to the sea with stacks of boards sticking out of them like quills from a porcupine." Murray's Malibu experience made him fluent in surfing, a sport he wrote about knowledgeably and often. It is not inaccurate to say the sport's growth was greatly influenced by his writing about it, especially in the 1960s and 1970s, when it reached its golden age.

Regarding his good fortune to be a sportswriter, Murray wrote of "hardships." He had to get up at noon and go to a ballpark at night, and thus missed *The Price Is Right.*

One of Murray's most effective techniques was comparing sports to highbrow culture, which he did in his column about Elgin Baylor of the Lakers. After speaking of his reaction to seeing "Barrymore when he was still Barrymore," he compared Baylor's skill on the court to the opera *Carmen* and the artistry of the great tenor, Enrico Caruso.

His column on Bob Cousy mentioned the Mona Lisa, Sarah Bernhardt, Caruso, and the Polish pianist Ignacy Jan Paderewski in the first paragraph. Cousy was "more Boston Pops and Arthur Fiedler than Arturo Toscanini, more comic strip than a candidate for the Louvre, a rhyme, not a poem."

Murray also liked to invent "conversations" between caricatured sporting figures, often football players at Notre Dame and Michigan with Eastern

European names like Bratkowski, an old-school reference to the kind of people who came to Americanize themselves.

Of golf Murray wrote, "Perfection is monotonous"; he preferred the weather-aided vagaries of the "Crosby clambake." Of the University of Houston, in the 1960s better known as the "University of Golf," the "entrance requirements are a 64 on an accredited course and a sound short game."

When famed jockey Eddie Arcaro decided to retire, Murray wrote that among his competitors the news was received with "the feelings of the crew of the *Bounty* when they put Captain Bligh to sea on that lifeboat, or the Russians when they got word Stalin was running a temperature." The use of Joseph Stalin as a sports metaphor resonated with many writers, who copied Murray by writing phrases like "the rest of USC's schedule fell like Eastern Europe under Stalin."

According to Murray, Rudolph Walter Wanderone, the man on which Minnesota Fats was based in *The Hustler* (his real nickname was the "Fat Man"), "has seen the sun come up redly through drawn blinds at the end of 50 hours of steady pool, a stubble of beard on his cheeks, his lips cracked and dry but his wrist as sure and steady as a piston." Fats also came up with a line worthy of Yogi Berra: "I don't miss no place. I like wherever I'm at. But when I'm gone, I don't miss it."

Of baseball statistics Murray wrote, "I think it was Mark Twain who first said, 'What do you want—the truth or statistics?'" As with Bear Bryant's supposed 1970 statement that Sam "Bam" Cunningham was "what a football player looks like," Twain may not have said it, but "he should have." Regarding the game's penchant in the 1960s for change and injuries, Murray satirized that in his day, "we never got sore arms." He loved poker references, as in "a guy who bets into a pat full house with a pair of eights and a kicker is a piker," a line he included in a column about the high bonuses paid baseball players. "Is baseball a business?" he asked. "If it isn't, General Motors is a sport."

He made up names and created scenarios using characters he called "Harry Hardthrow," "Jackie Shorthop," and "Barney Bullwhip." Of baseball promotions like "egg-throwing, wheelbarrow-racing and the like," Murray joked that a special contest should be held to determine the batter who "can make himself the most invisible" when called on to pinch-hit against the headhunting Don Drysdale or the relief pitcher "who can fake a back injury most convincingly when asked to go in and get Henry Aaron or Willie Mays out."

Murray enjoyed underdogs and sympathized with men who got the dirty end of the end stick, as did Roger Maris when he threatened Babe Ruth's home run record. Murray wrote that Maris was "baseball's answer to John Wilkes Booth." When Commissioner Ford Frick asterisked Maris's record, Murray criticized him roundly—with satire.

Mickey Mantle, previously disdained for not being Joe DiMaggio, suddenly discovered he was loved. In a column on Mantle, at the time considered a player not living up to his talent, Murray quoted former Dodger Jackie Robinson: "Look, we got plenty of guys worse than he is. Trouble is, we ain't got anybody as good." This was the sort of wisdom occasionally spouted by Winston Churchill, who once said, "Democracy is the worst form of government known to man . . . with the exception of all other forms of government known to man."

Murray's famed, biting humor shone through in a column titled "Pun My Word": "Sarcasm, it is said, is the lowest form of wit," Murray wrote. "But, even so, puns have to look up to it. My puns are half-backed but not hot or cross. And served up for the groaning."

In the big leagues, junk ball relief pitcher Stu Miller was "like a boy walking through Indian country with a Boy Scout knife and his lunch in a bag" (the phrase "Indian country," quite politically incorrect actually, was often copied by Vin Scully, sometimes to describe Walt Alston). His "fast ball" could be caught "in your teeth." Someday, Murray wrote, a rookie would swing and miss twice at a single Miller slow ball and be the first batter ever to strike out on two pitches. Watching Miller pitch was "as exciting as chess."

Monster Dodgers slugger Frank Howard, in contrast, was so imposing that when he arrived in New York, "the Army is called out, the United Nations meets in emergency session and they begin to fire bombs at it, which it catches and throws back." Howard's home runs "don't need a tape measure, they need an aerial survey." His shaky defense, however, was as suspenseful as an Alfred Hitchcock chase scene. He "is so big, he wasn't born, he was founded." Murray's puns, sarcasm, and hyperbole in describing Frank Howard's size were so over the top that in this particular case he became redundant. One of Murray's great gifts was knowing when to cut it out, but in Howard's case he committed a rare error in overdoing it. "There were many times he'd have bad days, when I would cringe at something he wrote," said his editor, Bill Dwyre. "So sometimes he went overboard, but Jim Murray batted .920."

Murray liked "nice guys." Everybody who knew him said that was what he was. In "Nice Guy Also Wins," Murray refuted the notion set forth by Leo Durocher that "nice guys finish last." As an example, he cited the "Castilian from Tampa," Chicago White Sox manager Al Lopez, who was highly successful without blowing his stack.

The great scribe also favored literate athletes, poet-warriors of a sort. Of Cincinnati Reds pitcher Jim Brosnan, who wrote a diary of the 1961 season, Murray wrote, "Broz is the only pitcher I know who thinks of Homer as a Greek poet and not a lucky swing by a banjo hitter." Brosnan had this humdinger on Don Drysdale: "The way Drysdale throws, he might as well throw a grenade with the pin out." This reference to Big D made it into a Murray column: when he had his control he was not around the plate but "around the head."

Murray brought to light the mysteries of sports at a time (before Jim Bouton's *Ball Four*) when nonathletes did not understand what "the life" was. In "Life on the Road," Murray dissected the baseball routine. Players were "in a town but not of it." No matter how great the cultural attractions of any given city, they lacked the slightest curiosity. They read *The Sporting News*. The main attractions were women in bars or a parlor game in which the players had to make sure they did their drinking where and when the manager was not, often a tricky proposition. The road was, he wrote, a difficult place to win baseball games: "A road game is like a knife fight in a room in the dark—only it's the other fellow's room." Road trips were a form of existentialism, or as "Schopenhauer once said," the road was a form of "peaceful non-existence."

Then there were the Trojans of Southern California, perhaps the inspiration for and happy beneficiary of Murray's greatest, most over-the-top hype. In *The Best of Jim Murray*, they were so prominent a subject that they rated their own special chapter, "Fight on for Old $C." If Grantland Rice turned Notre Dame into the nation's most popular football team, Jim Murray was every bit as responsible for the epic glamour of USC. The University of Southern California was already a huge college-sports powerhouse prior to Murray's arrival at the *Los Angeles Times*. An old-timer still writing for the paper, Braven

Dyer, had written of Trojan lore for decades and was singularly responsible for making Doyle Knave the most popular guy in America in 1939.

But Murray's arrival came a mere year after John McKay's, and the two had a symbiotic relationship that launched thousands of words. Murray, the Irish Catholic who grew up rooting for Notre Dame, understood and respected USC not merely as an opponent worthy of the Fighting Irish but as a team as responsible for Notre Dame's place in history, and vice versa. Perhaps because Murray wrote about Hollywood and John "the Duke" Wayne, he intrinsically understood that USC was not merely a university, but a Hollywood production. In some strange ways, outsiders understood this kind of thing better than the jaded Los Angelenos who were raised with Tinseltown at their fingertips. Everybody in the town lived near, or grew up with, or saw at the grocery store, somebody in the movies. To Jim Murray and other out-of-towners, the sight of stars never lost its luster.

Murray loved USC but did not bow down at the school's altar. Many worshipped USC. Some hated it. Association with UCLA often determined such idolatry. But his placing a $ (dollar sign) in place of the "S" in SC indicated his opinion. In 1965 he used the school as example number one that collegiate football was now at least as much big business as a football game in "Gold Line Stand." It certainly was a change of pace from the "raccoon coat crowd" of his Ivy League youth. In "The 'Heart' of Football," he continued the theme that college football coaches were not coaches but caretakers of a school's bank account. In "De-emphasis—'82 Style," he wrote a satirized, futuristic story in which college football is no longer the big deal it had been when they "broke it up in 1965."

His 1961 column, "Color Me Purple," described Jim Owens and the highly favored Washington Huskies entering the L.A. Coliseum like Romans conquering Gaul. Poor "Johnny McKay" and his Trojans were badly overmatched, better called "Faith, Hope and Charity" or, as he suggested, "they might throw in 'Surrender.'" Neither Murray nor anybody else at the time predicted that McKay, rather than being fired in his second straight losing year (as many assumed), would over the next two decades lead Troy to unparalleled dominance.

Some of Murray's favorite subjects were personalities on rival teams. One of the best was Ohio State coach Woody Hayes, whose Buckeyes overwhelmed

USC 20-7 in the 1955 Rose Bowl. After the game Woody let it be known that at least six Big Ten teams were better than Troy. This was a clarion call for some knight on a white horse to come forward and slay Woody and the Big Ten bullies. It took years, but that knight turned out to be McKay.

Before establishing the Pacific-Eight Conference as the dominant player in the Rose Bowl rivalry, McKay had to slay an even bigger dragon—Notre Dame. In a tongue-in-cheek column that had many Trojan fans declaring, "Finally," Murray wrote that Notre Dame was a top-notch educational institute, but nobody cared about improvements to the library or 99 percent graduation rates. "A formula for beating Army was all they wanted."

In "What's in a Name?" he recalled as a kid being fascinated with the high-brow names of USC football stars: Morley Drury, Homer Griffith, Grenville Lansdell, Gaius Shaver, Irvin Warburton, Orville Mohler, Ambrose Schindler, Aramis Dandoy, "Field" Marshall Duffield, Garrett Arbelbride, Courtney Decius, Orlando Ferrante, Volney Peters. "You had to sneer when you thought of other teams with a lot of guys named 'Mike' or 'Butch' or 'Pug' on them," he wrote. USC's coach should have been Sir Walter Scott, he theorized.

Growing up in the cold of Connecticut, Murray's uncles told him that the players were "two inches taller and 20 pounds heavier in California. They were all Olympic sprinters. They all had blond hair and swam to Catalina before breakfast every morning." In his youth, scientists and sociologists posited the notion that something in the water, the sunshine, and the food out West were responsible for the athletic success in the region. But by the 1960s Rose Bowl failure and losses to Notre Dame had people reversing their thinking. Now, amid theories that tougher conditions back East—coal mines and snow—created better grid stars, Murray was happy to report on Coach McKay leading his team back to the promised land in 1962.

Murray naturally gravitated to boxing, a subject of his Runyonesque youth. In a piece about the Floyd Patterson–Sonny Liston match, he wrote, "A 'journalist' was identified by a member of the British press on hand here as 'a gentleman who borrows money from a newspaperman.'" Sonny Liston "would be an 8-5 favorite over the Marines," he wrote. "He already has beaten more cops than Perry Mason." He was "the best argument I know for schooling." In "Sad Song for Sonny," Murray described miscreants of the fight game like Sonny Liston, Jake La Motta, and Rocky Graziano, who did time at Leavenworth.

"Anyway, the moral of the story is Jack the Ripper would be forgiven if he had a good left hook," he wrote. In 1963 Murray saw a boxing match in which Cuban Mexican Sugar Ramos beat Davey Moore so badly he died. In his column, he wrote, "A ringsider pointed out it was not a fight, it was Russian roulette with six-ounce gloves."

"Jim kind of soured on boxing," recalled promoter Bill Caplan. "He got very negative on it, but he said many of his best columns were on boxing. He had an Uncle Harry who would take him to the fights, and he always had a feel for the game."

Murray's second collection of columns, *The Sporting World of Jim Murray*, was dedicated "To the Swarthmore backfield, to Unknown Winston, to Dancer's Image, the Harvard Eight with Cox, the son of Frank Merriwell, the Walter who was not camp, Vincent and Al Lopez and every guy who tried to fill an inside straight while behind in his alimony." Murray was ironic and self-deprecating to the extreme. By 1968, he was getting more political. That made sense. The world was exceedingly political. Murray wrote that the benefits of his profession were overrated. He could watch Sandy Koufax take a shower, but "believe me, Elke Sommer is an improvement." Murray told readers he was advised to be cynical, but it was not his nature. He was too lucky and loved sports too much to not find amazement even in the routine. Somehow he was able to find as much wonder in Babe Ruth's called shot as in "Dempsey and Firpo fighting like animals," all with "a squirt of humor and a twist of irreverence."

Murray never wrote a column about Bo Belinsky, even though his biographer (Maury Allen) estimated that between 1962 and 1964 more words were written about the Angels southpaw than any player in the world. One reason for this was a platinum blond B-movie starlet who never made it but still stood out as a camp actress and sex siren representing the post-Monroe age. Her name was Mamie Van Doren. She was engaged to Bo in 1964. After having dated, and presumably gone to bed, with a who's who of Hollywood beauties for the previous two years, Bo getting hitched was big, big news. That year the Boston hotel where Bo was staying burned down. Everyone thought he was in it at the time of the fire—until he showed up "reeking of booze and broads" after a night on the town. He punched Braven Dyer in the Shoreham Hotel in Washington. Finally, he broke up with Mamie. The split was given more play than Elizabeth Taylor and Richard Burton.

Bo was interviewed incessantly. Murray always preferred to make his own way, not follow a well-worn path. He did write a column on Mamie, though. He never mentioned Bo's name. It was satire but so skillfully played that Mamie probably thought it straight journalism. He made fun of the busty actress, who took herself seriously on matters ranging from the Olympics to the Cold War. It was probably just a chance for Murray to be around a curvy broad, reminding him of his "date" with Marilyn, which ended with her in Joe D.'s arms.

Murray loved to invent fake conversations. In "One Day in April," Murray fashioned April Fool's Day "interviews" with Cassius Clay, Sandy Koufax, Frank Howard, Yogi Berra, Leo Durocher, and Sonny Liston, each saying the opposite of what he'd say in real life. For example, Sonny Liston: "I have always tried to model my life after Albert Schweitzer and St. Thomas Aquinas," while respecting the law and women.

Murray's long tirade against Cincinnati continued in "A Taste of Rubble." "You may remember the Reds from the 1961 World Series," he wrote. "On the other hand, maybe not." His treatment of Florida was little better. The state was "a body of land surrounded on three sides by sharks and on the fourth by Alabama and Georgia if you like to think of that as better." He called it like he saw it when it came to social inequity. Many black Dodgers players were complaining about spring training in Vero Beach. Dodgertown was a self-contained spring training wonder, but to venture beyond its walls was perilous. Black players could not find suitable hotels for their families. They took to cutting their own hair because local barbers posed a threat. They took their complaints to Jim Murray. Owner Walter O'Malley had little sympathy. Murray wrote columns that ranged from obvious to subliminal criticism of racism. Many Southerners did not know whether Murray was laughing with them or at them. The old rule was that sportswriters stayed clear of these sorts of issues. Murray was breaking that rule, little by little.

Murray had a growing family but was too busy to give them his undivided attention. His solution was to write about them. When Murray's sons played in the Malibu Little League, he found much fodder for his columns. Most of it was sour. He was no fan of little league. Murray despised the proverbial "little league parents," one of whom was Dean Martin. "When I was a kid we had little league for the Mafia," Dino recalled. "You don't get any uniforms, you just learned to steal in your regular clothes. To tell the truth I'm just surprised they don't have little league polo."

Occasionally Murray wrote columns in the Ring Lardner tradition, creating unique characters that might have appeared in Mark Twain books seventy years earlier. His columns were increasingly cutting and highly satirical. Take this from "Goof Balls Find Niche" about the Mets' Marv Throneberry (kind of): "Boss, he's been pronounced dead so many times there are doctors in this town who believe in ghosts when they see him up and around."

But while Murray could be humorous and sharp when making fun of mediocrity, he was at his best when describing excellence. When Sandy Koufax reached the height of greatness, he wrote a column called "Worker of Art" that was typical of his use of classical artistes as metaphors for athletic prowess. He opened, "If you want someone to play piano for you, get Horowitz." A doctor? He suggested Jonas Salk. It went from there. A golf partner? Sam Snead. A conductor? Leonard Bernstein, of course. Into dancing? Get Fred Astaire. This all led to his suggestion that if winning the World Series was your bag, "you hand the ball to Sandy Koufax."

Walt Alston had to decide whether to pitch Koufax or Don Drysdale in the World Series, a choice tantamount to deciding "whether to date Elizabeth Taylor or Jane Fonda." It was no disgrace to Big D that he was not as good on three days' rest as Koufax was on two, Murray wrote. After the Dodgers captured the 1965 World Series, he added, "All baseball, like Caesar's Gaul, is divided into three parts, the American League, the National League—and Sandy Koufax." After Koufax and his team defeated the St. Louis Cardinals, Murray wrote that the Cardinals' "attack" consisted of aiming "the bat where they thought they heard the ball go by."

Koufax was an intellectual, but Murray also enjoyed writing about athletes who were strictly "dese, dem and dose" guys who "never believed in prying into the affairs of Julius Caesar." Deron Johnson, raised in a bad San Diego neighborhood, was "the only white kid whose mother should have bused him to colored schools for a better shake in education." Johnson was "so painfully honest he could spot George Washington two answers in a lie detector test," he wrote.

When Dodger Stadium was built in 1962, Murray dubbed it the "Taj Mahal of Sport." The *New Yorker*'s Roger Angell picked up the moniker, calling the new stadium the "Taj O'Malley" after owner Walter O'Malley. Dodger Stadium, however, seemed too beautiful to waste on baseball games. Murray figured it was better suited to "the ballet Russe or the road company of *The Marriage of Figaro.*"

Likewise, although Murray loved college sports, he was not above pointing out its academic hypocrisy. On the issue of football recruiting, Murray wrote, "Anyone who thinks you can get a football team out of students must think you can get a debating team out of a backfield." But he truly admired the athlete-as-warrior. Of USC's 1965 Heisman Trophy winner, Murray wrote, "The only time Mike Garrett looks like an All-American is when he's got the football. After a game, he always looks like a train wreck." His uniform and his body were identical, both covered in blood. He was "willing to suffer for his art."

Golf had been a favorite foil of Murray's since his early fascination with Ben Hogan in the 1940s. Murray loved Hogan, who was a detailed golfer. He used to call Riviera "Hogan's alley." When Arnold Palmer once asked what Hogan would have done, Jim said, "Hogan wouldn't be in this situation."

Murray wrote that members of the Los Angeles golf crowd "range from the truant-playing bank president to the arrogant movie hero, blindingly decked out in checked coat, smoked glasses and trailing billowing fumes of cologne as he sashays down the fairway followed by a chattering band of sycophants in collars that look like sails in a good wind." The Los Angeles Country Club was "so lush, it seems a shame to waste it on golf." The place was "as hard to get into as Windsor Castle, so exclusive you can get the bends just driving by it." Palm Springs, California, was "an inland sandbar man has wrested from the rodents and the Indians to provide a day camp for over-privileged adults." Mickey Mantle "did speak to me once," Murray wrote: "You're in my way," he said on the fourteenth green at Palm Springs.

In an "only in L.A." piece about auto racing, Murray wrote, "The greatest stock car races in the world take place every afternoon about five on the Hollywood Freeway." The winner gets "an early dinner. Second prize is an early grave."

Murray once accompanied the Lakers on a flight to Ft. Wayne. At the airport somebody groaned, "Lindbergh crossed the Atlantic in equipment better than this." But the plane was not all bad. It had "won the Civil War." "Tell me, can he find Ft. Wayne in the dark?" Jerry West asked nervously as the plane rambled in. They arrived at four o'clock in the morning "and the temperature is a balmy zero." Murray knew that stories about freezing weather read by

Southern Californians waking up in seventy-five-degree sunshine fed nostalgia and worked up a sense of self-superiority. He later reported in a byline from St. Louis, "It's 8:30 and nine degrees."

Murray contemplated writing a book called *The Power of Positive Drinking*, an idea, like *People* magazine, that was appropriated at no recompense. He wrote that sports were so important in the American psyche that he half-expected to hear a news report announcing, "We will bring you the latest reports on the Arab-Israeli War right after Major League baseball." He railed unsuccessfully against delayed sports broadcasts. All things considered, as the 1960s came to a merciful close, Murray and his paper were the best in the world at what they did. Both portended the future. Both were on the cutting edge. Both were a perfect match of old and new, of traditional and modern.

Art Spander was a young writer out of UCLA who wrote for the *Santa Monica Evening Outlook* before moving to the *San Francisco Examiner* in the mid-1960s. He knew Murray well. He had been assigned to drive Murray when he was still a student. "Mel Durslag of the Hearst *Examiner* was also an excellent writer," Spander recalled of the sports writing scene when Murray arrived at the *Times* in 1961.

> Before Murray came to the *L.A. Times* and became syndicated, they had a very boring sports section. Jim came over from *Time* and *Sports Illustrated* and became syndicated, and at some point the *Times* announced that he was the first syndicated columnist in Los Angeles, but Durslag was syndicated as far back as the 1950s. Durslag could write, but before these guys came along L.A. had a bunch of hacks. There was a guy named Morton Moss who wrote for the *Examiner* who was always looking for puns. He was okay, but the quality was not great until the 1960s.

Spander was just breaking into the business in 1961. "Murray was writing at the time for *Sports Illustrated*," he recalled. "They could not hire Durslag. He was already established but under contract to the *Herald-Examiner*. I had to go in the Army for six months when Murray started, and people are sending me his stuff. He wrote like non-sports writers. There were these old guys like Braven Dyer, Paul Zimmerman, Charlie Park, a baseball writer, Frank Finch.

There were writers who tried to write sports but couldn't pull it off." After that, the *Times* under Otis Chandler consolidated.

"Murray was pretty liberal but not in a Democrat-Republican way," said Spander.

> By standards of the day he was liberal. He was liberal if you believe the term applies to fairness. He believed in equality and fairness. If the rules were unfair he wanted to change the rules.
>
> It bothered Murray if people didn't adhere to standards. He'd buy a nice pair of shoes and see people come into the press box in sneakers or with their hair all over the place. He was old fashioned and didn't like change.
>
> He had a Hollywood flair. He wrote comedy, he wrote some for *The Andy Griffith Show*. He tried his hand at screenwriting with Ben Hogan.
>
> In 1967 at the PGA in Denver, we were waiting for a bus or a cab to the airport. His suitcase came open and he could not put it back together, and he kept swearing, "Those damn engineers; why don't they just leave things the way they are?" He hated change.

Murray, Spander said, would often write, "DiMaggio would have had it."

But as great as Murray was in the 1960s, perhaps his and his newspaper's finest hour came in September 1970. He would cross over, above and beyond previous efforts, into the world of sociopolitics, landing on the right side of history. For a guy who loved history as much as he did, he would have it no other way. It did not come without criticism.

10

Civil War

Jim Murray was in his first year as an *L.A. Times* columnist in 1961. The Big Ten had not signed a contract to continue sending their champions to the Rose Bowl. They were weighing their options. At the time, the Pacific Coast Conference was struggling. Big Ten teams were not so sure they made themselves look much better beating PCC teams at Pasadena. Maybe another bowl, against a Southeastern Conference or Big Eight squad, would have more impact. Maybe they could talk Notre Dame into rescinding their bowl ban. Woody Hayes and Duffy Daugherty against the Fighting Irish? That beat a matchup against Washington or Oregon or Cal.

For several years the Big Ten accepted the Rose Bowl invitation, but on a freelance basis. In 1961 Woody Hayes and Ohio State felt they were positioned to win a vote for the national title from somebody. If the Associated Press or UPI would not give it to them, then maybe the Touchdown Club or the Columbus Quarterback Club could give them a plaque, and they could call themselves "national champions." Hayes figured if he went to the Rose Bowl and lost to Washington, he would not receive the Touchdown Club's nod.

Word went out for an alternative. Alabama was unbeaten and untied. An invitation came from the Southern California Football Writers Association, the Los Angeles Rotary Club, and others. They voted to extend a Rose Bowl bid to the Crimson Tide. Alabama's hallowed football history had been built on the Tide's winning trips to Pasadena, where they won Rose Bowls en route to national titles in the 1920s and 1930s. In 1946 they walloped Southern California in the first bowl loss ever absorbed by the Trojans.

Woody Hayes figured that if 'Bama came to Pasadena and lost, he would win the national title vote. In the end, neither Ohio State nor Alabama stepped up. Big Ten runner-up Minnesota played UCLA in the Rose Bowl. Ohio State sat at home. Alabama beat Arkansas, 10-3, in the Sugar Bowl. Alabama tried to spin its decision. The Sugar Bowl was Alabama's bowl. It was easier for their fans to travel to New Orleans than to Pasadena. It was a regional thing. "Hogwash," said Jim Murray.

Alabama was segregated. Images of Birmingham Public Safety Commissioner Eugene "Bull" Connor's troops using fire hoses and other strong-arm tactics on civil rights protestors were being broadcast across the nation. After a group of black students at UCLA announced plans to boycott and protest if Alabama played in the Rose Bowl, Murray weighed in. "The University of Alabama just about wrapped up the all-white championship of the whole cotton-picking world," he wrote after the Tide defeated Georgia Tech. Murray wrote positively about Alabama's on-the-field play but condemned the idea of inviting Alabama to play in the West Coast's prized bowl game.

The situation was a conundrum. In the eyes of Jim Murray and many outside the South, Alabama could not win for losing. There was vociferous criticism of any invitation for them to come to the Rose Bowl. And they were criticized for not accepting the invitations. Murray held nothing back. It was a white-and-black issue. The only way Alabama could redeem itself was to integrate.

Between 1965 and 1970 racial anger spilled into northern cities, with riots in Newark, Chicago, Detroit, and elsewhere. After the assassinations of Black Muslim leader Malcolm X and Dr. Martin Luther King Jr., the California-based Black Panther Party helped move the civil rights movement to a more militant direction. The *Los Angeles Times* covered all this as thoroughly as any newspaper in the nation. Many, even in the South, felt the *Times*'s coverage was the most fair-minded. Southerners viewed the *New York Times*, the *Washington Post*, and network television as "New York liberals"—old Civil War enemies. Because Los Angeles was outside that tradition, its media coverage of politics and sports was more acceptable to southern palates—except for Jim Murray's columns. Murray spoke his mind. He admired Bear Bryant and the skill of his athletes but found nothing good to say about Alabama's racial politics.

Murray was a man of pathos. On January 30, 1962, when Jackie Robinson was elected to the Hall of Fame, his column, "Jack Be Nimble," pointed out something profound about Robinson's impact on his team. For forty-six years before he became a Dodger, Brooklyn had won two pennants and no World Series. In his ten years with them, they captured six pennants, lost one in a play-off, lost another in the last game of the year, won one World Championship, and never finished lower than second. In all five of those Series losses, the Dodgers scraped until the end. In the five years that had passed since Robinson retired, they had won only one pennant. Yet it was Robinson's social role that continued to define him. "But the trouble Jackie made was good for the country like the trouble Lincoln made," Murray wrote. Robinson chided the Yankees for discrimination. "The Yankees denied it," wrote Murray. "But went out the next year and got Elston Howard."

In 1964 Murray wrote a piece about Negro League Baseball. He was one of the writers advocating that former Negro Leaguers such as Satchel Paige and Buck O'Neil be elected to the Baseball Hall of Fame. Paige eventually was. In a column called "Lot of Character," he praised the black umpire Emmett Ashford. He also wrote a laudatory column about black golfer Charlie Sifford. No black Dodger, Laker, Trojan, or other L.A. athlete ever found any fault with Murray. Many became close friends with him. He was willing to do what was right, but he was also willing to go beyond that. On January 21, 1969, Murray wrote a "Tribute to Abe" for Harlem Globetrotters founder Abe Saperstein. His team, he wrote, was as "powerful a lever at toppling prejudice as the Constitutional Amendment."

In 1964 and 1965 many Americans were aghast at the sight of the all-white Alabama Crimson Tide not only winning consecutive national championships but, in the most illegitimate of manners, being awarded the title prior to losing to Texas in the 1965 Orange Bowl.

Enter Jim Murray. Calling his column "'Bama in the Balkans," he opened,

So Alabama is the "National Champion," is it? Hah?

"National" champion of what? The Confederacy?

This team hasn't poked its head above the Mason-Dixon line since Appomattox. They've almost NEVER played a Big 10 team. One measly game with Wisconsin back in 1928 is all I can find. They lost.

This team wins the Front-of-the-Bus championship every year—largely with Pennsylvania quarterbacks. How can you win a "national" championship playing in a closet? How can you get to be "Number One" if you don't play anybody but your kinfolks? How do you know whether these guys are kicking over baby-carriages or slaying dragons?

Murray went on to write that he might respect Alabama's "national championship" if the team played Ohio State in Columbus, Michigan in Ann Arbor, or Notre Dame "anywhere." Bryant claimed his schedule was the best in the country, but Murray said there was no way to prove that because none of the other SEC teams played anybody "you couldn't invite to the Cotillion." He excoriated the conference and Alabama for letting great black athletes—who were "Americans" too, in case anybody forgot that—go to the Big Ten, the Pacific Coast, or Syracuse every year. *'Bama's* version of Old Glory, he said, should be "all white," absent the red, the blue, and the stars. Murray freely stated that 'Bama, and the SEC in general, played "ferocious" football in Dixie but added that the adjective could also be applied to a Balkan war. Bulgaria, he said, could not slaughter England, "just because it obliterates Mesopotamia."

Then Murray did the unforgiveable. He made fun of Bryant, who actually "walked on water" in a Coca-Cola billboard along the Alabama highway. He tied him to segregationist governor George Wallace, who was already touting himself as a presidential candidate. Here Murray made a rare misstep. Bryant and Wallace did not get along. Bryant mistrusted him, but Wallace knew he needed to look close to the coach to win votes.

For Alabama to be given real national title consideration, Murray wrote, they needed to "venture up in the snow country where the field is white but the players not necessarily. . . . Until then don't make me laugh."

Murray once called the Sugar Bowl the "White Supremacy Bowl." Bryant, he wrote, was "tired of winning the Magnolia championship." Murray's chidings did not go unnoticed by Alabama fans or Coach Bryant. While most in the region simply took umbrage, Bryant was smart enough to know that Jim Murray was a nationally read sports columnist who was highly respected and influential. He needed the likes of Jim Murray to create national respect for his football team. He needed the Jim Murrays of the American sporting scene to give his team the number one vote in the polls when they were in contention. He and USC coach John McKay were close personal friends. Bryant knew that McKay had great respect for Jim Murray. Murray could not simply be brushed aside as a "Connecticut Yankee" or a "liberal." He was a man of substance and needed to be dealt with.

In 1965 Bryant granted an interview to *Look* magazine. He may very well have been thinking of Jim Murray when he indicated that change was in the air and that black players were coming to the Southeastern Conference. Bryant was looking for the right time, the right opportunity. The George Wallace situation, his alumni base, and the politics of the times made the introduction of black players to the team perilous, but he had a plan. He said he would not be the first to integrate, "but I won't be third, either."

Murray riposted, "The South asks for terms." "Thems was fightin' words" in Alabama, and by proxy, Murray's challenge made the Trojans a rival of the Tide. USC was the one school in Murray's Los Angeles that would play anybody, anywhere.

The stage was set for more fireworks, and in the fall and winter of 1966 they exploded. Alabama was unbeaten, untied, and won the Sugar Bowl but finished third in the polls behind Notre Dame and Michigan State, both of whom tied each other and did not play in a bowl game. Alabama fans unfurled banners accusing Notre Dame of playing politics. A 'Bama newspaper showed a disgruntled Confederate soldier holding the AP poll and saying, "NUMBER 3—*HELL!*"

The fallout was tremendous. Not since the Civil War had the South felt as cornered as it did during the 1960s. Every pundit in the nation weighed in. None were so opinionated and open in their disdain of the University of Alabama as Mr. James Murray, the Irish Catholic gentleman from Malibu, California. His columns were read far and wide. In an age before the Bowl Championship Series and computers, sportswriters wielded incredible power, perhaps none more than Murray. There was no question in the minds of the Alabama football faithful that Murray was everything wrong with the world: Irish, Catholic, an East Coast native, and a West Coast liberal from the land of war protestors, hippies, and dilettantes. He could not have engendered greater hatred had he flown to Hanoi and taken photos of himself on a North Vietnamese tank, but of course nobody would be that crazy . . . would they?

"Jim Murray wrote a lot about this issue," Art Spander recalled in a 2007 interview. "He had a real social conscience. . . . He once wrote that Alabama was 'the King of the Caucasians.' There was debate about Alabama winning the national championship one year, and Jim influenced the votes by emphasizing that Alabama didn't have any blacks and didn't play any teams with blacks. There was a lot of stuff in the papers about that."

In the aftermath of the 1966 season, there was much soul-searching and blame-gaming in Alabama. The fans and the press tended to hunker down, taking an us-versus-them attitude. Southerners were in the right, their traditions were intruded on, the Feds had no right to come to their state, these were states' rights issues, et cetera. But Bear Bryant proved his leadership and took responsibility. He said he needed to put together a tougher, more diverse schedule. He said he wanted to prove on the field that Alabama was the best and not leave it up to the opinion of pollsters. He was already meticulously planning a drastic change. He just needed the opportunity.

Bryant had been born dirt poor in Arkansas. He identified with the plight of poor, rural blacks because he, too, came from nothing. His childhood friends had been black. He had served in the navy and managed a blues band. He had coached at Maryland, Kentucky, and Texas A&M before coming to Alabama in 1958, and he had attempted to integrate each program. The alumni and administration had rebuffed him at each turn. "That's the last thing we're gonna do," he was told at Texas A&M. "Well, last's where we'll finish then," Bryant drawled.

The politics of Alabama made it impossible to integrate when he arrived. A 1959 Liberty Bowl game with integrated Penn State was treated like it carried the plague. After that game, Bryant did something that set integration back years: he won three national titles. True, the 1964 title was not legitimate, as the Tide lost to Texas in the Orange Bowl, but the team's incredible success in the 1960s led everybody in the state to conclude that they simply did not need to integrate in order to win.

Enter John McKay. Cigar-chomping, iconoclastic, whiskey-drinking, conservative, Republican, Irish, Catholic, and Southern—from West Virginia—he was a good ol' boy tempered by military service and his years on the West Coast, at Oregon and USC. Because they were Catholic, his family had once had a cross burned on their lawn in West Virginia by the Ku Klux Klan. McKay turned USC from a mere power into a dynasty, largely on the strength of increased integration in the 1960s. John Wooden did the same thing with UCLA's basketball team during those years. The country took notice. Alumni at colleges everywhere realized they could have championship teams if they, too, recruited the next Jim Brown, Ernie Davis, Mike Garrett, Bobby Bell, or Lew Alcindor.

By 1970 Wallace was no longer governor of Alabama, and attitudes were changing. The tiniest of stirrings within the Alabama sports media began when Clarence Davis, born in Birmingham, made All-American as O. J. Simpson's replacement at USC in 1969. Bryant decided this was his moment to recruit a black player.

As he spoke to young black prep stars in the South about taking on the challenge of breaking 'Bama's "color barrier," he heard the same thing over and over. If they were to play for the Tide, they not only wanted fellow black teammates, but they also wanted to play games against integrated teams in integrated settings. Blacks were not keen on playing all their games at hostile, all-white campuses in Oxford, Mississippi, or Columbia, South Carolina. Could a game in Los Angeles, or Syracuse, or Ann Arbor be arranged?

This request ultimately catered to Bear Bryant's most powerful motivation: the national championship. The voices of a nation, led by Jim Murray, told him if the vote were at all close, he would be denied a championship so long as he continued to play all-white opponents. He was also persuaded by the fact that all-white Texas was awarded the 1969 national championship only after beating integrated Notre Dame in the Cotton Bowl.

In January 1970 the stage was set. Alabama's first black recruit, Wilbur Jackson, would be a freshman in the fall, and the National Collegiate Athletic Association unexpectedly announced that an eleventh game could be added to the schedule. Bryant called McKay, met him at the Los Angeles Airport's Western Airlines Horizon Room, and over cocktails, arranged a home-and-home game. If USC won, he could tell his alumni he needed to get the kind of "horses" they had in order to compete. If he beat the Trojans, his task would be trickier. He would face the old question, Why do we need to integrate? But he knew the Jim Murrays of the world would react to a failure to integrate with more righteous might than ever before. Bryant was counting on the sight of a classy, well-coached, highly disciplined Trojans squad impressing upon the 'Bama faithful a visual feast they could get used to seeing—a successful, integrated team. More than thirty years before, the sight of integrated USC-UCLA games had been exactly this kind of self-evident social statement.

But why the Trojans as opposed to Stanford, Syracuse, Michigan, or even Oklahoma, a quasi-Southern college that had successfully integrated a decade earlier? "I can see that Bryant chose McKay out of friendship, more so than choosing somebody else, based upon being less bitterly divisive than a school from the Yankee North," said *L.A. Times* sportswriter Jeff Prugh.

"I know my dad and Jim were very close and my dad had the greatest respect for him," recalled McKay's son, John K. "J. K." McKay, a Trojan star of the 1970s who played for the Tampa Bay Buccaneers, became an L.A. attorney, and is now USC's associate athletic director. "I can only imagine there was pressure in those times to speed up integration as it relates to sports. I was not frankly aware that Murray was writing those columns but he carried a lot of weight. He was a friend of my dad's, so that gave him credibility in Bear's eyes."

Aside from the Bryant-McKay relationship, USC represented a politically viable choice. USC was a conservative private school. Alabama fans would not have taken kindly to losing to a Northern California school, like Cal, whose campus fomented privileged anti-Americanism, while the South filled the ranks of Vietnam-era soldiers at a much higher rate than any other region. Moreover, right-wing Republicans such as Nixon and Reagan came from Orange Country—a place known as "Trojan country" for its significant alumni identity with USC—and lent the area a strong anticommunist image. Finally, USC and Los Angeles were Jim Murray's team and city. He would write about the game. If Murray got on board, the by-product might just be the deciding AP and UPI votes giving the Crimson Tide a national championship in the next few years.

When game day rolled around, "Jim Murray and I went to Birmingham—me first, Jim second, on Wednesday," recalled Prugh.

> The next day, we drove to Tuscaloosa, and Jim good-humoredly described as "elephant disease" our appointment with Bryant. We went in at 10 a.m. and his office looked like [it belonged to] the president of General Motors: mahogany paneling, Oriental trappings, with Bryant sitting at his desk in a dress shirt and tie, and the shirt looked like he had slept in it. As he talked, he spat into a large ashtray. Whether it was snuff or not, I don't know.
>
> It was very clear in talking to Bryant that he understood the social implications of this game. He volunteered that he was bemoaning the fact that USC had Clarence Davis at tailback, that he was born in Birmingham, and he was one who got away. Davis was the symbolism

that Bryant was trying to convey. If Davis had stayed in Alabama all those years, he'd've been at [the University of] Alabama.

Bryant made a big play of impressing Murray. There was no question he understood he needed Murray on his side. Many in the media did not quite grasp the social importance of the game. Bryant knew that Murray did. "My dad's relationship with Jim, a man of such stature, widely respected, I can see where Bryant would have wanted to have the opportunity to sit down and explain his position," said J. K. McKay.

Some have argued Bryant wanted his team to lose. He figured if 'Bama lost it would force his fans to realize they needed to change their ways in order to keep up with the USCs of college football. But Bryant did not want to lose—he was too competitive. He had a contingency plan in case his boys made good, but when USC trampled Alabama, 42-21, it turned out to be the best result he could have asked for.

Not only was USC integrated, with a black assistant coach (Willie Brown), the team also featured a black starting quarterback, Jimmy Jones. It had the only all-black backfield in history up until then (Jones, tailback Clarence Davis, fullback Sam Cunningham). Their defensive core, particularly at linebacker, was big, black, and imposing. They were a visual metaphor for an integrated society.

Jones was a fine field general and Davis played a great game, but the star was the sophomore from Santa Barbara, Cunningham. He rushed for 135 yards and two touchdowns, but his numbers belie his awesome effect. He literally bounced off 'Bama defenders. He could not be tackled. By the fourth quarter, members of the Birmingham crowd were so quiet, they could hear the shouts of USC players on the sidelines, or the cheers of a few black fans, rooting not for the Tide but the Trojans, given high end-zone seats. Finally, toward the end, the sound of gospel hymns rose above the crowd. A group of local blacks had gathered outside Legion Field with Bibles and candles to witness a kind of deliverance. They sang songs of Christian joy.

When the game was over, a throng of reporters, administrators, and alumni crowded into the USC dressing room, spilling out in the hallway. The sense of excitement and exhilaration was marked by a little bit of confusion. Then Bryant entered the dressing room, asking to "borrow" Cunningham. USC assistant coach

Craig Fertig accompanied them. Friendly alums and press diverted Fertig's attention. According to lore, Bryant took Cunningham into the 'Bama dressing room. Glistening with sweat, shirtless, and wearing only hip pads, the fullback was propped up on a stool and looked down on the beaten white boys of Alabama.

Bryant was said to have stated, "Gentleman, this ol' boy, I mean this man, Sam Cunningham, number 39. This man and his Trojan brothers just ran us right out of Legion Field. Raise your heads and open your eyes. This here's what a football player looks like." Then, the coach is said to have instructed each Tide player to shake Sam's hand. Various phrases such as "You're a better man than me" (attributed to 'Bama quarterback Scott Hunter and others) were offered to Cunningham. This story was repeated by McKay, Fertig, assistant coach Marv Goux, announcer Tom Kelly, and others in the media and at alumni banquets for years. There is no evidence that Murray ever repeated it, perhaps because the canny Irishman sensed that it was malarkey.

It was not until 2004–2007 that the truth, as much as can be divined, came out. Murray was gone by then. Not a single Alabama player or assistant coach who was in that dressing room said that it happened. Cunningham said, "I hate to be the one to admit it didn't happen, but it didn't." Fertig admitted he had been busy yakking with others and missed whatever happened. Time, a deadline, excitement, passion, heat—all these factors played into the fuzziness of memory as the story was repeated over the years.

What most likely happened is Bryant took Cunningham into the crowded hallway. There, in front of press, alumni, and administrators, he told him he was "what a football player looks like." He shook his hand as an object lesson to reactionary elements in his state. He probably repeated the phrase Cunningham was "what a football player looks like" in that hallway several times and, later, within earshot of writers. Cunningham himself said the door to the 'Bama dressing room was open and he could see players inside, quiet and beaten. A few of those players could see and hear what Bryant was doing with Cunningham in the hallway. A few, according to Cunningham, came into the hallway to shake his hand. The fullback himself did not hear the story until his pro career ended more than a decade later. By then the legend was complete and his own memory fuzzy.

How it went down was rather immaterial. "No, it didn't happen," said Scott Hunter, "but it should have happened. The story was too good not to be true." He was right. The spirit of Bryant's words somehow changed hearts and minds in the South.

It was a night game. The West Coast writers, including Jim Murray and Jeff Prugh, had three hours of leeway but were still under a deadline to get the interviews and postgame anecdotes and to compile game stories and columns for the Sunday, September 13 editions. The September 13, 1970, *L.A. Times* sports page featured a photo of quarterback Jimmy Jones throwing a pass next to the headline "Trojans Fall on Alabama; Bruins' Rally Defeats OSU." Prugh wrote, "It was a night when stars of Cardinal and Gold fell on Alabama. And the brightest star of them all—as USC's Trojans blasted once mighty Alabama, 42-21, Saturday night—was Sam Cunningham, a towering rookie fullback who runs like a locomotive."

The game was not televised, so what happened on Legion Field had almost a Gettysburg quality, requiring a Lincolnesque visual picture. Nobody was better equipped for the task than Murray. Of all the columns that Jim Murray wrote, however, the one printed across the top of the September 13, 1970, *L.A. Times* sports page remains the best of his career: "Hatred Shut Out as Alabama Finally Joins the Union":

BIRMINGHAM—OK, you can put another star in the Flag.

On a warm and sultry night when you could hear train whistles hooting through the piney woods half county away, the state of Alabama joined the Union. They ratified the Constitution, signed the Bill of Rights. They have struck the Stars and Bars. They now hold these truths to be self-evident, that all men are created equal in the eyes of the Creator.

Our newest state took the field against a mixed bag of hostile black and white American citizens without police dogs, tear gas, rubber hoses or fire hoses. They struggled fairly without the aid of their formidable ally, Jim Crow.

Bigotry wasn't suited up for a change. Prejudice got cut from the squad. Will you all please stand and welcome the sovereign state of Alabama to the United States of America? It was a long time coming, but we always knew we'd be 50 states strong some day, didn't we? Now, we can get on with it. So chew a carpet, George Wallace. . . . Get out of our way. We're trying to build a country to form a Democracy.

The game? Shucks, it was just a game. You've seen one, you've seen 'em all. . . . Hatred got shut out, that's the point. Ignorance got shut out, that's the point. Ignorance fumbled on the goal line. Stupidity never got to the line of scrimmage. The big lie got tackled in the end zone.

Murray went on to write that the previous time he had been in Alabama, the only black man in the stadium was carrying towels. But "a man named Martin Luther King" thought that if you paid for a seat on the bus, one ought to be able to sit in it. The only thing white folk in the state cared about was "beating Georgia Tech."

Murray pointed out that the citizens of Alabama took their football so seriously that they realized if they wanted to play in the big time, it would require integration. Otherwise, instead of invites to all the best bowl games, they would continue to be relegated to the Bluebonnet Bowl. "And," wrote Murray, "if I know football coaches, you won't be able to tell Alabama by the color of their skin much longer. You'll need a program just like the Big 10."

He was prescient, but remarkably few others were. Murray recognized what Coach Bryant was trying to do, something even the likes of McKay, Marv Goux, Sam Cunningham, and the fans in the stands did not fully understand. After this game, hatred was benched, and a nation lived up to its creed. Murray's turning of phrases—"Hatred got shut out. . . . Ignorance fumbled on the goal line. . . . Stupidity never got to the line of scrimmage"—were classics. His reference to a far away train whistle hearkened back to descriptions of his own youth, when the sound of a locomotive in the distance conjured images of a bigger world to conquer (this imagery also played heavily in speeches of the era by President Richard Nixon in describing his dirt-poor upbringing in California). In 2006 CBS and College Sports Television produced a documentary about the game with a title that was pure Jim Murray: *Tackling Segregation*.

"I can't say for certain, but I think Murray got involved in this whole debate, but when I heard that Sam Cunningham 'integrated' Alabama football, then all the South, well Jim influenced those events," recalled Art Spander.

"A little anecdote is, I reported this on the Monday follow-up, I was at the Holiday Inn in Birmingham, and men were sitting around the table, obviously football fans," recalled Prugh. "I overhead both men say, 'I bet Bear wishes he had some of them nigra boys on their team.' That was the new sentiment, the post-mortem, and it was revolutionary. It was obvious that things were going to change from that day forward, but I could not anticipate the pace and speed of change."

"Jim Murray was one of the writers who got me excited about being a sports journalist out of college," said Keith Dunnavant, author of *The Missing Ring: How Bear Bryant and the 1966 Alabama Crimson Tide Were Denied College Football's Most Elusive Prize* and *Coach: Life of Paul "Bear" Bryant.*

I started at the *Times* in 1988. I was on the Orange County staff, a mere punk of 22, for less than a year. He was the master of simile with an incredible turn of phrase.

In 1961 he had a big impact on Alabama not being invited to the Rose Bowl. There was no doubt that this was a turning point in the program, causing new thinking to enter into the process. It certainly inspired them to change with the times.

Dunnavant was asked whether Bryant scheduled the game to appease the likes of Jim Murray and whether Bear Bryant made a purposeful decision to host an extended in-office interview the week of the game with Murray and Jeff Prugh. "Coaches did more interviews with the media in those days," he replied.

Let's clear up a myth. Alabama was already integrated, but Jim's 1970 column was a huge part of the process. But let me be on the record on saying that Wilbur Jackson already was on that team, but Bear was trying to change Alabamian minds, plus Wendell Hudson was a basketball player there. I agree with the premise that he had to change hearts and minds in his fan base in order to help smooth the path for Wilbur. Teams were already being integrated. 'Bama was not on the leading edge of this, but not that far out.

There were several reasons they did not win in 1966. One that tipped the balance in a contentious struggle was the Alabama football team was in a struggle for the meaning of the name of Alabama in the nation's consciousness. Is it Wallace or is it Bryant? It was both. Lots of people assumed certain things, but even though 'Bama was segregated, it was more complicated than, pardon, black and white.

Another issue that comes to mind, and I guess I am liberal on the racial question—I never went to segregated schools, never saw violence—but they looked at a guy like Jim Murray and said he was acting hypocritically. He was right on the larger point that Alabama had no blacks, but there were no blacks on the news staff of the *L.A. Times* at the time of the 1965 Watts riots. Racism was a stain on America, but it looked different in the South than in the North and West at the time that Murray was writing about the issue.

I was in grade school, four years at an integrated school when rioting broke out in South Boston over busing. The horror of all that stuff; I'd never experienced anything like that not in my little town. People like Wilbur Jackson and Sylvester Croom were transforming the culture of Alabama.

Let me stress what an admirer I am of Murray, an incredible wordsmith, one of the twentieth centuries' iconic names in sports journalism, right near the top of the list. I grew up with Murray and Dave Kindred of the *Atlanta Journal-Constitutional*, Frank Deford; if you lived in a big city with at least one newspaper and were a sports fan, you connected with that guy three, four times a week. You saw his picture, felt you knew him. He was the identity of that paper, and Murray was the *Times* shining light, a beacon.

"With Jim, civil rights was a moral issue," said his widow, Linda McCoy-Murray. "It was not a religious issue really, but just the right thing to do. He hated injustice and used his position when he saw a wrong being perpetrated."

In 1971, Alabama indeed came to L.A. Bryant had recruited more blacks in addition to Jackson, and his team defeated USC in the rematch, 17-10. By 1973 Jackson was voted team captain, and the roster was dotted with black players now regarded as all-time greats in the Crimson Tide pantheon. Asked in 2005 about his time at Alabama, Jackson said, "If it was not as great as it was I never would have sent both my daughters there," which is, as Murray might have said, voting with your feet—or your pocketbook. Fully integrated, the Alabama football team enjoyed its greatest decade in the 1970s, winning national championships in 1978–79. Bryant retired in 1983 as the winningest coach of all time.

Jim Murray became a fan of Bear Bryant, even a friend. He wrote of him often, glowingly. The South came to realize that Murray was merely prodding them to listen to the better angels of their nature. Incredibly, his voice remains the only one that really got it then and there. No Alabama media outlet made mention of race in the immediate aftermath of the 1970 Alabama-USC game. There were no editorials suggesting that integration might help the Tide roll faster. If Alabama had been hoping to sweep the race issue under the rug, it would not have been able to because, to use another cliché, the "horse was out of the barn."

Murray had vision. "Birmingham will never be the same," he wrote. "And brother, it's a good thing. The point of the game will not be the score, the Bear, the Trojans; the point of the game will be Reason, Democracy, Hope. The real winner will be the South. It'll be their first since the second day at Gettysburg, or maybe, The Wilderness."

The following Thursday, in a column titled "Language of Alabama," Murray wrote, "Time to time, when I visit a neighboring country to the South, I try to pass on to you some of the key phrases which will help you to get along in a strange tongue. . . . Alabama is a body of land separated from the main body of the United States by a century." Murray continued with a "non-Berlitz course" that prompted a flood of pro and con letters to the *Times* over the next couple of weeks. In the years after he wrote about the game, Murray was happy to discover that the South indeed had grown up, and he was more than pleased to eat any uncomplimentary words he wrote about 'Bama and the region.

Birmingham-born Florida State coach Bobby Bowden thought that the USC-Alabama game was able to "change the minds of Alabama fans." Indeed, he was right. Not Murray's admonitions, federal troops, legislation, speeches, or protest marches could change "hearts and minds." The Catholic Murray did not like to trumpet faith in his columns, but in private he might have agreed, at least to some extent, that God used the players, coaches, even himself, as vessels to effect change. The second civil war was over.

It could be argued that the American South between 1970 and 1973, and then over a more prolonged period, changed faster and for the better more than any region in history. In so doing, it "rose again." The region became an economic juggernaut. Pro franchises flooded into big southern cities— Jacksonville, Nashville, Charlotte—and their college sports programs became the envy of a nation. Atlanta hosted the 1996 Olympics.

Husbanded into the union and mainstream American politics by Richard Nixon and Ronald Reagan, the South became a "Republican lock," to the consternation of Democrats and the Left. Consider the 1978 football season. USC returned to Birmingham. The Trojans were loaded with black stars as always, but so was Alabama. Writers and players making that trip do not recall that the racial issue was ever raised. In this respect, the success of the integration of Alabama football is most obvious. It was subliminal, quiet, and peaceful, just as Bryant planned it. It was self-evident, manifest. It needed no champion, no loud voices.

USC again defeated Alabama; it was the Tide's only loss that season. USC likewise lost one game. Both teams won their bowls and finished with even records. Logically, the national championship should have been awarded to the Trojans. Instead, USC had to share the championship, capturing the UPI (coaches) poll while Alabama took the AP (writer's) poll.

Twelve years earlier the vote had so famously gone against the Tide. Now, having successfully integrated, Bear Bryant was a beloved figure, his team a source of pride and joy to people of all colors. Nobody said it at the time, but Bryant and his team should have called a press conference to thank Jim Murray. Murray's exhortation of the coach and school to do the right thing and his praise of them when they did as much to change the minds of voters as Sam Cunningham's touchdown runs.

Jim Murray continued to write about race, politics, and social issues, although never with the religious urgency he felt compelled to exhibit in the 1960s. He wrote a chapter in his autobiography called "Some of My Best Friends Are . . .":

> In the decades since Robinson, baseball's integration is taken for granted. It is sometimes a non-issue. But it surfaces from time to time where you least expect it. An Al Campanis takes to the air to spout a lot of nonsense about black capabilities—managing or general-managing a baseball team is probably the easiest thing to do in our society next to being a guard at a railroad crossing where two trains a week come through.
>
> But the integration, astonishingly, has never become total. You would have thought by now these would be fast, permanent interracial friendships. That players of different colors would become cronies after years of dressing and playing and showering alongside each other.

If so, I have never observed it. Back in the days when players slept two to a room, some clubs endeavored to hasten the mix by rooming blacks with whites. The facts of the matter are that neither the blacks nor whites were happy with this arrangement.

There are still some clubhouses where there seems to be two teams, one white, one black. Sometimes, there's a third: Spanish-speaking. On occasion, when teammates get in a barroom fracas or otherwise on a police blotter, you can read the resultant story and find the miscreants are either all white—or all black.

A Utopian society was not in the cards. It was not unlike the 1971 Alabama victory over USC. John McKay graciously granted his friend's team a game that he needed to effectuate change. In 1971 at the Coliseum, the first 'Bama player to run past him on the opening kick was John Mitchell, an African American star from Alabama ticketed for USC until Bryant integrated and "stole" him away. "Well," McKay said wryly as he turned to Craig Fertig, "that's what you get."

So too with the 1978 split national title decision. Murray, the Trojan fan, undoubtedly voted USC number one, but his work had contributed to conditions making it possible for the Tide to get the vote they previously did not get. Well, that's what you get.

11

Halcyon Days

Steve Bisheff was a young USC graduate making "no money" writing for Bud Furillo's *Los Angeles Herald-Examiner*. He and another USC man, Allan Malamud, were part of a new wave of young talents who had arrived on the scene in the 1960s and 1970s. Malamud, a veteran of the *Daily Trojan*, started professionally at the *Herald-Examiner* but later became a respected colleague of Murray's at the *Times*, where he wrote a popular item called "Notes on a Scorecard."

"I met Murray at a young age in L.A.," Bisheff recalled.

> I was with the old *L.A. Herald-Examiner* and got to know him [when I was a] "rookie" on the Rams' beat. He traveled to road games and the play-offs. Everyone was a little in awe of the guy. To those of us in the sportswriting business, he was our hero. I remember being nervous sitting down to dinner with him on the road, or at Dodger Stadium or the Coliseum, but he'd put you at ease. He was completely unpretentious and could not have been nicer. He and Mal Florence had been around forever, and we really looked up to these men.

Bisheff said Murray was a "master at hype" who "overwhelmed you with knowledge of history. The man was so literate, nobody wrote that way before." Everyone coming up through the USC journalism school "tried to copy him." His style was "like punching, with quick shots." Murray was "very liberal related to the stuff that needed to be written, but not many were willing to write that way," Bisheff said in reference to racial issues. "He was unpretentious, but I remember once he was sitting in the press box after a game, and we're both writing our stories. It occurred to me, 'I'm trying to compete with Jim Murray.' He would look over and smile and say, 'Well, we fooled 'em again,' and you'd say to yourself, 'Yeah, right.'"

Writing for Bud Furillo, Bisheff was aware of a *Times-Herald* rivalry. The *Times* was big, while the *Herald*, except for Mel Durslag, struggled.

We were always the underdog so we tried to be more irreverent, more fun. The *Times* was the "paper of record," and that made the fact Murray was different, more loose and funny, stand out in their paper.

Furillo and Durslag talked every day and sure, the subject often was Jim Murray. What was he writing? How do we respond? Murray played a huge role at the *Times*. We had nobody quite like that. We all said, "Did you read Murray today?" You constantly referred to Murray. He quickly reached people outside of L.A. People picked up on his quotes. He had the background of a national magazine and the Hollywood connection.

Bisheff agreed that Murray created what could be called the "L.A. style," which was jaunty, lively, and looser than, say, the staid *New York Times*. The *L.A. Times* had been stodgy before Murray arrived. The columnist, however, was not afraid to write anything.

■ ■ ■

As bad as the 1960s and '70s were domestically, for California sports fans they heralded a golden age. New York in the 1950s was a pale comparison. The greatness started in 1962, when the Dodgers and Giants battled for a pennant and USC captured the national title on the gridiron, and ended in 1994, when the San Francisco 49ers won their fifth Super Bowl. In between were three decades of unmatched football glory for USC; twelve years of basketball greatness at UCLA; five straight College Series wins for the Trojans; Olympic Games in which USC and UCLA, had they been countries, would have been among the medals leaders; Dodger greatness and near-greatness; Lakers "Showtime" and even a Golden State Warriors title; "the greatness that is the Raiders"; perhaps pro football's best dynasty (49ers); and numerous moments of excitement for the Rams, Angels, Kings, colleges, and preps.

What a cornucopia for Jim Murray! In Los Angeles, enthusiasm and success reigned supreme. Attendance was down at many sports stadiums. Many arenas were old, decrepit, or poorly constructed, ill-advisedly designed to serve more than one sport and serving none of them well. Dodger Stadium and the

Dodgers were often referred to as the big leagues. Players wanted to be traded there. Their beautiful stadium, spring training facilities, private plane, huge crowds—no other team in baseball came close to matching their class.

Real estate values in Southern California shot through the roof. The armament business, still humming away next to the 405 Freeway from the airport to the Long Beach Naval shipyards, was in full swing thanks to an out-of-control nuclear arms race. Business was centered on the Pacific Rim. Computer technology was peaking, and California was its hub. In film, never before or since has Hollywood rivaled its production. Just as the 1970s were halcyon days for the city, so too were they a great time for Otis Chandler, the *Los Angeles Times*, and its star columnist Jim Murray.

■ ■ ■

The year 1971 was big for Los Angeles. In January the *L.A. Times* blared the headline, "Manson Verdict: All Guilty." Shortly thereafter, on February 10, an enormous earthquake hit the Southland. The front page featured a photo of patients evacuated from a San Fernando hospital, near the quake's epicenter.

In June, Gene Blake and Jack Nelson covered one of the most controversial stories in U.S. history, with profound implications. Daniel Ellsberg, once a Defense Department strategist tasked with defeating communism in Vietnam, had leaked the "Pentagon Papers," a long history of government secrets, to the *New York Times*. The decision to leak to the *New York Times*—after the *Times* staff was ordered not to print the Pentagon Papers, the *Washington Post* did—is worth noting. Ellsberg lived in the Los Angeles area. He was a consultant at the Rand Corporation in Santa Monica. He may have thought that the *L.A. Times*, owned by the conservative Chandler, would choose not to break such a story because it could be considered treasonous.

The era was one of huge government revelation, and more was on the way. The My Lai massacre had rocked the public's perception of the Vietnam War. By 1971 most Americans were firmly opposed to it.

The *L.A. Times* September 28 front page featured a story by Dial Torgerson, "Whew! Now It's Smog, Blackouts with Fierce Heat," critical of Los Angeles's lousy air quality. To those who experienced it, the smog and pollution were almost mind-blowing, and yet, incredibly, some of the greatest athletes, teams, and games ever played were performed under these horrid conditions.

■ ■ ■

The year 1972 was probably, up until then, the high point in the history of Los Angeles, in almost all ways people might measure such a thing. It certainly was for the Republicans, although that year it seemed as if everybody in America had voted for the GOP. On the strength of opening up relations with China and bringing the Vietnam War to an end, the Southern California native Nixon recaptured the White House, winning forty-nine of fifty states. The Right convinced itself that the election results were a complete repudiation of everything the 1960s stood for. It was the biggest landslide in presidential election history, coming with a popular vote of more than 60 percent in a sweeping win over South Dakota senator George McGovern.

If 1962 was a "California year" in sports, 1972 was *the* California year. USC was in the middle of the most dominant run in the history of collegiate athletics and won national championships in a variety of sports. What USC did not win, UCLA did. The 1972 basketball season in particular was almost above comprehension. Sophomore center Bill Walton was sensational, unquestionably on the same level as Lew Alcindor had been. He led the Bruins to an unbeaten year in which they were never challenged en route to another NCAA championship, achieved at the L.A. Sports Arena. The '72 Bruins are on anybody's short list of the best teams in collegiate history.

After the season, Murray wrote a column about Coach John Wooden called "Hoosier Hotshot." It was classic Murray sarcasm, leading off with the image of a typical college basketball coach as a guy with lots of diamonds, an entourage, an ego the size of New York, and nicknames like "the Baron" or "the Bear." The "American Gothic" Wooden, Murray wrote, put championship teams together with "elements as diverse as a Democratic ticket." They had to play in "Venice High gyms, on City College parking lots and at auditoriums built for auto shows, not zone presses" until "his monument," Pauley Pavilion, was built a good ten years after he had been promised when he was hired in 1948. Someday, Murray conjectured, a photo of Raquel Welch in a bikini would replace Wooden's Pyramid of Success, but "the Wizard" would be frowning, someplace.

When the National Basketball Association season began, fans checking out the box scores to see how many points Lew Alcindor scored were surprised to see that he was not in the lineup. Instead, some guy named Kareem

Abdul-Jabbar was making up the difference, scoring thirty points a game with fifteen rebounds most nights. Alcindor, a Muslim already, had publicly changed his name to honor his religion. Murray was unimpressed. "He didn't like Kareem Abdul-Jabbar," said Art Spander. "He came into the league with his stuff shot and different way of thinking, and Jim didn't like things that were away from the norm. He didn't like Muhammad Ali."

The Lakers ran up an all-time professional record thirty-three-game winning streak and finished with the best record in NBA history, 69-13. Then they knocked off New York in five games. Jerry West finally had his title. At least until the 1995–96 Chicago Bulls, the '72 Lakers were thought by many to be the best team of all time.

But the best was saved for the last. The 1972 USC football team is still believed to be the finest collegiate gridiron squad ever assembled. Such luminaries as Dan Jenkins, Keith Jackson, and Lee Corso are a few of the experts who agree on this assessment. The Trojans rolled through the season without challenge at 12–0, annihilating Ohio State, 42-17, in the Rose Bowl. Against Notre Dame, Anthony Davis rushed for six touchdowns in a game that could go down as the best single-day performance ever.

But sports news in 1972 was not all good. The baseball players had the audacity to strike from April 1 to 13, and for the first time regular season games were canceled. But that was nothing compared with the Munich Olympics, when Black September, a Palestinian terrorist organization formed by Yasir Arafat, kidnapped and then murdered most of the Israeli Olympic team. It was the most blatant intrusion of war, politics, and terror into the world of sports that had been seen in the modern era.

Dwight Chapin covered USC and UCLA sports for the *L.A. Times* in the 1970s. He and his friend and partner, Jeff Prugh, were both assigned to the Bruins' basketball beat, which was at its all-time high mark during this period. Chapin shared the same name as Dwight L. Chapin, Richard Nixon's appointments secretary. Because the political Chapin was a USC graduate, many confused the two. When sportswriter Chapin traveled to Maryland for the NCAA basketball tournament, he was given a friendly White House tour by the appointments secretary.

Both Prugh (who passed away in 2009) and Chapin were heavily influenced by Jim Murray. Their shared desire to write not just about sports, but also about the world, to incorporate sports into their larger observations, came directly from the cutting-edge Murray. Chapin and Murray were together when the ultimate crossover between politics and sports took place at Munich in 1972.

"I have a strong memory of him when we were the only *L.A. Times* sports-writers assigned to the 1972 Munich Olympics, and we flew to Munich together," recalled Chapin.

> He rented a car at the airport and asked me to ride with him to our quarters in the Olympic Village. The only problem was, his eyesight already was not the best, and I assume he missed a turn or two. Anyway, he was soon wandering around in what looked like marshes and it was getting dark quickly. We both started laughing because we could see the headline, "*Times* Writers Lost on Their Way to the Olympics." We eventually found our way back to the right highway, but Jim would bring up that wandering day/night every time I saw him.

Chapin also recalled working another event with Murray. "I was working desk shift one night when he was covering the Indy 500. He had planned to go back to his hotel to write his column after the race but the track was hit by a strong rainstorm before he left and the parking lot was so snarled he couldn't get out. So he had to dictate his column, cold. I took the column from him over the phone, and it was letter perfect. I've never forgotten that."

Jim Murray moved from Malibu to a section of Brentwood just east of the 405 Freeway in December 1972. Located in the Los Angeles 90049 zip code, it was one of the most prestigious addresses in the city, a part of Brentwood some referred to as lower Bel Air. Near Sunset Boulevard, it was a few blocks from the UCLA campus. Brentwood is generally thought of as the neighborhood west of the freeway, adjacent to Pacific Palisades at the bottom of the Santa Monica Mountains, where O. J. Simpson lived with his wife before her murder. Technically it snakes across the freeway to an area many think of as Bel Air, which is actually a gated community across the street from the UCLA campus, extending into the hills and canyons and rising up toward Mulholland Drive.

Murray's eyesight was declining. Driving was becoming a problem, and the trek from Malibu was becoming more and more crowded on the Pacific

Coast Highway. Brentwood was in the middle of the action, relatively near Dodger Stadium and the Coliseum and next door to UCLA. It was obviously a comfortable, wealthy part of town, but for the writer, the move came with reservations. He had fallen in love with the beach life—not just girls in bathing suits and the "woodys" traversing the surf route, but the winter conditions, the fog rolling in to meet the Santa Monica Mountains, and the mournful fog horns out at sea.

He wrote his ode to Malibu, to which he did not awake on Christmas morning for the first time in eighteen years. He preferred the ocean, but by 1973 getting to places like Anaheim Stadium and the Forum was becoming too difficult. He wrote that he would miss the rain sweeping in from an ocean storm, "leaving the temples of the mountains with the hoar of mist, what the poet calls 'compassionate sweet laughter of the rain, gray-eyed daughters of the mist above the flawed and driven tide.'"

■ ■ ■

The year 1973 started out with the U.S. Supreme Court handing down its decision on *Roe v. Wade*. The court determined that a woman's right to have an abortion could not be restricted by individual states without strict scrutiny of the law.

Jim Murray, the student of history and product of parochial schools, could have predicted based on his studies that hubris and arrogance were the great equalizers of a fallen, corrupt humanity, that "pride goeth before the fall." For a brief period, the United States of America stood astride the world like a colossus. Richard Nixon was not a president, he was a potentate, a puppet master pulling the world's strings. Then came Watergate. The May 1 *Los Angeles Times* blared the headline, "Knew of Burglary, Ehrlichman Says" under "Ziegler Offers an Apology." The June 18, 1972, *Times* headline "Five Held in Plot to Bug Democratic Office" and article by Alfred Lewis were given scant attention at the time. The crime was denied by all; Nixon called it a "third-rate burglary." Zealous supporters, rabid Cuban anticommunists, well meaning in their desire to fight evil, were deemed responsible. Initially Nixon skated.

Beginning in March 1973, a drip-drip-drip of accusations and revelations began. Quickly, the story unraveled, and the guilty rushed to save their skins. A single "good soldier," G. Gordon Liddy, remained tight-lipped, paying for his silence with a long prison sentence. But Chief of Staff H. R. Haldeman and top aide John Ehrlichman had known about the crime from the beginning. Former attorney general John Mitchell was also in on it. Legal counsel John Dean spilled the beans. A host of other powerful men went down for the count. They were *All the President's Men*, the title of a book by intrepid *Washington Post* reporters Bob Woodward and Carl Bernstein. The *Post* scooped the *L.A. Times* for much of the Watergate scandal, but not always. Jack Nelson was able to outfox Woodward and Bernstein on at least one or two key stories.

The *Times* found itself in a difficult position in 1973 because Otis Chandler faced government accusations of wrongdoing in an oil investment scheme that had been orchestrated by his old Stanford pal, Jack Burke. "I knew him the last two years at Stanford," recalled Chandler. "I will never forget that: Jack Burke sitting there destroying all my hopes and dreams." Nixon was not happy with Otis Chandler as it was because he was not the supporter his father had been. But Watergate swallowed Nixon up. He was not able to exact any major price against Chandler, the *Times*, or the rest of the media, almost all of whom were on his infamous "enemies list." Chandler's reputation was damaged by Burke, but not irreparably.

Naturally, the *Los Angeles Times* covered Watergate with a fine-tooth comb. History records that it was Woodward and Bernstein, Ben Bradlee and the *Washington Post* who broke and expanded the story. But many of the players were Southern Californians. That proximity, and the personalities arrayed, made the *Times* a paper of record when it came to Watergate. Nixon was caught on tape infamously ordering his men to go after Chandler and the *L.A. Times*. The president said that he knew how they operated, he was from there, and "those sons of bitches" would pay via tax audits and other forms of government abuse of power.

Then there was the Nixon administration–USC connection, which the *Times* gleefully exploited. Many Trojans were among the administration officials. First Lady Patricia Nixon was a USC graduate. Haldeman attended USC before transferring to UCLA. Appointments secretary Dwight L. Chapin, press secretary Ron Ziegler, aide Bart Porter, and legal counsel Gordon Strachan were all USC men. Kissinger's aide, Mike Guhin, and Michael Woodson, who coordinated Nixon's 1969 inaugural, attended USC with Donald Segretti (who supposedly coined the phrase "USC Mafia"), a young lawyer recruited by

Chapin to disrupt the 1972 Democrat primaries. Longtime aide Herb Klein attended USC as well.

This no doubt delighted many over at UCLA, as Watergate proved to be a major bone of contention in football rivalries and halftime demonstrations. Bruins fans took to calling USC the "University of Spoiled Children," a privileged Republican school. Stanford's band, eschewing traditional uniforms in favor of cock-eyed red jackets, untucked shirts, and fishing hats, employed a Nazi salute when USC's band played. They mocked Troy as somewhere between the Third Reich and the Roman Empire, meanwhile performing a "Tribute to Chairman Mao" that left announcer Chris Schenkel speechless. Mao's Cultural Revolution was at that time at the height of a killing spree that ultimately left about 55 million Chinese murdered. University of California–Berkeley students dumbly waved their credit cards when USC's band played "Conquest." Sports had become sociopolitical.

The sports year started on a sad note when Pittsburgh Pirates superstar Roberto Clemente was killed in a plane crash while trying to fly relief supplies to earthquake victims in Nicaragua. On January 3 Murray paid homage to the Puerto Rican hero, the man who created a breakthrough for Latino stars, in a column called "Clemente: You Had to See Him to Believe Him." Clemente was the type of guy who would claim his back was broken and then "go three-for-four with a stolen base and three outfield assists," he wrote. The worse his supposed ailment, "the worse the pitchers felt." Clemente often argued with Murray because Murray did not believe Clemente was as sick as he claimed to be. It was good-natured. Clemente sensed Murray was a kindred spirit, a supporter of his cause, which at the time was equality for Spanish-speaking ballplayers.

"He didn't answer questions so much as he delivered orations," Murray wrote. "He could lecture brilliantly on osteopathy, orthopedics or the anatomy. But he was Calamity Jane of the dugout. He was always playing the last act of *Camille*. It was funny to be sitting there talking to this figure that looked as if it had just walked off a Michelangelo pedestal and hear it talking like something in a TB [tuberculosis] ward."

Murray said Clemente was the best World Series player (star of the Pirates' 1960 and 1971 title teams) he had seen since Babe Ruth and Lou Gehrig, quite a statement since he had also seen Joe DiMaggio, Mickey Mantle, Whitey Ford, Sandy Koufax, and Bob Gibson.

Also in 1973, one of the greatest boxing matches ever fought almost didn't happen. The legendary Joe Frazier squared off against formidable challenger, George Foreman. The 1968 Olympic champion, Foreman entered the pantheon of boxing superstardom by knocking Frazier out almost as soon as the fight began on February 5. Murray thought it a disaster, theorizing that in giving Foreman his shot, Frazier blew the economic benefits of a rematch with Ali. In this rare case, he was wrong. His miscalculation was comparable to that of the guy who "bought into the market on October 29, 1929." The Foreman-Frazier fight, which produced Howard Cosell's famed "down goes Frazier" quote, did as much for boxing as any other match. It expanded interest. Instead of just two champion-contenders, now there were three. Over the next few years, the fight game would see some of the greatest matches ever, involving Ali, Foreman, and Frazier. They became international events.

They became international events in 1973, as was the performance of the greatest racehorse who ever lived, Secretariat. Before this horse captured the Triple Crown at the Belmont Stakes, Murray wrote that after the race was won, "His stud book will be busier than a sultan's."

During the 1973 NBA play-offs, Murray wrote a fanciful column in which he featured Bill Russell of the Celtics as a sort of medieval knight, tasked with stopping the "giant," Wilt Chamberlain. Using metaphors from *Jack and the Beanstalk, Gulliver's Travels*, and the Old Testament, Murray spun a literary cautionary tale about Chamberlain's constant challenge. After Russell came Abdul-Jabbar and Willis Reed. In the end Murray concluded, "Wilt, You Can't Win." The Lakers were again favored in the NBA Finals but were unable to pull a repeat against New York.

Around Thanksgiving, Murray wrote a column titled "Thankful, But . . ." It was typical of his iconoclasm and included a return to an old issue, the South and civil rights. "I'm thankful the Old South finally got blacks in university backfields and lines—but I'd be more thankful if the rooting sections would put away those Confederate flags."

■ ■ ■

Amid worldwide gas shortages—the Arab world's reaction to two wars lost to Israel within six years—1974 brought more bad news. The May 18 *Times* front page informed readers that India was now a member of the "nuclear club." At the time, the country had not yet decided whether to ally itself with the United States or the Union of Soviet Socialist Republics, so this news was particularly disturbing.

On that same front page, blaring headlines and shocking photos described a shoot-out between the Los Angeles Police Department and a leftist terrorist organization, the Symbionese Liberation Army, along the 1400 block of East 54th Street in South-Central L.A. "SLA Hideout Stormed, 5 Die," screamed the headline above a story written by Al Martinez and Robert Kistler. The SLA was infamous for having abducted newspaper heiress Patricia Hearst in Berkeley. Supposedly indoctrinated to hate her role as a rich white girl and therefore "responsible" for the plight of minorities and the poor for time immemorial, Hearst was said to have become a participant in the SLA's bank robberies.

Jack Nelson covered in excruciating, day-by-day detail the Watergate mess, which never seemed to end. Throughout the spring and summer near-daily revelations about the cover-up were exposed, to the consternation of conservatives who saw all their gains crumble like a house of cards. Finally, on August 8 a *Times* extra blared simply "Nixon Quits." Nixon flew to San Clemente, and the paper wrote a series of aftermath stories with a local flavor to them. Staff writer Kenneth Reich found the former president sheltered at his two-hundred-acre state. After being pardoned by President Gerald Ford in September and now living by the sea, Nixon said he had a new perspective on his presidency. He added that Watergate was "a burden I shall bear for every day" until he passed away.

In November the Democrats swept into office. Ronald Reagan set his sights on the 1976 presidential race. Reagan's plans, however, were thrown into turmoil by Watergate. When Vice President Spiro Agnew resigned, Reagan became the most likely Republican to succeed Nixon. Yet Gerald Ford's ascendancy meant he would have to face a sitting Republican president in the 1976 primaries. Former governor Pat Brown's son, Jerry Brown, was elected governor of California. A hip, handsome young man, he was said to be the model for Robert Redford's film *The Candidate*. Brown dated the singer Linda Ronstadt.

While 1974 was a disaster for Republicans, it was possibly an even greater, more exciting year in athletics than 1972 had been. It did not start out well, however. The UCLA basketball team returned all its seniors. They were considered unbeatable until they took their all-time record eighty-eight-game winning streak into South Bend and managed to blow an eleven-point lead with just a few minutes remaining. They lost that game and a few more after it but still made it to the championship game, a rematch with North Carolina State. The Bruins were forced into overtime but were soon up by seven. North Carolina State rallied to win. After seven straight NCAA championships (1967–73), the streak was over. Across town Rod Dedeaux's Trojans won their fifth straight College World Series.

It was certainly an all-California big league baseball season. Los Angeles and the two-time defending World Champion Oakland A's met in the World Series, with Oakland winning in five games.

In football, the 1974 Southern California Trojans were far from the best team in the school's history. They were, however, the most exciting, not only in USC annals but perhaps among all collegiate teams ever. Trailing Notre Dame, 24-0, they scored fifty-five points in seventeen minutes to destroy the Fighting Irish, 55-24. Tailback Anthony Davis earned the moniker "the Notre Dame killer" after scoring six touchdowns against Notre Dame in 1972; he added four more in 1974, including a return of the opening second-half kick for a score. His performance made him the easy choice for the Heisman Trophy, but the game was played just as the ballot deadline was approaching. In those pre-Internet days, most of the writers had already returned their ballots by mail. Ohio State's Archie Griffin won instead.

"I saw the wildest football game I have ever seen in 1974," wrote Murray. The columnist was in his rarest form when writing about Woody Hayes and the Buckeyes prior to their Rose Bowl three-match with USC. "Ohio State is not a squad, it's a horde," he wrote. "It is going through the Big 10 like Attila the Hun through the gates of Rome." When somebody wanted to know how the team returned from a Rose Bowl practice session, Murray wrote, "The usual way—by goose step." This kind of commentary inflamed Hayes. In 1974 it reached its climax, at least by Rose Bowl standards (a few years later Hayes's career ended when he punched a Clemson player at the Gator Bowl).

If Hayes felt in 1968–69 that a trip to Los Angeles was a descent into moral depravity, that sense was heightened threefold by 1974–75. Hayes was a tremendous Nixon supporter. Watergate, in his view, was a liberal conspiracy to destroy all that was decent and true and open the door for debauchery and communism. News of the convictions of Haldeman and Ehrlichman were announced on TV at halftime of the Rose Bowl game. Hayes felt the world was against him. He punched a *Los Angeles Times* photographer who got too close to him.

During the game, Pat Haden hit John McKay with a desperate heave into the corner of the end zone, followed by a two-point conversion, and Troy scored a remarkable 18-17 victory over the Buckeyes. Coupled with several high-ranking losses in bowls that day, the win gave once-beaten, once-tied USC and Coach McKay his fourth national championship.

"Jim wrote about me in December of 1974, in between the comeback over Notre Dame and then the Rose Bowl win over Ohio State," said J. K. McKay, who starred in USC's comeback game over Notre Dame.

I don't really recall that he interviewed me for the article, but he wrote a sort of tongue in cheek column that might have been called "A Case for Nepotism." It was about the advantages and disadvantages of being the coach's kid. I was really honored. He wrote about Pat and me. . . .

My impression of Murray was that there was a great deal of admiration between him and my dad. It was a matter of mutual respect. Murray was as good as it gets. It meant a lot if my dad had a column written about him by Jim Murray.

[Murray] played a huge role in the mystique of USC football. He had great respect for USC football. I think he wrote about it in a clever and interesting way, with a certain amount of reverence.

After the 1975 Rose Bowl, when my dad went for two against Ohio State, he wrote a great article extolling his willingness to go for two at a time in which there was no overtime and coaches did not always do that. He had high compliments of my dad and referred to other games, like the loss to Purdue [in the 1967 Rose Bowl].

Pat Haden was an English major who had the utmost respect for his unique ability, but Murray was a *writer*, he could have been a novelist, he could have written anything and do it well.

"In an odd kind of way, Jim was a USC guy," said Linda McCoy-Murray.

He liked the athletic program. He had a lot of respect for John McKay and enjoyed his company, but he'd say, "I don't have a favorite team. I root for the guy who ran the wrong way, 'Wrong Way Riegels.'" Notre Dame was never his beloved team. He grew up Irish Catholic on the East Coast, so naturally Notre Dame was the team, but I would agree that since USC was the team that rivaled Notre Dame, and had an equal tradition with them, that helped him as a point of reference when he arrived on the West Coast. Ara Parshegian [the Notre Dame coach] was one of his favorites. He liked him a lot, as a person.

Jim said that when you get too close to a player or coach it causes trouble. "I can't crawl in bed with a coach or owner because one day I'll have to write something about that guy and it will rear its ugly head," he'd say.

Jim's admiration for McKay and USC shone through in his writing. There was *enthusiasm* in his words. He depicted Troy and their stars as human. While he certainly recognized that the New York Yankees were the greatest sports dynasty of all time, he had no love for them. He had viewed them almost as automatons going back to his attendance at Yankee Stadium, when the Bronx Bombers humiliated the Chicago Cubs in the 1938 World Series, four games to none. Even their own fans booed the heartless Yanks, probably the genesis for Murray's—not Red Smith's—quote that, "Rooting for the Yankees is like rooting for U.S. Steel."

On January 20, 1974, Murray wrote a column about Mickey Mantle's induction into the Hall of Fame. There was something missing in it. It lacked the joie de vivre of his 1962 ode to Willie Mays. Murray could not come around to the Yankees. In his mind, they were not a poem but a bank statement.

Similarly, Murray never truly came around to auto racing, which always evoked the Grim Reaper in his columns. Murray wrote about race driver A. J. Foyt. "Death is always on the pole in this game," he wrote. "No 500-mile guarantee comes with these cars. Neither car nor driver has a warranty." On March 12 he wrote that hockey star Bobby Orr "could score on the German Army."

In July Murray went to Anaheim to catch up with Baltimore third baseman Brooks Robinson. In his column he quoted ex-Angels manager Bill Rigney, who said he swore Robinson sold his soul to the devil; there could be no other explanation for how he was always positioned in the right place to make catches. All balls that go over third base are called foul, Rigney explained, "because they figure if it was fair Brooksie would have caught it." It was a takeoff on the old Ted

Williams line that if a pitcher threw him a strike, "Mr. Williams would let you know it."

When Dizzy Dean passed away on July 17, 1974, Murray put the loss in perspective, describing the pitcher's era (the Great Depression) as "the *Grapes-of-Wrath* America." He was as "vain as a movie star, as amiable as a dolphin." "Son," Dean once said to a hitter, "what kind of pitch would you like to miss?"

In "Catchin' Up With Satch" on August 11, Murray left little doubt that in his mind former Negro League ace Satchel Paige was baseball's greatest all-time pitcher. Coming four years after the famed USC-Alabama football game, it was another distinctly sociological piece advocating fairness and equality. As he did whenever he came across someone who really had something to say, he broke from his usual standard of not quoting his subjects much. This time he captured Paige's many homilies.

He addressed his own personal ambition on August 25 ("Blasting a Golf Trail") when he wrote, "Some guys want to climb the Matterhorn. Others dream of singing opera. Still others wish they could quarterback the Rams. But my life's ambition has always been to hold the course record somewhere." As in, "That's Jim Murray. You know, he holds the course record at L.A. North. Shot a 56. In the rain."

In "Weird Site for a Fight," Murray managed to write an entire colorful column about the incongruity of a heavyweight title match fought in the old Belgian Congo, in the city of Kinshasa in what was then called Zaire, in "darkest Africa." He never once mentioned the two fighters, Ali and George Foreman, instead lacing the column with references to *Robinson Crusoe* and Henry Morton Stanley's initial meeting with David Livingstone ("Dr. Livingstone, I presume."). Eventually Ali upset Foreman, completely changing the dynamics of boxing. The victory put Joe Frazier back in play and made Ali a legend once and for all.

In "Woman of the Century" on November 17, he wrote a delightful piece about Mary Sutton Bundy, whose husband had Bundy Drive (later the infamous street where O. J. Simpson allegedly killed his wife) named after him. "I interviewed the Rose Queen the other day," he wrote. "Only this one was from 1908." She also won Wimbledon in 1905. The piece was a throwback to "more graceful days in the life of this state."

"You certainly have compiled a monumental library of humorous and serious writings," crooner Bing Crosby wrote in a 1974 letter to the writer.

■ ■ ■

The year 1975 may have been the worst of a bad decade. New York declared itself on the verge of bankruptcy, and President Ford refused to come to its aid. It was a rotten year for the Big Apple. The greatest of American cities was a mere shadow of its once-proud self. Sports victories by the Jets, the Mets, and the Knickerbockers provided temporary hiatus from its troubles, but crime, corruption, racial strife, and union strikes brought New Yorkers to their knees. By 1975 their teams were in the doldrums too.

After a seemingly unending string of marvelous sports years for Southern California teams, 1975 was relatively down. Most regions of the country, like Chicago and even New York, would have gladly traded for L.A.'s success, but the local fans were spoiled. Ultimately only UCLA reached the mountaintop when John Wooden's last team rebounded from the disappointment of 1974 to win his tenth NCAA championship in twelve years. After the victory, Wooden announced his retirement.

Murray wrote eloquently of the Wizard of Westwood at the end of his career in "He Dared Stand Alone" on April 4. "This is not old Blood and Guts or Old Hickory, this is Mr. Chips saying goodbye," he wrote. All Wooden wanted was a schoolroom with pictures of "George Washington, Christ and a pair of crossed flags." He was "St. John," straight out of the New Testament. Murray half expected to see him walk to work "across Santa Monica Bay." Wooden's rules were "real easy to follow—if you lived in a convent."

Wooden once won an NCAA title with "nothing more than 6-5 centers and the Book of Leviticus." UCLA was a campus surrounded by "Gomorrah by the Sea," a place where half-naked coeds looked like Barbi Benton (who was one of those coeds when Wooden coached there), sorority parties were sometimes junior varsity tune-ups for the real thing a mile or so away at Hugh Hefner's mansion, and rumors of a cheerleader sex-fest ran rampant. Regardless, "Wooden quietly went his winning way with the Bible in one hand and a basketball in the other."

In "Death of an Heirloom," Murray addressed the passing of Casey Stengel. Stengel had spent the last decade of his life living near his friend, former Brooklyn Dodger Rod Dedeaux, in Glendale, California. He had a cushy job at a local bank. Murray created a humorous scenario in which

Stengel's entrance to heaven is announced by "The Owner," who directs him to a press conference of sorts with "my writers, Matthew, Mark, Luke and John, so he can tell them how he won the 1953 World Series by holding Robinson on."

In 1975 Murray revisited a favorite old subject, Willie Mays. It was a whimsical slap, probably in part his own vision of personal morality. It was a sad reflection on a player he admired greatly but who had played past his prime and was now an embittered "victim" laboring under the lie that somehow the world did not treat him as he deserved.

Murray also wrote of race in a column about the black golfer Lee Elder. Elder just plain "earned his way in." He was not there because of legislation or protests or even flowery columns written by a talented writer with a social conscience. "Lee Elder's soap box is the first tee," he wrote. "His sermon is a first at Monsanto, an appearance at The Masters, a play-off with Nicklaus. I don't know of any rhetoric that could be more penetrating or meaningful. A 69 is plenty of militancy for whitey in this game."

When Julius Erving made his Los Angeles debut, Murray wrote, "He can hang in the air so long on a jump shot, they say, he could jump out of a one-story building and take an hour to hit the ground. If he jumped off the Empire State Building, he'd hover indefinitely."

In a 1975 piece on Bill Veeck ("Baseball's Showboat"), he wrote that Veeck bought a Cleveland Indians team that had not won the pennant in years and "couldn't have cared less. They were as passionless as cost accountants, a locker room full of nine-to-five guys who correctly understood their function in life was to lose gracefully to the Yankees and go home." But Veeck made them exciting, fun, and good; they won the 1948 pennant while setting the big league attendance record of 2,620,627 (subsequently broken by the 1962 Los Angeles Dodgers).

■ ■ ■

Murray's February 22, 1976, column on golf's newest star, Ben Crenshaw, was titled "Baby-Face Bomber." Comparing the fresh Crenshaw with his hero, Ben Hogan, Murray wrote of Crenshaw, "He looks as if he came direct from a Christmas pageant." Hogan "played golf as if it came wrapped in tinsel" and "walked up on a green as if he intended to arrest it."

In a column about USC baseball coach Rod Dedeaux, Murray wrote,

> But the greatest farm club in the history of the Major Leagues . . . and the most consistent supplier of Major League talent the past 10 years is a franchise maintained at no cost to baseball. It finds and signs its own prospects, suits them up, develops them, refines them, weeds them out—and then turns them over to the big leagues fully polished and ready for the World Series.
>
> The University of Southern California baseball team is to the Majors what the Mesabi range is to steel or the forest is to Weyerhaeuser—a seemingly limitless supply of basic ore or timber.
>
> . . . Rod Dedeaux went to bat only four times in the big leagues. Nevertheless he probably should go to the Hall of Fame as a man who has done as much for the great game in his own way as Babe Ruth.

Murray's May 4, 1976, column on Muhammad Ali was a bit over the top with one-liners and hyperbole following each other, paragraph after paragraph, with little purpose. In his column about jockey Bill Shoemaker, he wrote that most riders rode their horses home "in filets, 1,500 pounds of frightened, bullied flesh," whereas Shoemaker brought the steeds through the finish line "as if it were a date." Handsome race car driver Johnny Rutherford "looks as if he had just stepped out of the pages of *The Great Gatsby*." Huge Detroit Pistons basketball center Bob Lanier's size-22 feet were so big they looked "like supertankers."

When leukemia took the life of Minnesota Twins infielder Danny Thompson, Murray wrote about how the word "courage" was loosely thrown around, describing guys who played "with a limp" or pitched "with a sore finger." Thompson was "up against the 1927 Yankees of diseases." Murray admired Thompson's Christian faith, which he maintained until the end.

Nineteen seventy-six was another good Olympic year for Los Angeles athletes, particularly USC and UCLA track stars and swimmers at the Montreal Games. Murray wrote a column about Romanian gymnast Nadia Comaneci. He said it was her Olympics, as 1932 belonged to Babe Didrikson and 1936 belonged to Adolf Hitler, until Jesse Owens "struck a blow for black self-esteem that never did subside thereafter." Nadia was "the most famous collection of syllables to come out of Romania since Magda Lupescu."

■ ■ ■

The Lakers under Jerry West burst back onto the pro basketball scene in 1977. Kareem Abdul-Jabbar was at the height of his career. Murray's May 1 column, "A Rejected Landmark," depicted the superstar as "a national monument. The real Civic Center." He "belongs to the ages like Yosemite," a part of California lore as much as Jack London. "Kareem Abdul-Jabbar was put together by the same forces that made Mt. Whitney. Or Farrah Fawcett." He then went on to analyze how a guy who was arguably the best athlete Los Angeles ever had, essentially a homegrown product since he had played at UCLA, was not popular because of his association with the Black Muslims. Kareem tried to "explain" the religion to Murray, who in turn tried to write it down. It was still a mystery. Abdul-Jabbar never achieved the popularity of Jerry West or Magic Johnson.

Seattle Slew thrilled horse race fans and was the feature of Murray's June 12 column, "It's a Fairy Tale Finish." Murray also hailed the debut of John McEnroe, a teenager from Long Island, then entering Stanford. He somehow extended Jimmy Connors to four sets after defeating a host of opponents at Wimbledon. "The gateman thought he had come to get autographs," Murray wrote. "The linemen thought he was the ball boy." Murray correctly determined that McEnroe's decision to stay an amateur at Stanford was a good one, predicting greatness for him. He was right.

After beating Philadelphia in the Championship Series, Los Angeles took on the New York Yankees in the Fall Classic. It was a return to the glory days of a rivalry starting in 1941, transferred to the West Coast in 1963, and now entering a new era dominated by George Steinbrenner, Billy Martin, Reggie Jackson, Thurman Munson, Sparky Lyle, Tom Lasorda, Steve Garvey, and Don Sutton. It did not fail to thrill. In game six at Yankee Stadium, Jackson unloaded with three home runs, finishing with five in the Series to carry his team back into the glory halls after a twelve-year absence. Murray was at Yankee Stadium and up to the task. "Excuse me while I wipe up the bloodstains and carry off the wounded," he wrote. "The Dodgers forgot to circle the wagons.

"Listen! You don't go into the woods with a bear. You don't go into a fog with Jack the Ripper. You don't get in a car with Al Capone. You don't get on a ship with Morgan the Pirate. You don't go into shark waters with a nosebleed.

You don't wander into the Little Big Horn with General Custer." His "nose-bleed" in "shark waters" became a cultural touch phrase.

Reggie Jackson, who once said if he played in New York he would have a candy bar named after him, was such a superstar in the Big Apple he might have had "an entire chocolate factory named after him." The Yanks again were a "bunch of guys who go for the railroad yards in bombing runs or shell Paris with railroad guns."

One of Jackson's home runs "would have crossed state lines and gone through the side of a battleship on its way to the seats." The home run "is to the Yankees what the Raphaels are to the Vatican and the Pyramids to the pharaohs—symbols of glory and tradition." Murray reverted to his memory of Dizzy Dean struggling in the twilight of his career at Yankee Stadium in the 1938 World Series. It was an opera with Reggie the star of the last act. "The 1977 World Series is Reggie Jackson's fee simple."

When stuntman Evel Kneivel beat up a press agent for writing a paperback tell-all, it was Jim Murray he asked to write a column helping his public image. "He had to be put back together more often than a museum dinosaur," Murray wrote. "He had more broken bones than a slaughterhouse. He was either in a spotlight or in traction."

In December Murray wrote about ex-football star Alex Karras, who was now an actor and pro wrestler. "The guys in the white hats always win," he wrote of the wrestling game, "but the black hats make all the money."

After the bowl games, which were becoming more numerous, Murray wrote about a series of high-scoring games. The teams in contests like the Gator Bowl and Bluebonnet Bowl did not scout each other as the Rose Bowl or Orange Bowl teams did. "Are USC alums going to turn in their pompoms if they lose the, for crying out loud, Bluebonnet Bowl?" he wrote. "But if they lose to UCLA—now, *that's* serious!"

Prior to the Super Bowl between Denver and Dallas, Murray introduced much of the world to Lyle Alzado, a street-tough New Yorker then starring with the Broncos. Later Alzado became the face of the L.A. Raiders.

After moving to Los Angeles, writer Alex Haley read Murray "now or then" until he "perceived—this guy is damn good! And for a long time I've just had it in mind to tell you that. You are a fine writer, my friend!" he wrote to him in 1977. *Star Trek* star William Shatner also wrote a letter to Jim, stating that his July 3 column was "the funniest piece of writing I've read anywhere. . . . Your genius is undeniable."

■ ■ ■

Then came 1978, a year of both tragedy and triumph. Pope Paul VI died. His successor would help end the Cold War and usher in a new era of world Catholicism. *Times* readers were shocked to pick up the paper on November 21. In a story covered by Charles Krausse, Robert Barkdoll, and Leonard Greenwood, the headline read, "Jones Ordered Cultists to Drink Cyanide Poison" under "Started with Babies." Aerial photos showed hundreds of dead bodies, the result of a mass suicide ordered by the Reverend Jim Jones of his followers in Guyana. In December, the United States recognized full diplomatic relations with China, a process begun in 1972 when President Nixon visited the communist country.

It was another one of those California years in the world of sports. USC's baseball team was believed to be the best in college history. They finished 54-9, capturing the school's eleventh national championship. The Dodgers captured the National League pennant but fell again to New York in the fall classic. USC earned the national title after beating Michigan in the Rose Bowl game.

"Jim was the kind of figure people did not see very much," recalled USC's Hall of Fame coach, John Robinson.

In twelve years I was interviewed by him three times. He came and sat down with me, and occasionally we talked by phone call. I would briefly tell him something he needed for his story. For the most part I just picked up his column and read it. He was like reading Hemingway, that kind of guy. He never reported on an event, but rather on a kind of condition.

His commentary was always on point. There was some distance between him and the average athlete. He liked the mystique of USC football.

New Rams coach Ray Malavasi was at the helm of a fine team in 1978. They finally slayed Minnesota, 34-10, but were no match for Roger Staubach and Dallas in a 28-0 drubbing in the National Football Conference title game. Before the Super Bowl in Miami, Murray wrote, "The Same Old Song." In it he complained that previous Super Bowls had been boring. He wrote about "one of those guys from an acid-rock paper who drinks up all your drinks" and then writes what a "phony hype it all is." It was a reference to Hunter S. Thompson, who in 1973 wrote a freaked-out, half-true, half-psychedelic piece for *Rolling Stone* including an interview in a limo with President Nixon that many claimed was made up but that Pat Buchanan said actually occurred.

Dallas lost to Pittsburgh in the Super Bowl. Instead of "one of those 12-9 games" that Murray had complained about, it was a 34-28 barnburner. The game lived up to the hype.

Murray wrote a column featuring Steelers wide receiver Lynn Swann titled "Graceful as a Swann." He said the first thing to consider was whether "Swann" was his "name or a description. You wonder whether the Pittsburgh Steelers found him on a pond in Holland or in the third act of *Lohengrin* or *Siegfried*. He could be a ride at Disneyland. Tchaikovsky would build a ballet around him." He was what Vaslav Nijinsky would look like if he could catch passes, Murray continued. Of his sixty-one catches in 1978, "only about five" were caught with his feet on the ground. On a team of bullies representing the steel town they played in, the USC-educated Swann, who went to a fancy Catholic high school in the Bay Area, was miscast. Swann was "ethereal," a man who wrote poetry, danced tap, and composed music. He was to pass-catching what Lord George Byron was to reading (Murray never tired of literary analogies). If Michelangelo were around, he would have sculpted him. At USC, instead of majoring in eligibility, he wrote a term paper on plantation slavery. To Murray, Swann was comparable to Claude Monet or the Louvre. "If everybody played football this way they'd soon move the Super Bowl to the Met," he concluded. "Nureyev would be second string, and they would have to play Super Bowls with Swann in them to the strains of *The Nutcracker Suite*."

As great as the decade was for football, or boxing, the 1970s may have been the best decade in the history of horse racing. Murray wrote about the tremendous steed Affirmed on May 7, 1978. Against a sterling field—"These were the kind that won the wars, settled the West, delivered the mail"— Affirmed made the Dempsey-Firpo battle look like a "debate." Murray compared Affirmed's "bored efficiency" with Joe DiMaggio drifting after a fly ball. If the Kentucky Derby winner were human, "he'd be Robert Redford."

Murray wrote a self-deprecating column on April 6 ("The Hall of What?") about being elected into the Hall of Fame—the National Sportscasters and

Sportswriters Association (NSSA) Hall of Fame in Salisbury, North Carolina. He tried to pretend he was undeserving and even admitted he had never heard of the NSSA. He went on to say that they never heard of him either.

When longtime Dodger Jim Gilliam passed away, Murray wrote a tribute to the journeyman. He called him "my favorite all-time athlete." He also wrote a great retrospective of the little-known 1930s boxer, Jim Braddock (the subject of Ron Howard's 2005 *Cinderella Man*).

On November 23 he wrote the "Laws of Murray," a sports take-off on Murphy's Law: "If it can go wrong, it will." Among his laws was "Whatever can go to New York, will. Whatever can't will go to Philadelphia." The Rams' quarterback "is the one that's not in there." If it does not move, "it must be the Rams and Atlanta." Rhetoric, he wrote, "is the art of being loud." Nixon "not only admitted he was wrong, he set out to prove it."

■ ■ ■

On March 31, 1979, the *L.A. Times* startled readers with two front-page articles by Bryce Nelson, Penny Girard, and Ellen Hume about a nuclear power plant in Pennsylvania called Three Mile Island. An equipment failure at the plant caused a core meltdown in one of the reactors, and this resulted in the release of radioactive gas into the environment. The Three Mile Island incident combined with the film *The China Syndrome* all but doomed the nuclear power industry.

On May 26 the front page was dominated by headlines about 270 people killed in a Los Angeles–bound jet airline crash. On that day in a front page article by Robert Shogan, President Carter admitted his "shortcomings." His problems were only just beginning. After the ouster of the shah of Iran by Muslim fundamentalists, the cancer-stricken deposed ruler was given shelter in the United States, where he eventually died. Enraged Muslims stormed the U.S. embassy in Tehran on November 4, seizing hostages. It proved the eventual end for President Carter.

In "Trouble Hits Tape" (March 16), Murray wrote of the great Olympic sprint champion and Dallas Cowboys star Bob Hayes, who was in jail on drug charges. Of the drugs, he wrote they were "one baton Bob Hayes should have dropped." Later in the year he wrote about Hayes's teammate Roger Staubach. After spending four years "mapping the Gulf of Tonkin" and on a "gunboat in the Mekong," while his team "got good at losing to Green Bay and the Cleveland Browns," Staubach defied all odds by becoming a superstar. The Dallas quarterback, as outlined in numerous novels and movies, was supposed to be nicknamed "Broadway" or "Dandy" or "Whiskey." Instead, the former Navy officer and NFL legend claimed that he was never invited to the wild parties depicted in those books, or that they were "figments of the authors' imaginations."

Murray's 1979 column on former Oklahoma football coach Bud Wilkinson referred to his retirement in order to run for office. "And, when the voters rejected him for the Senate in 1964, no one was sure whether it was because they didn't want him as a Senator or because they wanted him back as coach." It was probably a little of both. Jesus would have been in trouble running as a Republican in 1964.

Murray's December 30 column, "Recruiting Sales Talk," made fun of college football coaches and their efforts to bring in blue-chippers. In the article, he paraphrased a famous Bear Bryant speech, given after his success with Joe Namath and Ken Stabler. "No, old man, if you've got some whiskey-drinking, women-chasing graduates of a Birmingham jail or Altoona pool hall, you send them to yours truly," Murray wrote, quoting a speech Bryant once made to a group of California high school football coaches. Kids who want to be doctors or lawyers? Send them to "Muhlenberg or Susquehanna or Amherst." Bear would welcome the D students.

From Banning High in Carson, the Rams picked up a journeyman quarterback named Vince Ferragamo. Surprisingly, he led them all the way to a "home" Super Bowl at the Rose Bowl, versus Pittsburgh.

A few days before the game, Murray captured the essence of Steelers linebacker Jack Lambert in a column: "The first time you see Jack Lambert, you're tempted to ask what he did with the fangs," he started in "First Test-Tube Linebacker" (January 17, 1980). He was "the NFL's resident Jack the Ripper." He played football "the way Attila the Hun sacked villages." Murray wrote that if Genghis Khan were a football player, he would have resembled either Lambert or other linebackers such as Dick Butkus or Ray Nitschke. The position required the same compassion as "a Chinese war lord or a Mafia hit man." Lambert, he wrote, needed hours after games to come down so he could mix with "polite company, where you can get one to 10 for doing what he does to Roger Staubach."

The Rams, in their last year at the L.A. Coliseum, led the Steelers and had victory in their sights. Behind Terry Bradshaw and Lynn Swann, however, Pittsburgh took control of the game, beating Los Angeles for their fourth Super Bowl title of the decade.

12

Visionaries

By midsummer of 1979, Jim Murray was an institution. He had been the star sports columnist of the *Los Angeles Times* for eighteen years. His rise, popularity, and success mirrored that of the paper Otis Chandler had taken over and the city they both loved. The 1960s and 1970s were a period of astounding growth in Southern California. But this growth came with setbacks. Air quality was abysmal. Traffic, overcrowding, crime, and illegal immigration from Mexico had become major problems. However, over two decades during which much of America had suffered, its major cities in terrible decline, Los Angeles stood atop the nation. Its in-state rival, San Francisco, could see its best days only in the rearview mirror.

San Francisco had little of the panache and Old World charm that had marked its heyday right after World War II. Its sports teams were all dominated by champions in L.A. Politically, the city had no power, no influence.

But the world was changing. A new decade beckoned. Tremendous changes in sports, politics, and culture would be ushered in. Los Angeles would experience major changes, some for the good, some not so much for good. Its influence would not wane. Politically, its major protagonists, men shaped by the city's uniqueness, would shape the world.

For Jim Murray and his boss, Otis Chandler, the '80s would be different. By the mid-1970s Murray's eyesight was poor enough that he occasionally missed a turn while driving and often was the passenger in a car by mutual agreement. The move to Brentwood in 1972–73 was meant in part to accommodate his condition, but his failing eyesight became a major challenge in 1978.

In his 1993 autobiography, Murray wrote a chapter called, "On My Blindness, with Apologies to Milton." "1978 pretty much started out like any other year," he wrote.

The Open was in Denver, the World Series was in Yankee Stadium. Bad luck, as usual, was keeping its hand hidden, its cards at its vest.

You learn in this game of life that you can go along on a winning streak only so long. Slumps are inevitable.

But I don't remember any foreboding when I took off for the World Cup golf tournament in Hawaii that December. A week in the sun, ukeles, drinks with umbrellas on them, Pacific sunsets, Bali'hai.

Paradise is a terrible place to get your life ruined. But that is what happened to me.

He was in his hotel room when the phone rang early in the morning. Scrambling to answer it, he broke his foot against a piece of furniture. The pain distracted him from the blurriness in his left eye. He ascribed it to tiredness. His right eye was already filled with cataracts.

Six weeks later at the Super Bowl, he kept rubbing the eye. A good friend, Dr. John Perry, gave him eyedrops. "John, I don't think this is anything eyedrops can cure," Murray said to him.

"Washington Boulevard" looked like "W-A-X-Q-H-V-S-P." He thought Miami was engulfed in a dust storm and mentioned this to Thomas "Hollywood" Henderson of the Cowboys. "There's no dust in the air here," said Henderson. "It's as clear as a bell out." Murray realized it was his eye. "By now, I was going through the hotel lobby by Braille. Trying to put a quarter in the Coke machine was brain surgery."

His egg salad sandwich "looked as if it were growing red worms." His eye was bleeding. The TV looked like it was covered in blood. So, he went to the emergency room. The doctor told him his eye was OK. "I think he was the guy who told the captain of the Titanic not to mind the ice," Murray recalled. "I not only hope they take his license away, I hope they take it away from the school that graduated him."

John Perry found another doctor for him: Dr. Dave Sime, an ex-Olympic sprinter. Ironically, Murray had once written a story about Sime for *Sports Illustrated*. The doctor determined that he probably had a detached retina and had been suffering from the debilitation for the better part of four years. The situation had recently gotten worse, most likely because of his fall in Hawaii.

When Dr. Sime determined that that part of the eye, called a scleral buckle, did not hold, he ordered further tests. Half the doctors said it was a retinal detachment. Half said it was caused by trauma. Murray noticed that the doctors were divided in their diagnosis based on their age, and he speculated that a recent medical school theory had entered into the younger doctors' thinking. As he watched *Operation Cicero* on TV one day, James Mason started to melt. It was as if he had flowed off the screen onto the floor. Murray went to bed blind.

The cataract in his "good," right eye had gotten dense, and it was not centered in the eye. Murray could no longer read. He had had the cataract since 1978, and it had left him with only peripheral vision in that eye. A four-hour operation ensued, followed by four other operations on the left retina over the course of a year. Unfortunately, the doctors could not put the retina back. Murray lost sight in his left eye, was blind for a year, and began to suffer claustrophobia. The cataract worsened, but the doctors did not recommend another operation, which would risk pulling the retina down in his right eye too. Murray dictated into a cassette or called his stories in by phone, giving them to a copywriter word for word. "At that point, I did not care," Murray wrote. "I would like to have died, actually. When you're blind, there's no quality to life."

Like many *Times* writers, Dwight Chapin vividly recalls taking Murray's dictation. Other writers were in awe of him and considered it an honor, redundant or not. Most were amazed at how precise his language was, even though it was not written down. His accuracy added to his legend. Murray did not recall his writing as being nearly so precise. He said dictating forced him to learn his craft all over again. "I had to be careful I didn't interview Dave Parker thinking it was Willie Stargell even though I knew Willie well," Murray wrote in his autobiography.

The *Times* supported the columnist by assigning a young man named John Scheibe as his chauffeur and assistant. Scheibe recalled his apprenticeship with Murray in a 2007 interview with *L.A. Observed* and in a book, *On the Road with Jim Murray*. "I didn't hear him complain very much," he recalled.

I remember once we went to an Angels game. They were going to play the Yankees, and we had just pulled into the parking lot. It was one of his first trips to a ballgame after he came back to work. He said something like, "The way things are, it's not easy being funny."

I think going to the ballpark cheered him up, seeing all his colleagues and all the players. The atmosphere was a good thing for him. And, he always had hope that the cataract would be taken care of. He had the best doctors at Jules Stein at UCLA.

Murray obviously had to make major concessions to his condition. "It went several ways," said Scheibe.

If he was at home and, say, had talked to Maury Wills, he'd pre-write it in his head and dictate the column into his tape recorder. Then, he'd play the tape to the transcription department at the *Times*.

Another way was, he'd write it in longhand on scratch paper, in giant letters. It would take him, like, 10 pages for a column. I'd re-type it on regular paper and send it to the paper. Anytime he was covering something live, he'd write it in longhand.

He and some of the editors noticed that the columns he tape recorded tended to go longer in length. He couldn't see what he was writing, and it kind of got away from him sometimes.

Readers never noticed any difference, and neither could Scheibe.

"Writing a column with only the sound of your voice is something like assembling a 1932 Ford roadster wearing boxing gloves," wrote Rick Reilly.

"It wasn't very good," Murray says. "But to me, it was a hell of an achievement."

With no chance to repair the left eye, in December 1979 doctors decided to remove the cataract from his right. That worked until the retina detached from it too. "Retinas 2, Murray 0," wrote Reilly. The right retina was finally repaired on January 18, 1982. Murray's vision, albeit tunneled, one-dimensional, and precarious, came back.

Scheibe's assistance was a lifesaver, or at least a career-saver, for the scribe, but Murray still had his share of problems. At the Los Angeles Rams' training camp, he crashed into a rusty pipe. Dr. Bob Woods said it almost cost him a leg. "Friends told me the leg looked like the *aurora borealis*," Murray said, managing to make a joke of it. At Massachusetts General Hospital, he could not tell if the doors were open or closed.

During the course of these events, he came under the care of a group of doctors. Dr. Charles Schoeppens had once fought the Nazis in the "Belgian underground" during World War II. Otto Jungschaffer and Dr. Richard Kratz were among the top cataract surgeons in the world. Murray underwent Kelman phacoemulsification, a cutting-edge method of extracting the cataract and lens with a small incision and supersonic drill. The doctors liquefied and pulverized the cataract, removing it with minimal trauma. The procedure was a success.

Years later Murray saw a Charles Kelman at the Bob Hope Desert Classic. He approached him and asked if he was the renowned doctor who developed phacoemulsification. Kelman said no, he owned "frock shops," but later Murray found him in golf pairings under the name Dr. Charles Kelman. He wrote a column about him.

The day after the surgery, Murray was lying in his hospital bed with patches over his eyes. He saw what he thought was a spotlight. It was a TV set. The patches were then removed. He looked up and saw Craig Morton, number seven of the Denver Broncos, on *Monday Night Football*. He recalled it to be the "most beautiful sight" ever: Craig Morton on channel 7. "I never look at Craig Morton without recalling that thrilling moment," he wrote.

At first the doctors gave Murray binocular-type eyeglasses because they thought he needed to see every detail of the sporting events he wrote about. Murray explained that he needed to see only enough to get the general idea. He could look up the rest. What he really needed to be able to do was read.

"It's not 'courage' that makes a cornered animal fight," he recalled of the experience. "It's necessity. Depression." At first, he admitted, he asked himself, "Why me, God?" but then he endeavored, with the support of his employers, family, and colleagues, to not "go gently into that good night," to quote Welsh poet Dylan Thomas. "I could not have made it without Gerry, my lovely wife, one of the greatest people ever put on this Earth," he wrote. "I shudder when I think what this must have put her through."

A few years later the retina in his other (right) eye began to tear. He looked at the L.A. skyline and saw another "dust cloud." He looked in the mirror and saw "floaters," or what he called "dogs in the neighborhood." Murray missed the 1982 49ers-Bengals Super Bowl in Detroit. Dr. Jungschaffer tried a "cryo" technique to freeze the retina into place.

Murray's eyes were still bandaged from the operation when he received a call in his hospital room from Reggie Jackson. He was not supposed to take any visitors or calls, but Jackson talked the switchboard operator into putting the call through. "He'll want to talk to me," the slugger pleaded. "I'll buck him up." Jackson was right.

The operation was a success. Murray's retina held and stayed intact. Later when the capsule behind the eye became opaque, Jungschaffer gave him laser surgery. The columnist's "all-stars" were now doctors, a "line-up to hang on my wall forever."

Those close to Jim Murray knew of his predicament. The public did not. Despite being plunged into darkness, he found a way to write his column, which continued to be printed five days a week, syndicated in more than two hundred newspapers, and read by more than a million subscribers in Southern California alone. He did this without being able to see the game he was covering, the person he was interviewing, or most important, the words he was writing. Jim Murray was blind. A sportswriter's job requires sitting in a press box, observing the great doings on a field or court below, and Murray could not see that which was placed before his eyes. Doctors had improved his vision to the point where he could function, but he was handicapped nevertheless.

In 1999 editors David Halberstam and Glenn Stout selected the finest sports articles, columns, and essays from a century of newspapers, magazines, and "assignment" writing for their book *The Best American Sports Writing of the Century*. They selected Murray's column from July 1, 1979. On that day, in "If You're Expecting One-Liners, Wait, a Column," the great writer told the world of his predicament. Many would argue that Murray had written better columns. His piece "Hatred Shut Out as Alabama Finally Joins the Union," after the 1970 USC-Alabama game, certainly must rank. But his "blind" column remains among the most personal and poignant in a career filled with the personal and poignant.

His impaired vision became one of his defining characteristics. He painted a picture with words. Readers for decades had visualized what happened on a field even though they could not actually see it. Now, neither could the artist, the wordsmith who brought them the game. After all, Murray had learned from his first observation of Babe Ruth hitting a homer at Yankee Stadium that the description of an event was often more exciting than seeing it happen.

"Jim didn't see well for much of his life," said sportscaster Roy Firestone. "His eyes often failed him, but his heart never did. And so he 'saw' with his brain, his heart, and his soul. And he wrote what he saw. He wrote with passion. He wrote with insight. He wrote about the soaring human spirit, and he wrote about the parade of life's most accomplished and flawed individuals. And he wrote funny!"

"Courage and strength and hope and humor have to be bought and paid for with pain and work and prayer and tears," said Vin Scully. "Jim Murray had all those virtues during his lifetime. And he also had those crosses to bear. There was a decency about him that was glorious to behold. There was an indomitable spirit. And he gazed upon life and the world with sort of a bemused sense of humor."

■ ■ ■

Once Otis Chandler firmly affixed his imprimatur upon the *Los Angeles Times*, "it was like a comet in constant ascent, nothing but growth, bureaus opened, reporters hired, the world conquered, old friends alienated, new friends made," wrote David Halberstam in *The Powers That Be*. The *Times* opened a San Diego bureau. Chandler ascended to heights previously reserved only for Henry Luce, William S. Paley, William Randolph Hearst, Phil Graham, Arthur "Punch" Sulzberger, and later Rupert Murdoch, titans of communications, movers and shakers of the American Century.

Richard Nixon thanked Norman Chandler for his support in 1968. He did not thank Otis Chandler. But Chandler did not turn to the Left. He supported the Vietnam War with reservations. He hated it but was not blinded by ideology. Chandler and his paper recognized the brilliance of the Nixon-Kissinger strategy of triangulation, which ultimately earned Kissinger the Nobel Peace Prize. Before Watergate, Nixon was wildly popular, at least from a purely electoral point of view. Otis and Missy Chandler, California royalty in a world dominated by Californians, accepted White House invites.

Chandler was invited to the western White House in San Clemente. He sat on a promontory overlooking some of the wildest surf on the coast and was even allowed to surf the breaks. He was embarrassed because other surfers were barred from riding the popular point. Chandler did not like privilege, even though he had spent his life in privilege.

Editorially, his newspaper in the 1970s more resembled a daily magazine. It was a tour de force, a massive accomplishment manifesting itself day after glorious day. Chandler's rise met a bump in the road in the form of Watergate and the oil deal he entered into with an old college pal that went bad. Nixon and H. R. Haldeman were infuriated over Watergate coverage. The *Washington Post* had a news service partnership with the *L.A. Times*, but the *Post's* editor, Ben Bradlee, put distance between his paper and the other in order to grab Bob Woodward and Carl Bernstein's spotlight. If Nixon thought his Chandler connection, so much a part of his legacy, would protect him, he was wrong. Still, Halberstam wrote that the *Times's* L.A.-based editors were not plugged into Watergate; they headed to the tennis courts, not fully aware of the massive implications of the scandal in D.C.

Chandler and his paper were investigated to some extent during the Watergate hearings but, after some nervousness, both emerged stronger than ever. After Watergate Chandler consolidated the family's holdings, expanded, bought new publications, and made the *Times* one of the richest and best papers in the world.

Richard Nixon gained a measure of revenge to some extent when Otis's father, Norman, was diagnosed with throat cancer. While staying at the Chandler family compound in Dana Point, not far from San Clemente, Norman learned during the last days of Watergate that the president would visit him before he passed away. A visit was planned twice, and both times Nixon was a no show without immediate explanation. It was rumored that Haldeman canceled the visits as retribution for the *Times's* coverage of Watergate.

■ ■ ■

Fifty years after William Mulholland's St. Francis Dam collapsed, the *Los Angeles Times* won its tenth Pulitzer Prize for its coverage of shoddy and unsafe dams in the United States. Gaylord Shaw did most of the investigative reporting.

The change in quality and culture at the *Times* reflected the times. By 1980 the Right generated much of its mojo by criticizing the "left-wing media." After the *New York Times* exposed the Pentagon Papers, the *Washington Post* exposed Watergate, and Hollywood dramatized the cover-up in the film version of *All the President's Men*, conservatives considered the "dominant media culture" to be the enemy. Conservative talk radio, not to mention the Internet, were far from coming into being. The Right was alone. Conservatives had few allies. The odds seemed stacked against them.

No Republicans were touting the *L.A. Times's* friendliness. Chandler hired cartoonist Paul Conrad, a vitriolic liberal. His depictions of Nixon, Republicans, and later, Ronald Reagan were vicious. The Right felt he crossed the line, that there was no middle way, no fairness, just left-wing hatred. But Chandler hired him, kept him, and defended him. None of his ancestors would have let Conrad in the building.

In the late 1970s a new presidential candidate, also a Los Angeleno, Ronald Reagan, was making his mark on the political scene. He, too, paid attention to the *Times*. His wife, Nancy, was known to call Chandler personally, often complaining about Conrad. But Chandler's paper was considered fair and balanced overall. It was by no means considered partisan akin to the *New York Times*, the *Washington Post*, *The Nation*, and even *Time* magazine, since Henry Luce's 1967 passing.

In 1980 more than eight thousand people worked at the *Times*. Its average weekday circulation was 1,043,028, second only to the *New York Times*. Around that time, Chandler noticed that Punch Sulzberger of the *New York Times* and Katharine Graham of the *Washington Post* were still holding onto their positions. He thought they had been in place too long and figured if they had overstayed their welcome, so had he. He decided it was time to give someone else a chance. "I didn't want to continue as publisher until death or retirement," Otis said. He wanted to work on his health.

His son Norm had started at the *Times* in 1976, but there was no assurance that he would inherit the paper. "What he really wanted was to be a surf bum," Norm's wife, Jane Yeager Chandler, said. "His passion was surfing and if he could have figured out a way to make a living at it I think that's what he would have done." Norm's brother, Harry, wanted to be a filmmaker. Both had graduated from Stanford. Unlike their father, neither ever had any military training.

Ultimately, Chandler's choice to replace him was rooted in new sensibilities. He picked Tom Johnson, a Georgia native, and directed him to "move it forward." In his retirement speech, Chandler said he left the paper "a better company than when I came in 20 years ago." Chandler was a self-described "fighter, a gambler." His marching orders to the newspaper were to "push the *New York Times* off its perch." Many felt he had already done so.

Chandler made himself chairman. He would remain as involved as ever before in the first half of the 1980s. Journalist Carey McWilliams wrote that many visitors and pundits came to L.A. to find out how it all happened, what drove the city, what made it tick. "But it was, of course, the *Times* that put the city on the map, that made it known—at the dawn of what I suppose can fairly be called the age of the media," McWilliams wrote.

Chandler's stepping down as publisher freed him to express his political views more openly. "To Otis, Ronald Reagan seemed the perfect guide to sleep-walk America through the 1980s; a former actor with a good, conservative heart who was never faced with a Vietnam or an assassination," wrote Dennis McDougal in *Privileged Son: Otis Chandler and the Rise and Fall of the L.A. Times Dynasty.*

"He did some good things," said Chandler of Reagan. "He was very articulate when he spoke. He knew California well. I think he made some booboos too, like when he said, 'If you've seen one Redwood tree you have seen them all.' Things like that." But Reagan "came across the radar at the right time." Chandler concluded that Reagan was both lucky and good, a combination Napoleon Bonaparte always said made for greatness.

Tom Johnson's tenure as publisher was not met by infighting or a Chandler family struggle to regain control. Harry Chandler preferred to try and work in Hollywood. He did not have the acumen for the newspaper business that his predecessors had. Otis himself said so in cutting interviews that roiled the family. Regardless, any remote hopes that Norm Chandler would take over were dashed when he suffered a brain seizure.

Otis Chandler slowly drifted off to do other things. He engaged in a range of oft-dangerous Hemingwayesque activities, while lending the family name and money to a variety of philanthropic organizations. It could be argued whether the *Los Angeles Times* was still nominally a "Republican paper." If it was, its Republican leaning lasted only through Reagan's landslide 1984 reelection and possibly the election of his successor, George H. W. Bush, in 1988. Reagan was a wildly popular local hero, and California voted for Bush in 1988. It was the last time the state went Republican. By 1990 the *Times* was decidedly not conservative and would shift further to the Left in succeeding years.

The effect of the *Times* on Reagan's political career was far less important than it had been on Nixon's. The paper, particularly articles edited by Kyle Palmer, along with the Chamber of Commerce and business interests, seemingly built Nixon, brick by brick, beginning with his recruitment and first congressional campaign in 1946. Reagan was a movement, an idea. He tapped into the zeitgeist, and no newspaper could control it.

■ ■ ■

Chandler wrote in 1987 that he had created several new sections of the paper, with two goals in mind. One was to make it the best paper in the United States. If the *Times* attained "best paper in the U.S." status, it invariably meant it was the best paper in the world. If indeed by the 1980s and 1990s the *L.A. Times* fulfilled Chandler's goal of superiority, it could well be argued the edge came in the sports section and, particularly, with the hiring of Jim Murray. If Murray's newspaper were a baseball team, he was the free-agent slugger whose triple-crown season pushed a great team to dynasty level or a pitcher whose twenty-seven wins and 1.73 earned-run average (as in Koufax's 1966 statistics) made the difference between average and ultimate greatness.

Chandler's second goal might answer the question, how did he achieve the first? Chandler's background as a businessman from a conservative family informed his second goal: to make his paper "the most profitable in the world." Many in the newspaper game, then and now, would argue such a goal is mutually exclusive from the paper's "greatness." Many would go further to say if a paper is highly profitable, it automatically cannot be great. But Chandler was an aggressive, hard-charging, optimistic publisher. He saw the future.

Murray became a benefactor of Chandler's profit motive, a rich man in a business not known for producing rich men. In fact, Chandler's business model made many wealthy. By 1987, when *Front Page: A Collection of Historical Headlines from the* Los Angeles Times was published, the paper's net revenue increases were $400 million, or 650 percent. Daily circulation would grow by 520,000, or 104 percent. The Sunday circulation would increase by 400,000 (45 percent). Advertising, the lifeblood of all newspapers, went up by 87 million lines (110 percent). The staff increased by 1,900 employees (40 percent), 417

(140 percent) in editorial. Operating costs went up by $27.5 million, an increase of a staggering 820 percent. This was a sign of growing unionism and high-tech costs, which ultimately did not bode well for the post-Chandler years. In 1970 Chandler's vision of regional site expansion began in Orange County and San Fernando, along with modernization of the downtown plant, at a cost of $220 million over five years.

The year 1984 symbolized the L.A. renaissance. With Reagan in the White House and the Olympic Games held in Los Angeles, Hollywood, sports, politics, and culture all came together with a California theme. That theme could be summed up in Chandler, the athlete who loved the mountains and the ocean, who had an eye for pretty women, who did not see any logic in the concept that intellectual stimulation can be promoted only amid dirty urban settings, in cold weather, by frail academicians eschewing physical vigor in favor of deep thought.

Who better than Jim Murray to demonstrate that sports was not mutually exclusive from philosophy?

13

The Poet of Brentwood

Scott Ostler was the new breed of young sportswriter influenced by reading Jim Murray. A graduate of the old Pepperdine University, when it was near downtown Los Angeles, before its relocation to Malibu in the early 1970s, Ostler was considered a Murray clone. His columns appeared in the *Los Angeles Times* sports pages alongside the great man's. Steve Bisheff said that "many tried" to imitate Murray but failed. Ostler, however, appeared to have succeeded.

"I really admired Murray's writing," Ostler said, "and tried to copy it in high school. But by the time I got to the *L.A. Times*, I knew I couldn't write like Jim, and I had evolved my own style, which certainly owed a lot to his influence. Mostly what I 'stole' from Jim was the concept of writing to have fun and entertain the reader, to be as non-boring as possible."

Readers picked up on Ostler's jaunty witticisms. It was a challenge, a dare, to try to write like Jim Murray. It could open up a writer to criticism, but readers generally liked Ostler. He pulled it off.

"I worked with Murray and was a huge fan of his, but I can't say we were tight pals or anything," Ostler recalled. "I got to sit next to him on occasion at games, and rub shoulders at an occasional company party. Delightful guy; smart, funny, absolutely nonpretentious. If he realized he was a journalistic pioneer, and that he made sports fun for millions of readers daily, he didn't act like he knew."

By the time Ostler worked with Murray, the latter was a legend. He had rebounded from his blindness, which only added to his luster. He was syndicated nationwide, the best sportswriter in the world, and a towering figure no matter now unpretentious he tried to be. For the new generation, including Ostler, he was on a pedestal. Getting to know him was difficult, but not because Jim made himself inaccessible. It was a matter of respect.

Ostler recalled an early career break he owed to Murray. The famed columnist was in Miami to cover the Super Bowl when he suffered his detached retina. Ostler was asked to go and take over the great writer's duties, his first big assignment.

"One thing that always struck me, he would interview an athlete for a half hour, take notes, then when writing the column, would use maybe one little quote," recalled Ostler.

> He was like an artist, word-sketching his subject, then using his own art to create a word picture. He didn't fall back on the crutch of filling his column with bland quotes from his subject, as many writers did, and still do. Jim made each column a Murray creation. His output was prodigious. I think at one time he was writing six per week. Amazing.
>
> Writing "like Murray" is something you can carry only so far. I mean, coming up with these one-liners. "The guys' so skinny he has to jump in the shower to be wet." Later I developed my own style, my own voice. There's nobody else like him.

■ ■ ■

The rest of America began to catch up with Los Angeles in the 1980s. It was not a matter of L.A. slipping but of other cities and regions finally getting back on their feet after the economic disasters of the 1970s.

The *Times* and its city enjoyed all the advantages of having a Los Angeles politician in the White House, with none of the headache of Watergate and its subsequent disgrace. The power of Los Angeles and the state of California, politically, financially, culturally, and in all other ways, grew beyond previous eras, but other areas grew with them.

The United States did not participate in the Moscow Olympics, a much-criticized decision by Carter made to protest the Soviet invasion of Afghanistan. Murray, out of curiosity as much as anything, usually worked the Olympics, and did so in 1980 regardless of American participation. This was typical Murray; he did not relegate his columns only to L.A. sports and sports figures, and he found international sports worthy of his attention absent U.S. involvement.

While at *Sports Illustrated* in the 1950s, he was frustrated when a colleague traveled to the USSR for the U.S.-Soviet games and ended up reporting about "a track meet." Murray was determined to give readers the flavor and color of what he "saw," and a half-blind Jim Murray could paint a better picture than ten other scribes. On July 16, 1980, he wrote, "Ivan, you're not going to believe this but the American Olympians are here and they're an average of fifty-five years old, alcoholic, wear bi-focals, hearing aids, and they smoke in bed and complain of gas in the stomach."

The weather in Moscow that July was mildly cold as usual, but overall "it wasn't too bad." Murray wrote, "It's a handsome city. Oh, it's not Palm Springs. Or even Palm Beach." He noted that the homeless and the riff-raff were "floated out of town for the Olympic party." He saw no graffiti. The people were "neither friendly nor unfriendly, just unsmiling." The Russians, he observed, required a "special permit" to smile. Obviously they were the "happiest people on Earth" because they did not need to smile in the fake manner of Hollywood actors.

In the end, the Russians "won" the Games but not by the margins their propagandists had hoped for. "The rulers wanted the Soviet Union on page one for something besides troop movements," he wrote. He concluded, "It's a great place to visit—but you wouldn't want to live there."

■ ■ ■

In February, Murray wrote a piece advocating for Raiders owner Al Davis's right to move his team from Oakland to Los Angeles if he so chose. In it, he demonstrated what could only be called a laissez-faire economic philosophy. It was straight out of Alexis de Tocqueville's *Democracy in America*. He said previous leagues were formed by dint of men simply deciding to do it. Teams, including the Dodgers and the Giants of 1958, were moved on no more pretense than their owner's decision to make the moves. What, Murray asked, had changed? He did not like the idea of the government and the courts imposing themselves on a man's desire to operate his business where he liked.

Murray compared golfer Tom Watson to *The Adventures of Tom Sawyer*. Watson had always enjoyed the game, but now that he was a star, he had responsibilities, just as Sawyer hated being "sivilized." Murray saw Watson as an example of the new corporate nature of athletics. Watson handled this well, but some of the pure joy was gone.

On March 13 he revisited familiar territory: Alabama football coach Bear Bryant ("The One and Only"). The old recriminations about race were absent.

Bryant was a heroic figure, closing in on Amos Alonzo Stagg's all-time record for college football victories. Fresh off his second straight national championship (1978–79), Bryant was playing golf, one of his favorite off-season activities, in a celebrity tournament in Palm Desert. His voice was "an indistinct rumble," and he was a "refugee from a steam iron for 40 years." When he hit a golf ball in the water and did not walk "over the top of it," it was obvious he was an "imposter." After all, he "wouldn't need a boat to go to Cuba." This was a reference to the 1960s Coca-Cola ads in Birmingham that had shown him walking on water.

Murray wrote a column on April 16 about the emerging possibility of baseball going on strike. In it, he suggested that he felt sympathy for the players. He furthermore added that they no longer respected the press, even though the media drummed up the excitement and fan support that made it possible for them to become wealthy in the first place. It was a sign of the times.

Murray enjoyed revisiting his boyhood in a piece about former USC law student Buster Crabbe, whose life changed when he won a gold medal for swimming at the 1932 L.A. Olympics. Crabbe later became a movie star who earned starring roles in the science fiction matinees of Murray's youth in Hartford.

In "World Class Leprechaun" (May 8), Murray wrote of the champion miler Eamonn Coghlan, "There is no need to ask, did your mother come from Ireland? Aye, you can see, and his mother's mother's mother—and so on, all the way back to Brian Boru."

Later in the year, he wrote "All-Time Greatest Name," in which he waxed romantically over some of the best names in sports history. These included Napoleon Lajoie, Germany Schaefer, Dummy Hoy, and Van Lingle Mungo, who he saw pitch in Hartford in the 1930s. Murray wrote that the Dodgers of the era had a lot of guys "named Rabbit."

On July 13 Murray joined a growing chorus of pundits who believed the "Green Monster," the huge left field wall at Fenway Park, had ultimately hurt the Red Sox over the years. The team had had two great left-handed hitters in recent seasons, Carl Yastrzemski and Fred Lynn. "With the right field fence two zip codes away, they looked at the seductive left field fence—and became inside-out hitters," he wrote. "That's like teaching Dempsey to jab." Only two pennant-deciding games had ever been played in the American League, both at Fenway Park, "and the Wall won both of them." In a 1978 play-off, both Yaz and Lynn hit 375-foot shots to right. Both were caught. Bucky Dent of the Yankees, whose 314-foot shot to left was a homer, won the game. "The Wall," Murray concluded, "has done more damage to the Red Sox than Harry Frazee. Only the Berlin Wall has caused more misery to the home team, to the good guys."

"I remember he wrote an article where he called me a 'hitting machine,'" recalled Fred Lynn, an L.A. native, USC All-American, and 1975 American League Most Valuable Player with the Red Sox.

> He was a columnist I enjoyed reading a lot. He was a great writer. English is not my best subject, but he was a poet, very rare and fun to read, and if he wrote about you, you were special. I loved Jim. I considered him a friend and missed him when he passed. He was around a lot and he never forgot anything you said, but anything you told him always came out better in print.
>
> It was a privilege to be interviewed by him. The conversation always swung back to USC. He was a USC fan. To me, when USC recruited me I slammed the door on everybody else. Jim was an absolute USC fan. He favored them. He painted a picture of USC that made people want to go there. He helped create the mystique of the Trojans, an image that was very appealing.

In November Murray took on a different subject. Ken Uston was the world's greatest blackjack player. Eventually a screenplay, *21*, was written about his exploits. It was obvious, from Murray's Hartford background and his uncles, who were gamblers, that gambling was a romantic notion to him.

When a TV movie (starring Robert Urich) depicting the life of Rocky Bleir of the Steelers aired, Murray reviewed it. Murray had been at a press conference in 1969 when Bleir, a former Notre Dame captain, announced he was going to play pro football. He had just had his foot blown up in Vietnam, but he fought his way back. When he finally made it, Murray wrote, "You made us look good. You made America look good."

Shortly after Christmas, Murray wrote a charming column about his granddaughter, Danica Erin Skeoh, a beautiful little girl who stole his heart.

■ ■ ■

On March 30, 1981, the *Times* ran a screaming extra edition headlined, "Reagan Shot." Twenty-two-year-old John Hinckley had shot the president on a Washington street. A Shakespearean drama could have revolved around what might have happened had Reagan been killed or unable to resume his duties. The president's fortitude in overcoming an assassin's bullet made the Republican more popular than new policies ever could.

The year 1981 was desultory for sports. The Lakers failed to repeat, losing to Houston in the play-offs. Larry Bird and Boston captured the championship. Even the Dodgers' World Series victory will forever be marked by an asterisk. They were the toast of baseball in the first half of the year; led by a rookie left-hander, Fernando Valenzuela, who was the biggest thing to hit baseball in years. He was unbeatable and exciting. Attendance was up all over the league. Then the players struck.

While the players were on strike, Murray wrote a column in which he expressed his distaste for lawyers, agents, and unions ruining baseball, all the while quoting Supreme Court Justice Oliver Wendell Holmes, who said "baseball was a sport, not a business." The players finally returned, but so much of the season was lost that everything—statistics, standings, play-offs—meant little.

On February 15 Murray wrote "Master of the City Game," a column about the emerging superstar Larry Bird, then in his second year with the Boston Celtics. "You don't get basketball players out of French Lick, Indiana," he wrote. "You get them off the playgrounds. The projects. The sidewalks of New York. Or the sidewalks of Chicago. Or North Carolina. Marquette. UCLA. You get apple pickers out of French Lick, Indiana."

The Celtics were Bob Cousy, "cool cats" like Sam Jones, a "glowering" Tom Heinsohn, "street-smart immortals like Bill Russell. Hondo Havlicek." They wanted guys with nicknames like "The Glide" or "Dr. Dunkenstein" or "The Truck" or "Magic." Instead Boston had a farm kid, and they were well on their way to a return to glory, another NBA title. Bird did not even have a wristwatch because in French Lick "they tell time by the cows." Murray concluded his piece by predicting, accurately, that Bird's jersey would someday hang from the rafters of the Boston Garden.

After giving the *Webster's* definition for "legend," Murray started his piece on golfer Sam Snead,

Ever regret you didn't see DiMaggio hit? Gehrig homer? Hubbell pitch?

Feel cheated you never got to see Dempsey punch, Grange run, Jesse Owens jump, Nagurski block? Like to have seen Jones putt, Luisetti shoot, Sande ride, Seabiscuit race? Maybe you wish you could have seen Nijinsky dance, Barrymore act, Tilden volley?

Sam Snead, he continued, "belongs to the past." He was one of those guys. None was "a bigger legend than Snead." He was "pure Americana" whose "first golf club was a swamp maple limb with a knot in the end and the bark left on for a grip." He grew up in northern Virginia hollers so narrow "the dogs had to wag their tails up and down." He was "Dan'l Boone with a one-iron, Huck Finn in a hat. Mark Twain would have loved him. Sam Snead, coonskin golfer. We shall not see his like again. A legend past his prime."

Murray's March 18 column honored a fellow superstar of the media, albeit of the spoken word. Lakers broadcaster Chick Hearn was the best in the business (although Warriors fans argue that their guy, Bill King, was at least Hearn's equal). Hearn "talked so fast the game couldn't keep up. Most basketball announcers are telling you what happened two minutes ago. Not Chick. Chick tells you what's going to happen."

In "He Needn't Take a Number, It's His," Murray wrote a column about the auto racer Richard Petty. Noting that Petty was distinctively "number 43," he wrote that he dominated his sport more thoroughly than Babe Ruth or any other athlete had dominated his. "Twenty-four years of the most hairy wheel-to-wheel racing and he doesn't have a mark on him," wrote Murray. "He has all his teeth, marbles. Limbs, walks without a limp, can eat steak and corn, doesn't need glasses and his thick, black hair doesn't look as if it was ever set afire."

In a piece on the trend toward funky baseball uniforms, Murray belittled the odd looks of the Chicago White Sox and Oakland A's. Told the White Sox were holding a contest to determine what fans wanted future uniforms to look like, Murray suggested entrants simply find a 1936 newspaper photo of Joe DiMaggio "with his hat on straight, his shoelaces tied and his shoes shined.

Submit that to your contest board. That's what a ballplayer should look like. Always."

"The Eternal Cowboy" (July 13) Walt Garrison looked like "trouble just sitting there. He's coiled. You'd imagine the members of the Dalton Gang looked like this. He looked like he might have a price on his head somewhere west of the Brazos. Wyatt Earp would be nervous if he rode into town."

He opened up a column on track superstar Carl Lewis with

The last time the world had anybody who could run faster and jump farther than anyone else on Earth at the same time, Hitler was ruling Germany, Roosevelt was running for a second term, and the King of England was giving up his throne for love.

That's how hard it is to do.

Murray wrote a column just before Christmas in which he wistfully listed all the things he wished he saw in sports, among them referees who were bigger than the players and who beat them with one-two combos when they argued; a clown football player doing a "funky dance," only to fall, embarrass himself, and for good measure, incur an injury (not too serious); and maybe a baseball player who acts nonchalant about everything and thus commits a replay of the "Snodgrass Muff."

American track star Mary Decker Tabb looked so youthful that if you saw her in Disneyland you would "take her picture with a police cap and page her mother."

Murray did not realize he was seeing the steroid era, which reached its peak in track (particularly during communism) long before it hit in baseball. Noting the huge size of so many female athletes, he wrote that in a world in which most girls wanted to look like Bo Derek, the athletes more likely resembled Bo Schembechler. "In a world of perfect '10s,' they're 'minus threes.'"

Murray also wrote a satirical piece describing himself looking in the mirror every day and seeing a guy who was "much older than I." He said that in his fantasy he looked like Rudolph Valentino whereas the guy in the mirror had paunches; he could eat chile relleno and drink Dos Equis, but the guy in the mirror got heartburn. He said he was ripe and ready for the Sunset Strip whereas the mirror told him to go to bed. "If he says write nice about

Cincinnati—or Seattle, or Santa Clara—I tear into them," he concluded. "If this ol' geezer thinks he owns me, he's got another think coming."

After another perfect Rose Bowl game played on another sunny Chamber of Commerce day, Murray wrote the sort of column he was famous for. As a transplant, he captured perfectly the ambience of his adopted homeland in a piece called, "We Just Have It Too Good." He started out by writing that the Rose Bowl "is plotting the destruction of California as we know and love it." On New Year's every year, the weather at the Arroyo Seco is perfect. This had to be a plot. "Lush, sunny," he wrote. "Snow in the mountains. Orange blossoms blinking in the sun." This, he added, was "insidious" and "subversive." The problem was that millions of Americans who "look outside and it's Duluth" viewed this spectacular of bare-chested bodybuilders, tanned girls in shorts, and pretty cheerleaders. Consequently, they all moved to California, which of course would eventually result in the Golden State sliding into the ocean. The "Rose Bowl menace," he wrote, needed to be "neutralized." He briefly suggested getting the Japanese to attack again but nixed that idea.

Murray suggested that fans be mandated to wear ski muffs and mittens, that "tickets should not be sold to anybody with a tan," and that NBC "should be forbidden to zero in on anyone not wearing a shirt, even if it's Cheryl Tiegs." Sunglasses should be "confiscated on the spot." Views of the San Gabriel Mountains should not be allowed, "unless they are on fire." MGM, he suggested, could truck in a snow machine. The Rose Parade was definitely out. He certainly did not want to convey the impression they could actually "grow roses in January, for Heaven's sake." Leonid Brezhnev should be the grand marshal. No young movie stars should be allowed at the game to seduce viewers with their million-dollar Pepsodent Beach Boy smiles. Instead of the Big Ten and the Pac-Ten, who usually gave America the most exciting New Year's bowl game, he suggested "inviting Harvard and Washington."

San Franciscans thought Los Angelenos were just too smug, arrogant, and into themselves. Murray's column was the kind they hated, even though they had Herb Caen. Yet, where Murray was a poet, many victims of Caen's vitriol considered him a guttersnipe. But in 1981–82, a small chink was found in L.A.'s armor.

Joe Montana and San Francisco arrived on the scene with a thunderclap to capture the Super Bowl title. The victory recalled Charles McCabe's 1962 columns, in which he posited that San Franciscans were satisfied being second best, that just coming close was all they really wanted, that "ultimate victory" was some sort of jingoistic, too-American virtue, the kind of thing to be saddled on New York or Los Angeles, not the City.

When Montana, Ronnie Lott, and genius coach Bill Walsh beat the Cincinnati Bengals in the Super Bowl, everything changed. It was a turning point, perhaps not really understood at the time, but in retrospect a moment for the ages. It unquestionably was the first real championship San Francisco had ever experienced. And McCabe had been wrong: denizens of Baghdad by the Bay liked ultimate victory just fine, thank you.

Los Angeles would achieve its fair share of ultimate athletic victory in the 1980s, but its total dominance was gone. Politically, the Southland still controlled everything. California voted Republican. It was the home of the "conservative revolution." The *Los Angeles Times* was the greatest paper in the world. The *San Francisco Chronicle* was weak in comparison. But the success of the 49ers, symbolic as it may have been, ushered in an era of change. San Francisco would chip away at Los Angeles over the next ten-plus years, in sports and elsewhere. Its voices would be heard, its votes counted, its political heroes elevated.

■ ■ ■

In an April 1982 column about The Master's golf tournament, Murray wrote of its notoriously difficult holes, giving each a horror movie name such as "Five Graves to Cairo." In a piece about horse racing, he used statistics to show that "Breeding Counts but Doesn't Add Up."

The St. Louis Cardinals defeated the Brewers in the World Series. Ross Newhan, Jim Murray's colleague at the *Times* who is also in the Hall of Fame for his baseball writing, recalled,

> Jim wrote all those great columns. I remember we attended the 1982 World Series between Milwaukee and St. Louis. We were in St. Louis and because of the press overflow we were not all in the main press box. Jim and I were sitting in a special press section down the right field corner, right behind the foul pole. The wind was blowing and it was very cold in St. Louis. I had to go downstairs after the game but Jim was gone. I didn't know what he was going to write. The next day I read this absolutely

wonderful column he wrote about the right field foul pole. I don't know how he did it, but he found a way to write a funny column about sitting behind the foul pole. I always brought that up when speaking with him.

Murray was the recipient of the Red Smith Award for lifetime achievement by the Associated Press Sports Editors in 1982. He had written a tribute to Smith, the great New York columnist, after his passing in January. When Rudy York hit a home run just as a wartime blackout caused the electricity to go out at the Polo Grounds, Smith had written, "The scorer ruled it self-defense." Murray was obviously influenced by Smith's turn of phrase. He recalled the time Red accidentally came across a shady story involving controversial manager Leo Durocher. It would have been a big scoop for him to reveal it, but since he did not come across it on his own, he let it ride.

Murray's kind words for Smith came from a generosity of spirit. According to a colleague of Murray's who asked not to be quoted by name, Smith called Murray a "joke writer" when he first came on the scene. At some point he most likely realized Murray's talent, but his initial cutting words reflected a New York bias that took years for Murray, and many other things associated with Los Angeles, to overcome.

"Red Smith was by far the greatest of all writers," said the iconoclastic former big league pitcher Bill "Spaceman" Lee. "He was the Secretariat of writers." Lee is a talker. A California native and USC star, Lee grew up with Murray and was in his column on occasion. "I was with Expos when Jim Murray interviewed me and did a story about me," recalled Spaceman.

> I had gotten into trouble with Commissioner Bowie Kuhn because I said I sprinkled marijuana on my pancakes before I went jogging, and he wanted to shut me up, and it was a free speech issue. Murray approached it as such with the local angle of a flaky California southpaw from USC. I can't remember exactly what Murray wrote about me, but Joe Falls of the *Detroit Free News* also wrote about me at the time.
>
> I thought Murray's writing was spectacular. It was kind of like an Eastern writer writing in a Western environment. He should have been in the New York papers, he was above the California readers. No one in California reads.

He had the biggest Coke bottle glasses and it always amazed me that a guy who was so blind could see so much. I read him all the time, but Murray was the kind of guy who came around a little but he was always in the background, not striking up one-on-one conversations. He maintained good olfactory sense and always knew when someone stunk, or was in a state of decomposition [laughs].

I loved Murray's references to Rome conquering Gaul. I didn't always agree with him all the time but I always read him, but I consider Smith to be better. I rank him number one and Dick Schaap number two. Writers are basically guys who wanted to be ball players, who couldn't play, and most don't know anything about pitching except it's hard to hit.

On December 15 Murray wrote a classic, "Coach of the Living Dead." "It starts like a horror movie," he began. "The man comes into focus. It is the face of a man who knows there is no longer any use in screaming." The man, Chargers coach Don Coryell, was known for making pained expressions akin to those of Czech long distance champion Emil Zatopek. "His mouth is turned down . . . his eyes register sheer terror. His is the face of a man tied to a plank with a buzz saw slicing its way toward his torso. His eyes are slightly bugged, as though a tombstone just talked to him. He is a man looking at his own corpse." Coryell, the writer added, always had the look of a guy the cops were asking about the murder of a mother and her child.

■ ■ ■

In March 1983 Reagan made the speech that defined his presidency. Speaking to Christian evangelicals in Florida, he referred to the Soviet Union as the "Evil Empire," a movie term straight out of the *Star Wars* series. It was a shot across the bow. The Soviets were in the midst of a period in which several premiers took power, only to die in office. Reagan was promoting another "Star Wars," a missile defense system planned to shoot down Soviet nukes before they could land on American soil. He was actively arming "freedom fighters" defending against communist expansion in Latin America. He and his CIA director, William Casey, were formulating ingenious ways to disrupt Russia's occupation of Afghanistan. The Soviets were scared of him and installed a moderate,

Mikhail Gorbachev, to lead their nation. The idea was that Gorbachev might be less confrontational and therefore might appease the "cowboy" Reagan.

In 1983 the Christian Right was in ascendancy, and with Reagan in office, it was time to make a strong move. Priority one was *Roe v. Wade*, the decade-old decision that made access to abortion legal nationwide. On June 16, however, *Times* staffer Jim Mann reported from Washington that the Supreme Court, despite having been buffered by some of Reagan's choices, upheld *Roe* in its ruling on two related cases. The abortion issue was at the heart of a cultural battle that had long been growing in America and that would continue for decades.

The Los Angeles Raiders provided the kind of glory the Rams had never been able to. Featuring former USC Heisman winner Marcus Allen, Hall of Famer Howie Long, and reborn quarterback Jim Plunkett, the Raiders ran the table, clobbering the Washington Redskins in the Super Bowl.

Murray wrote of legendary ex-Dodgers manager Walter Alston. In a "great victory for apple pie, ice cream, soda, biscuits and honey and whole milk," Murray wrote, Alston's 1983 induction into the Hall of Fame was "a marriage made in Valley Forge or the Declaration of Independence. They're as made for each other as cider and donuts. As American as pumpkin pie with whipped cream." Alston, he wrote, was fearless, a man you wanted next to you in a lifeboat. As far as the columnist was concerned, the Dodgers' tremendous success from 1954 to 1976 was as much his doing as it was Duke Snider's, Jackie Robinson's, Sandy Koufax's, Maury Wills's, Steve Garvey's, Don Sutton's, or any other star player's. "He was a good manager because he was a good man, a walking advertisement for the Good Book, an Old Testament model," he wrote. "Players black and white knew him as a man of probity and character." Alston never had an agent, never asked for more money or a longer contract, and "redefined the meaning of the word 'man' . . . a Man with a capital M."

In lauding Alston as he did, Murray was saying something about himself. He was saying that quiet, dignified, religious folks were simply better people than blowhards, lechers, and money-hungry egomaniacs. He made it clear that the latter were far more prevalent than the former, that the likes of an Alston or a John Wooden were rare. The world was filled with Leo Durochers and Muhammad Alis, who might be entertaining but who were unimpressive beyond their specialty. Alston was the kind of Rock of Gibraltar for the ages, the salt of the earth.

Perhaps inspired by Alston's upcoming election to the Baseball Hall of Fame, Murray wrote another column, "Scully Handles a Mike Like Ruth Did a Bat." Vin Scully and Alston were two of a kind, moral arbiters in a sea of second rates, true quality in an ocean of athletes who were all but stealing money from their employers and fans. Murray was part of a tiny group of men who transcended this sort of character flaw. He, Alston, Scully, and John Wooden rose above other sports figures, not only in Los Angeles but also in the world. They were giants not merely because of their talents but because of their moral character. Each was a rare combination of the highest success in their chosen professions and a generosity of spirit rarely seen. A professional manager, a college coach, an announcer, and a sportswriter, each stayed with the same team until the end.

Of Scully, who announced other sports in the 1970s, Murray wrote, "Rembrandt could probably paint soup cans or barn doors, if it came to that. Hemingway could probably write the weather. Horowitz could probably play the ocarina. What a waste!" Baseball fans, Scully knew, were "ancestor worshippers, like the British aristocracy," and through his words, "we suddenly see knights in shining armor out there carrying on glorious traditions instead of two rival factions of businessmen trying to land an order." Whereas football required "screaming," baseball needed what Scully gave it, "humor, deft drama, a sprinkling of candor, mix well and served over steaming hot tradition." Scully's pairing with Joe Garagiola on the *Baseball Game of the Week* was inspired casting, as important as "Ruth and Gehrig or Tinker and Evers and Chance."

Los Angeles sports fans long realized how very lucky they were. The best sportswriters and sportscasters in the world plied their trades in the City of Angels: Bud Furillo, Mel Durslag, Mal Florence, Bob Oates, Dick Enberg, Bob Miller, Chick Hearn, and Tom Kelly were among them. But Scully and Murray stood head and shoulders above them all. Character and talent linked their names together. Two twentieth-century giants of Los Angeles cast a Rushmore shadow over American sports.

On August 21 Murray tackled one of his greatest subjects, the superstar pitcher Tom Seaver. The title, "Almost Too Good to Be True," said it all, for Seaver was. The timing of the piece was notable. It was not a coincidence that it came on the heels of Murray's laudatory stories about Alston and Scully.

Rod Laver and
Jim Murray in
their respective
primes. JIM SLOAN
AND JIM MURRAY
MEMORIAL
FOUNDATION

Stars all lined up: Jerry West, Mel Durslag, Vin Scully, Jim Murray, Roy Firestone.
ALAN BERLINER AND JIM MURRAY MEMORIAL FOUNDATION

Murray interviews baseball legend Roberto Clemente shortly before the Hall of Famer's untimely death in a plane crash while delivering supplies to Nicaraguan earthquake victims on December 31, 1972. THE TIDINGS

On the job at a sold-out Coliseum for a 49ers-Raiders game, 1980s. JIM MURRAY MEMORIAL FOUNDATION

Jim Murray's introduction to the Baseball Hall of Fame, 1988. JIM MURRAY MEMORIAL FOUNDATION

ABOVE: Jim with Roy Firestone in Hawaii (1994). JIM MURRAY MEMORIAL FOUNDATION

LEFT: The great Murray posed for this photo, used on the cover of his 1993 autobiography. JIM CORNFIELD AND JIM MURRAY MEMORIAL FOUNDATION

In 1995 with Gene "the Singing Cowboy" Autry, 1995. MARC GLASSMAN AND JIM MURRAY MEMORIAL FOUNDATION

In Ohio with native son Jack Nicklaus in 1995. JIM MURRAY MEMORIAL FOUNDATION

Jim poses with race legend Mario Andretti and actor James Garner, Beverly Hilton Hotel, 1996. JIM MURRAY MEMORIAL FOUNDATION

From left: Tom Lasorda, Linda McCoy-Murray, Jo Lasorda, and Jim Murray, "Sports Spectacular," Century Plaza Hotel, 1996. Lasorda had a heart attack the next day. JIM MURRAY MEMORIAL FOUNDATION

With hotel magnate Barron Hilton, 1997.

JIM MURRAY MEMORIAL FOUNDATION

Jim and Linda McCoy-Murray pose with Dodgers owner Peter O'Malley and his wife, Annette, at the Historical Society of Southern California Jack Smith Community Enrichment Awards, the downtown L.A. Biltmore (1997).
JIM MURRAY MEMORIAL FOUNDATION

Golfer Al Geiberger and Jim. JOHN ROUNTREE PHOTOS AND JIM MURRAY MEMORIAL FOUNDATION

"It's never over till the fat lady sings 'it's déjà vu all over again' at a place nobody goes to 'cause it's too crowded." With fellow wordsmith Yogi Berra during the twilight years.
JIM MURRAY MEMORIAL FOUNDATION

In the spring of 1998, the great scribe posed with ex-Trojan Mark McGwire at Dodger Stadium. Big Mac hit seventy homers that year to set the all-time mark. MITCHELL HADDAD AND JIM MURRAY MEMORIAL FOUNDATION

Two legends: Murray with tennis star Rod Laver at Indian Wells in 1998. JIM MURRAY MEMORIAL FOUNDATION

Jim and Linda McCoy-Murray with Chris McCarron at Santa Anita. McCarron was the subject of his last column in 1998. JIM MURRAY MEMORIAL FOUNDATION

ABOVE: The best of the best. Poets Murray (77) and Vin Scully (69), both recipients of the Richstone Caritas Awards, at the Beverly Hilton. JIM MURRAY MEMORIAL FOUNDATION

LEFT: Jim at the podium. JIM MURRAY MEMORIAL FOUNDATION

Seaver was past his prime and not a star on an L.A. team, but Murray wanted to include him in that hallowed group of special, high-character sports figures. As in his 1962 column on Willie Mays, it was the best meeting the best, a master writer given free rein to write about a larger-than-life subject. He began the piece exactly as he had the Mays column twenty-one years earlier. "The first thing to do with a person like Tom Seaver is to establish that there is one." Seaver was a real-life incarnation of the boys from the adventure stories of his youth. "You have to make sure he didn't just walk in off the pages of *A Lad's Pluck* or *How Frank Merriwell Saves the Day at Yale*." Indeed Seaver was one of the rarest of all athletes: an absolute superstar, one of the greatest of the all-time great, yet possessing the intelligence of the secretary of state, "collar-ad good looks," and the All-American background of Frank Merriwell.

Seaver, having starred for Rod Dedeaux at USC in the mid-1960s, had a Los Angeles pedigree. The Dodgers could have had him for fifty thousand dollars in 1965, but scout Tommy Lasorda only offered two thousand. He ended up with the New York Mets and was the greatest pitcher in the game, arguably as good as Sandy Koufax, all the while comporting himself as if running for the U.S. Senate. "You have to find out if he isn't a public relations hoax," Murray wrote of him. Many had thought early on that he was "too good to be true," but by 1983 he was nearing the end of his career and, indeed, he was that good, all the way around. Murray made the usual Seaver comparison, with Christy Mathewson, one of baseball's earliest heroes, credited with giving the game respectability. Seaver never got thrown out of bars and did not pay alimony to two wives.

It was an off year for the ace right-hander, though, and his performance on the field was not what made him a feature story. Murray saw nobility in his pitching. "What's a goody like him doing with a 97-mile-an-hour fastball?" he asked. His skin was clear. He did not even spit. With his tools he should look more "like Burleigh Grimes than Christy Mathewson." Seaver, Murray wrote, was that rarest of athletes, the true New York sports icon who "awed" the Big Apple, a place that was in awe of only the most elite of the elite, whether that be Babe Ruth, Dwight Eisenhower, or John Glenn. They called him "fearless, faultless, a hero out of the dime-novel era. The guy who would rescue the orphan from a burning building, warn the train trestle was out, capture the runaway horses with the heiress in the carriage. Thrash the bully. Tom Swift and his Electric fastball."

Seaver was as "motivated as a monk," who instead of discussing "booze, broads," enjoyed the merits of finger pressure and proper wrist snap. Now back with the Mets after a sojourn in Cincinnati, Seaver was closing in on three hundred career victories. Murray displayed as much admiration for Seaver as for any athlete he wrote about.

■ ■ ■

Los Angeles may have found ultimate glory in 1984. Everything the city, the region, the state had ever aspired to be seemed encapsulated by that magical year. Oddly, it was the year chosen by George Orwell as a period of gloom and oppressiveness in his 1948 novel, but it may have in fact represented the opposite of that: free market capitalism and democracy at their peak. Whatever 1973–75 was supposed to have been, when the Los Angeleno Richard Nixon gripped tight the reins of power but let it all slip away, 1984–85 offered the chance, a decade later, to regain lost ground. This time Ronald Reagan kept his grip.

USC, the school that produced so many Watergate conspirators and now many of Reagan's key aides, was unapologetic about its conservatism. When G. Gordon Liddy spoke on campus, he received a hero's ovation from an audience chanting, "USA! USA! USA!" A sorority woman asked Liddy how students should protect themselves, since the school was located in a rough neighborhood. Liddy told her they should round up swimmers, football players, and assorted "tough guys" and, in vigilante style, proactively walk the streets to "take back what is rightfully yours." O. J. Simpson never heard greater cheering.

Democrat Walter Mondale spoke on campus. He was met by the thunderous chant, "Reagan country!" He admonished the students, stating, "You should be ashamed of yourselves. This is the school that produced Donald Segretti." But no one could hear him over the chanting. Reagan had planned to address USC's 1984 graduating class, but he missed the event when it was scheduled too close to his return from an exhausting visit to China.

By 1984 America was flush with success and secure in "peace and prosperity," a phrase used by Reagan throughout his campaign. A simple advertisement called "Morning in America" captured the essence of Reagan's appeal. To Republicans at least, "the Gipper" was every bit as true and righteous as Walter Alston, Vin Scully, Tom Seaver, and Jim Murray, all of whom most likely voted for him.

"I think Jim was offended by Watergate," said his widow, Linda McCoy-Murray.

> He had supported Richard Nixon, he knew him, and Watergate was an affront, he felt betrayed as did all of America, but I think he continued to vote Republican. Later, he lived near Ronald Reagan and he just loved Reagan. He knew him personally and found great humor in Reagan. At some point the Reagans moved to Bel Air and Jim joked, "I live about $6 million from the Reagans."
>
> One night we attended a party. I chaired a dinner in 1992 honoring Jim, and the Reagans were on stage with Merv Griffin, who owned the Beverly Hilton. Griffin presented Jim an award. So yes, we socialized with the Reagans and were friends. Jim definitely loved him and voted for him. I'm a Republican but very independent. If I like a candidate I'll vote that way regardless of party and I think Jim was that way, but leaning to the right.

The *L.A. Times* was still at the height of its glory. Sports, culture, and political power seemed to congregate at the Los Angeles Coliseum when L.A. hosted one of the most successful Olympic Games of all time. On July 29 the *Times* featured the Games on its front page with articles by Peter King, Tom Gorman, Patt Morrison, and Mark Stein. An aerial photo of the Coliseum at night captured the magic.

Peter Ueberroth pulled off what for years many speculated would be a wasted effort. *Sports Illustrated* had written a dismal piece predicting that the Los Angeles Games would be a disaster, mired in smog, crime, heavy traffic, crumbling facilities, and lack of fan enthusiasm. They were wrong. The United States—led by track stars Carl Lewis, Edwin Moses, and Evelyn Ashford; gymnasts Mary Lou Retton and Bart Conner; diver Greg Louganis; swimmers Rowdy Gaines, Matt Biondi, and Tracy Calkins; basketball gold medalists Michael Jordan and Patrick Ewing; volleyball stars Steve Timmons and Karch Kiraly; and a host of other star athletes, many with Los Angeles ties—dominated the 1984 Olympics.

Dodger Stadium hosted baseball. The U.S. team, coached by the Trojans' Rod Dedeaux and led by USC superstar Mark McGwire, is still regarded as perhaps the greatest collection of amateur baseball players ever.

The USC campus was the marquee attraction of the Games, and millions of people from around the world marveled at its facilities, some of which were built just for the Olympics. Many Trojans and Bruins athletes captured medals in the L.A. Games. It was a showcase for both schools and for Los Angeles.

The attendance and financial success of the '84 Olympics belied the notion that the typical Los Angeleno was jaded and bored or unwilling to attend all the Olympic events. President Reagan presided over the opening ceremonies. Former UCLA and 1960 decathlon champion Rafer Johnson lit the torch. It was a high point not just for Los Angeles but also for America.

Murray was in his usual form when he wrote his August 7 column, "The Baryshnikov of the Barriers." "I like to see Edwin Moses run the hurdles for the same reason I like to see Rod Carew bat, Bing Crosby sing, Joe DiMaggio drift under a high fly, Joe Louis throw a left, Sammy Snead hit a drive, Swaps in the stretch," he opined. "Palmer putt, Koufax with the hitter in a hole, Marcus Allen hit a line—for that matter, a Swiss make a watch, an Arab sell a rug, a Manolete fight a bull or a Hemingway write about it, an Englishman do Shakespeare, or Roosevelt make a speech." (His line "an Arab sell a rug" may not have been "politically correct," but that term had not been invented yet.) In other words, Murray wrote that Moses was one of "those guys who make it look easy."

The Olympic hurdles champion, Moses was the best ever at what he did, "one of the great virtuosos." Knowing thousands of sophisticated Europeans and world travelers were in town reading his column at that time, Murray filled it with classic superlatives about Caesar inspecting the battlefield, Baryshnikov on the dance floor, and Tchaikovsky writing music. Naturally he made biblical references to Moses's seven undefeated years. Jim Murray was now a writer of the world.

The L.A. Games helped spotlight previously little known sports—and Southern California's tendency to dominate those sports. The world knew that California, and the Southland particularly, produced baseball, basketball, football, track, and tennis stars. But in 1984 swimming, diving, and many other smaller sports received due attention. TV viewers learned that the Mission Viejo Nadadores was the premier swim club in the world and that USC and UCLA were much more than just O. J. Simpson versus Gary Beban on the gridiron or Lew Alcindor and Bill Walton on the hardwood. The sexy sport of beach volleyball was a big hit. It had been around, but in 1980 the dour Moscow atmosphere and America's failure to participate meant it was not highlighted at those games. It was a natural success in Los Angeles, however, and Murray was more than happy to write about it.

Great sports coaches and managers had dotted the American landscape for a century. Amos Alonzo Stagg, Knute Rockne, Vince Lombardi, Bear Bryant, John McGraw, Connie Mack, Casey Stengel, Red Auerbach, John Wooden, Toe Blake—these and many others were legends, national heroes. Even more impressive perhaps was the record quietly compiled over the years by a fellow named Al Scates. "Al Scates?! Precisely. The one and only," wrote Jim Murray. At UCLA, John Wooden was a walking marble statue, football stars roamed the green plains, Rafer Johnson and C. K. Yang were international stars. It was the school where Jackie Robinson and Arthur Ashe had become men, where Jim Morrison cut his teeth arguing the merits of French New Wave cinema with Francis Ford Coppola, where Nobel Prize winner Dr. Ralph Bunche learned history and diplomacy, and where on some Friday nights sorority parties half-resembled the *Sports Illustrated* swimsuit shoot. Al Scates quietly operated in this atmosphere of excellence, champions, and glory, and he won more often over a longer period than any of his more famed colleagues. Al Scates "is to volleyball what Wooden was to basketball, [Red] Sanders was to football, Napoleon to artillery," wrote Murray. It is interesting that of all the many, varied columns the great scribe wrote, many remember this one, about a relatively unknown volleyball coach.

Of course, Scates was probably among the two most successful Division I college coaches in history. His only real competition comes from crosstown rival USC, where Dean Cromwell seemed to win the NCAA track and field title every year. Rod Dedeaux? John Wooden? Pikers in comparison with Cromwell and Scates.

Cromwell also coached the U.S. Olympic teams, which in his day were basically made up of Trojan athletes dressed in red, white, and blue. So it was with Scates, whose UCLA teams also seemed to win national titles as regularly as the swallows returned to San Juan Capistrano and whose Olympians might as well have been a bunch of Bruins gathered together on a Saturday afternoon at Manhattan Beach—and sometimes they were.

"Oh my, sure, I'm very familiar with Jim Murray's claim that I was 'to volleyball what Napoleon was to artillery,'" Scates said.

Our SID for volleyball, Rich Bertolucci, puts it in the media guide every year since that 1984 interview. "Al Scates . . . the one and only . . . what Wooden was to basketball . . . Napoleon was to artillery." I was just very happy he came to my office to interview me. I would open the *L.A. Times* and the first thing I always read was Jim Murray. I bought all his books. In fact one year at the California Sports Hall of Fame induction, Jim Murray and his wife were there.

He was waiting for me, almost blind, but after we met it was a great time. I walked him down the stairs in front of the building. I asked if he needed help negotiating the steps. Well, he hardly saw them, but it was an honor to be in his presence. Such a humble man. He put me completely at ease. He wrote such great articles. He did his homework. He knew a lot of the stuff in the article. He knew we beat SC 16 times in row. He'd gotten the run-down from Bertolucci and Marc Dellums and was prepared.

Of a "poison pen" columnist who followed him, Scates recalled, "He was so different from T. J. Simers. T. J. was controversial. Murray did it with his prose, comparing things to legends like Lombardi and Rockne. He was well grounded in the history of sports in this country."

Scates apparently had Murray's column readily at hand during the interview and read randomly from it:

Listen to this: "It's the best of the world, action packed, cut throat competition by guys and gals going at a breakneck pace. It's about as polite as an air raid."

I invited him to a banquet to see Coach Wooden. I taught elementary school most of the years I coached at UCLA. At first I'd not heard too much about Murray, but over time I did. After the season there was a lot of talk about that particular article. It helped put my program on the map and led to higher salaries and full-time positions in the secondary sports. I always made sure my wife read it. It changed everything for us.

Thanks to smart planning, both traffic and smog were reduced greatly during the 1984 Games. Murray wrote about freeway congestion and air quality from time to time. He laughed at the naysayers who had predicted Olympic disaster. Almost thirty years later, it is clear that the Olympics were the beginning of the cleansing of the Los Angeles Basin's environment. In the early 1980s, football fans could barely see the other side of the Coliseum. They often could not tell, because of dirty air, what was happening on the field. The Coliseum press box and adjacent veranda are particularly situated with unobstructed east, west, north, and south views of the Santa Monica Mountains, Hollywood hills, the Hollywood sign, the downtown skyline, the San Gabriel range, the entire L.A. Basin stretching to Orange County, the endless strand, and the Palos Verdes peninsula. Before the Olympics, unless it was a rare breezy winter day immediately following heavy rain, all these views and more were like the Holy Ghost: you knew they were there, but you could not see them. Today sharp-eyed press box denizens can pick out details of mansions in the Hollywood hills!

Aside from the Olympics, 1984 was an exciting year in California sports, although it was not as great as 1962 or 1972. In his February 28 column on Boston's Larry Bird, the decidedly unprovincial Murray wrote "Bird Really Turns Pale with Losing." He wrote that saying the Indiana native was "white" was tantamount to "saying a desert is 'sandy.' If Larry Bird were any more white he'd be invisible. You could read through Larry Bird. If you held him up to the light, you could see what he had for dinner. He's the only guy in the room who doesn't need X-rays. You just stand him next to a window and count the bones. He'd make a great Halloween decoration." While Murray did not mean it to be, the column—as with the Olympics reference to an Arab selling a rug—was at best "politically incorrect." Had he written of a black athlete, "He's so black he could be mistaken for an eclipse," he would have received angry letters. But after paragraphs of yucks and more yucks about "the White Shadow," Murray did finally say that, oh, by the way, Larry Bird was one of the best basketball players of all time. At the time, he was considered better than Magic Johnson, even though Johnson and the Lakers had captured two titles (1980, 1982).

Magic, Kareem Abdul-Jabbar, and the Lakers appeared to have the NBA Finals sewn up, but Bird and Boston launched a comeback to take the title. The Celtics win marked an intense mid-1980s rivalry, and further enhanced the "Bird is better" arguments. Magic held his tongue, but after retirement he revealed that the talk bothered him.

Murray's March 28 column on Mario Andretti included this prize: "Mario is the most successful Italian export since pizza."

■ ■ ■

By and large, things continued to go Reagan's way in 1985. This made his presidency unusual. Successful first-term presidents historically tank in the second term. Cultural anthropologists, who view the decade as one of extravagant wealth to the point of greed, view 1985 as its pinnacle best represented by the movie *Wall Street*, released in 1987.

Reagan met Mikhail Gorbachev in Iceland. The two got along well. British prime minister Margaret Thatcher remarked that Gorbachev was a man she could "do business with." That seemed to be the case when the leaders of the United States and USSR agreed to dismantle a huge payload of nuclear weapons. At the last minute, Gorbachev tried to spring one on the old man. He would agree to dismantle the weapons only if Reagan would defund his Star Wars program. Reagan knew the program was the ace up his sleeve and refused the compromise. The media blamed Reagan for blowing an opportunity to achieve world peace. He stuck to his guns, literally.

After the Soviet empire imploded, their leaders admitted publicly that they were afraid of Reagan's Strategic Defense Initiative and that the American president's refusal to give in was the ultimate kick that kept them down for the count. Archives of the Venona Project and interviews with ex-KGB agents, who expressed downright admiration for Reagan's skill in a documentary called *In the Face of Evil*, confirmed this.

The 1985 Lakers beat Boston and, in doing so, established themselves as one of the greatest teams in NBA history. Of a July 4 column about Bob Hope (who hosted famed golf tournaments), the iconic comedian wrote to say he was having wallpaper made of it "so I can kiss it every day," adding he did not know how to thank him. "If I was a girl I could think of something, but since I'm just a hacker, I offer you two at Lakeside for a nickel any day."

Murray wrote a column about Miami quarterback Dan Marino, whose good looks he compared to Warren Beatty's. He figured quarterbacks needed to be "hunch-backed, pigeon-toed guys in high-top shoes like Johnny Unitas," but Marino was so hunky Murray could not understand how he ever dragged himself "away from a mirror."

In a March 28 column, "Fernando Throws Age a Screwball," Jim Murray described the Dodgers' ace, Fernando Valenzuela, as "Grover Cleveland Alexander with an accent." Nobody knew how old the Mexican southpaw really was, "somewhere between 45 and infinity," according to the writer. Rival managers regularly demanded not just to see the ball after striking out a hitter whose swing looked particularly embarrassing (to check for foreign substances), they also wanted "to see his birth certificate." He was "part Pancho Villa, part Cisco Kid." Murray said his first year ("Fernandomania," 1981) was comparable to Ruth's in fan interest, a remarkable assessment. Valenzuela, Murray wrote, "might just disappear into the mountains some day, like Jane Wyatt in *Lost Horizon*."

When German teenage sensation Boris Becker won at Wimbledon, Murray called him, "The pro from the Brothers Grimm." He dreamt of militaristic headlines like "Boris Becker Went through Wimbledon's Seeds Like von Moltke through the Low Countries Here Today." He hit his shots with the "authority of a Reichswehr 88-millimeter field piece." German readers, unaware that Murray made similar comparisons to the German army when writing about USC's Thundering Herd or the Yankees of Mantle and Maris, probably thought he was going too far.

When Howard Cosell left *Monday Night Football*, Murray pulled no punches. He did not like the famed announcer. Cosell was everything Murray was not: vain, pompous, self-serving. Murray was also smart enough to let Cosell do the talking. The columnist often eschewed quotes, preferring his own words, but when writing of a guy like Casey Stengel or Howard Cosell, he used quotation marks. Cosell dug a huge hole for himself, complaining about his old *MNF* booth mates Frank Gifford and "Dandy Don" Meredith. Murray wrote, "Howard Has Much to Be Vain About."

■ ■ ■

On January 28, 1986, the space shuttle Challenger exploded above the skies of Florida. In October the Iran-contra scandal hit. Reagan's presidency had finally hit an obstacle.

In a *Sports Illustrated* profile, reprinted by the magazine in 1994, Rick Reilly noted, "Murray may be the most famous sportswriter in history. 'What's your favorite Murray line?' At the Indy 500: 'Gentlemen, start your coffins'? Or

'[Rickey Henderson] has a strike zone the size of Hitler's heart'? Or UCLA Coach John Wooden was 'so square, he was divisible by four'? How many lines can you remember by any other sportswriter?"

In a marvelous piece about Magic Johnson, Murray wrote,

> If I were an NBA player, the last sight in the world I would want to see is Magic Johnson coming down the court with the basketball. You imagine this is the way the captain of the *Titanic* must have felt when he saw the iceberg.
>
> It's like seeing Babe Ruth coming to bat with the bases loaded and your fastball gone. It's like having A.J. Foyt in your rearview mirror on the back straight with 10 laps to go. The feeling Al Capone must have had when he got on the intercom and they said, "There's a Mr. Eliot Ness here to see you. He's got three men with him and he says it's important."
>
> It's like seeing a hand come up out of the coffin, or hearing a wolf outside the castle in the moonlight.

Murray did his best work when describing the best individual athletes who graced the scene throughout his career. He used a Caesar metaphor to describe Johnson's looking over the floor, setting up a play. He was as "indefensible as a riptide." Magic "is a conductor. Magic gives you a symphony, not an aria. Magic is trying to win a war, not a medal."

The column was written as a warning to the Houston Rockets, but the Lakers' dynasty took a turn sideways when the Rockets upset them, four games to one in the Western Conference finals. After Boston beat Houston in the NBA Finals, Murray found a local angle, the Celtics' sixth man, Bill Walton. The sixth man was a long Boston tradition, going back to John Havlicek and before him. Walton, one of the two greatest college players in history, led Portland to the 1977 NBA title, but injuries prevented him from attaining the level of greatness he seemed destined for. Still, he was on a team that won the 1986 championship, happily contributing as Larry Bird's teammate.

Interviewing Walton at a celebrity event at La Costa near San Diego, Murray wrote that in between his championship years—1977 and 1986—the creaky, oft-injured 6-foot-11 center was "crystal ware on the ends of his legs." In Boston, Murray continued, Walton could now "rank with the Lowells and the Cabots and the cod. The Kennedys might not want to ride in the same car." Of the upcoming meeting with President Reagan, Murray quipped that politicians would say to him they knew who he was, "but who's that actor with you."

When former New York Giants and Minnesota Vikings great Fran Tarkenton entered the Pro Football Hall of Fame, Murray wrote, "This is the look of a guy asked to go through Indian territory with only a map and a canteen, which is a fair description of his life in the NFL." Murray quoted the eloquent Tarkenton extensively in the piece.

Before the 1987 Super Bowl, Murray wrote about superstar quarterback John Elway. Elway catapulted Denver into the championship game against Bill Parcels and the New York Giants on the strength of "the Drive," a legendary, last-minute act of field generalship still resonating in the glory halls. He moved his team down the field in winter conditions, defeating the Cleveland Browns and their increasingly despairing fans. Murray wrote that nobody knew anything about the Broncos; they only knew Elway. When the Broncos arrived, everybody turned, expecting to see a whole team, but it was only Elway. All the Giants could talk about was Elway, as if there were no other players on their opponent's team.

He continued with classic Murray prose:

There is only one story in the Mile High City. Elway is like Caruso in the opera, Paderewski at the piano, Nijinsky at the Bolshoi.

If he wins, it'll always be "Elway Slays Giants."

Elway could throw footballs through "two time zones." He could make a football "sing Dixie." He was the "nearest thing to a one-man show since John Wayne cleaned up the Burma Road." If the Broncos' bus went over a cliff, the headline would read, "John Elway, 44 Friends Hurt in Crash." When the Super Bowl was actually played, however, the Giants roundly smashed Elway and his team.

The Denver–New York Super Bowl was played at the Rose Bowl in Pasadena. Sports editor Bill Dwyre was authorized to hire a prominent non-sports writer, a prominent, world-class author, to pen articles from the game. "I hired Leon Uris, who wrote *Exodus* about the creation of the state of Israel," recalled Dwyre. "I think we paid him $5,000 apiece for 3,000 words each." As the game wound down, Uris "just looks up at me and says, 'I can't do this.' He was too intimidated by Jim Murray."

Dwyre said, "Murray had trouble seeing, the game was boring, and Uris sat next to him all game while Jim tried to come up with a column. Then all of a sudden when the heat was on Jim just pounded one out and Uris is sitting there, unbelievably intimidated. He spent two or three years to write the kind of stuff he did. I had to write the last 18 graphs for him."

In a column about golf legend Jack Nicklaus, Murray wrote that he was a man who could "bring a sense of order, stability to our world." To watch Nicklaus in the links made it "1963 again." The Masters, he observed, was now "the Dallas Cowboys of golf." "As the poet said, with Nicklaus winning the Masters, God's in his Heaven and all's right with the world," he concluded.

Of Greg "the Shark" Norman ("Shark May Have Bitten off More than He Can Chew," June 15), Murray wrote, "You could chop wood with his face." Of famed horse trainer Eddie Arcaro, he wrote, "He could do anything on horseback that Jesse James, Tom Mix, Buffalo Bill or the Lone Ranger could." On September 23 Murray wrote a column on tennis "brat" John McEnroe, quoting Revolutionary War governor Patrick Morris, who said that a man could be judged by who shows for his funeral. Presumably Murray did not think McEnroe would attract a very good crowd. At the time, he was one of the dominant players in the game but an incredibly controversial figure on the court.

■ ■ ■

Two events dominated American domestic news in 1987: the Iran-contra hearings and the October stock market crash, a record 508 points in a single day. Somehow, the crash was only a blip; the economy picked up again and kept going. In West Germany, President Reagan exhorted Mikhail Gorbachev to "tear down this wall" in a speech given before the Berlin Wall. Like John Kennedy's "Ich bin ein Berliner" speech of 1963, it was met with wild enthusiasm.

A CIA-sponsored war in Afghanistan, sparked in large measure by a rogue Texas congressman named Charlie Wilson, resulted in a Soviet defeat that historians dubbed "their Vietnam." The Cold War was all over but the shouting.

Of all the great Los Angeles Lakers teams of the decade, the 1987 squad was probably the best, comparable with all-time NBA powerhouses such as the

1967 Philadelphia 76ers, the 1972 Lakers, and the 1996 Chicago Bulls. Murray wrote that they, led by Magic Johnson, "took the game out of idle," comparing games with the Showtime Lakers with "nightmares, tidal waves, vampires, earthquakes or falling from great bridges" for opponents.

The 1987 football strike rendered the pro season inconsequential. It (the strike) was the kind of thing Jim Murray hated. The innocence of sports that he had cherished since his youth was now a thing of the past.

■ ■ ■

In 1988 Murray was awarded the Lifetime Achievement Award by the Southern California Broadcasters Association. He also published his third book, *The Jim Murray Collection*. Broken into sections such as "Personally Speaking," "Portraits," and "Fond Farewells," it was a collection of his columns going back to the early 1970s. He inscribed it, "For every guy who ever struck out with the bases loaded, took a 10-count, fumbled on the goal line, double-faulted, missed a lay-up at the buzzer, pulled a three-foot putt and bet into a pat hand of aces full . . . and every guy who ever closed a bar alone at two o'clock in the morning."

Murray joked that he often received letters from some "patch-elbowed, blue-jean college work-shirkers" asking him to "explain" the role of "sports journalism." He claimed that they asked only so he would do their homework for them. He wrote that the best educational institution for journalism was not some place with ivy on its walls but rather the *New York Daily News*. He said "great" was too often used for "mediocre," "sensational" for "poor," and "immortal" for "competent." Among books that influenced him, he joked, were *Modern Theories of Cricket*, Clifford Irving's biography of Duane Thomas, and *The Religious Experiences of Leo Durocher*. His favorite spectator sport was the all-nude Broadway revue *Oh! Calcutta!* He loved being assigned interviewing duties in the locker room of the ladies tennis tour. His advice to future journalists was to "do your own homework" because "you can't cover the Super Bowl by questionnaire."

Vin Scully was a huge admirer of Murray, his equal in the pantheon, and an exclusive member of the two-man mutual admiration society. According to Scully, "[Murray] can level cities with tongue-in-cheek descriptions, humanize by hyperbole, and puncture the pompous with his literary lance. . . . I marveled at his sensitivity when he wrote about losing the use of an eye as if he had just lost an old friend. . . . He is, without doubt, a star of the first magnitude in the firmament that is sports writing, and well worth the looking."

Nineteen eighty-eight was another wonderful year in California sports. The Lakers captured another NBA title, and Stanford won its second-straight College World Series championship. The Dodgers, led by the fiery Kirk Gibson (Most Valuable Player) and pitching ace Orel Hershiser (Cy Young), captured the division, and then beat a favored Mets club in the play-offs.

In a piece on manager Tommy Lasorda, Murray led off with about a page and a half of hype before he even mentioned Lasorda's name. He said when the movie of his life was made, Lasorda would be played by Vincent Gardenia (*Bang the Drum Slowly*). He invoked God and country. If Lasorda were a politician, his foreign policy would be "Beat Montreal!" Lasorda was not above fabricating stories if it would fire his team up. He was "Mr. Baseball" and "as perfect for the Dodgers as peanut butter for white bread."

Pitcher Orel Hershiser broke Don Drysdale's all-time record for consecutive scoreless innings with 59 1/3. He earned the record dramatically in 1988, rather than waiting until 1989, by going ten innings in a 0-0 tie against San Diego before being pulled. As he was closing in on the record, Murray wrote, "They Won't Call Him Dr. Zero for Nothing." "Norman Rockwell would have loved Orel Hershiser," the piece began. Murray wrote that the pitcher's name should be Ichabod and "he's so white you can read through him," a retread from his column about Larry Bird. While Don Drysdale pitched in rage, throwing the ball "as if it were a grenade," Hershiser did not use intimidation. His pitches resembled a "16-pound shot." It was obvious in the column that a Christian family man like Hershiser was the preferred kind of athlete in the Murray lexicon.

Los Angeles pulled off an enormous upset of the mighty Oakland Athletics in the World Series. In game one at Dodger Stadium, Gibson homered off Oakland relief ace Dennis Eckersley to give his team the win, propelling them onward. Hershiser was as great as Koufax or any other postseason hurler. He shut out the A's at Dodger Stadium in game two and then defeated them in a complete game 5-2 win at the Oakland–Alameda County Coliseum to wrap up the 4-1 Series win.

Doug Krikorian was a young writer groomed for the business by Bud Furillo at the *L.A. Herald-Examiner.* "I'll always remember as a young reporter covering the Lakers and traveling with Jim Murray on a train with the Lakers from New York to Baltimore," he recalled.

> He couldn't have been nicer. Also, I never will forget us sitting next each other in the Dodger Stadium press box and when Gibson hit his famous World Series home run. Both Murray and I had already concluded our columns for Sunday's papers, as he had written about José Canseco's early game home run that had staked the A's to a big advantage and I had finished my piece for the old *L.A. Herald-Examiner*. And, Murray uttered a curse when Gibson's home run landed into the right field bleachers. "Now I have to write another column, (bleep) it," he said.
>
> I was always around Murray at big Las Vegas fights and Super Bowls. Good guy, affable to young reporters, never took himself seriously.

The year's California theme continued during the college and pro football season. The college season was as heavy with Los Angeles influence as it had been any year since 1967. USC's Rodney Peete and UCLA's Troy Aikman battled each other for the Heisman Trophy (just as O. J. Simpson and Gary Beban had in '67), and their schools battled for the national title, with Peete and the Trojans winning. After Peete bombed on the big stage against Notre Dame, Oklahoma State's Barry Sanders ended up the Heisman winner, and USC folded in an uncharacteristic Rose Bowl defeat at the hands of a team they normally whipped, Michigan.

In the new year Joe Montana, Ronnie Lott, and the San Francisco 49ers defeated Cincinnati in the Super Bowl. Bill Walsh retired after the victory with three Super Bowl wins. By now Charles McCabe's old saw about San Franciscans being psychologically unable to handle the thrill of ultimate victory was rendered completely irrelevant.

During spring training, Murray wrote a column about Nolan Ryan in which he compared his statistics in various seasons when other pitchers had beaten him out for the Cy Young Award. The way Murray framed the argument made it almost ludicrous to conceive that Gaylord Perry had been better than Ryan in 1972, Jim Palmer in 1973, Catfish Hunter in 1974, or any of a number of other years. Ryan had consistently posted a high number of wins, more than three hundred strikeouts, microscopic ERAs, and annual no-hitters over the course of three hundred innings and twenty-plus complete games. "Give him the Cy Young Award?" wrote Murray, miffed. "Don't be absurd! Not when you have pitchers like Pete Vuckovich, Steve Stone, LaMarr Hoyt and Steve Bedrosian to give it to. You don't give the Cy Young Award to a guy just because he has set or broken 38 Major League records. After all, did Chaplin ever win the Academy Award?" His arm "should go to the Smithsonian," Murray continued. Ryan did not "rob banks, kill kittens, sell government secrets, set fires," or "drink, smoke, chew or swear" for that matter. Other than that he was a pretty good guy. "He's polite, approachable," believed in God, was unimpressed with himself. "The Cy Young voters have managed to stay pretty *blasé* about it, too," Murray wrote. "Maybe they're waiting for him to cure cancer."

Also in 1988 Murray wrote columns about horse trainer Chris McCarron and race driver Richard Petty. He revisited the story of Bob Beamon, who set the long jump record in 1968 with a mark so outrageous the column was titled, "He Landed Somewhere in the Future." He also did a retrospective on 1948 and 1952 Olympic decathlon champion Bob Mathias (a teammate of Otis Chandler's at Stanford), whom he called a "one-man track team." His bad javelin form resembled a guy throwing a "spear like a guy killing a chicken. He went over the vault like a guy falling out of a moving car, and his high jump looked like a guy leaving a banana peel. All he did was win."

When hockey legend Wayne Gretzky signed with the Los Angeles Kings after years of dominance with Edmonton, Murray wrote flat-out that it was because he desired to be recognized on a large stage. His wife was an actress, and "you can't be an actress" in Edmonton. "Trust me." Gretzky "wants to play the Palace."

■ ■ ■

The last year of the decade has gone down in history as a "game changer," to use a sports term. In June the Chinese fired on demonstrations by citizens who wanted democracy. Thousands died. The sight of a faux Statue of Liberty, dubbed the "Goddess of Democracy" by the demonstrators, enraged the Chinese leaders. The world noticed the Chinese protests at Tiananmen Square. The quest for freedom, inspired by Reagan, who had been succeeded by George H. W. Bush in January, was moving all over the world. In November Reagan's exhortation from two years previous finally came to fruition when the Berlin Wall was torn down.

Afghanistan had turned against the Soviets two years earlier. It was a moment of triumph for the United States, and now Eastern Europe was free.

In 1989 the Detroit Pistons ended the Lakers' run. Kareem Abdul-Jabbar retired, and Murray wrote that he had finally shut his many critics up. "God made him more than seven feet tall," he wrote. "He took care of the rest." He was finally "winning with class."

It was a defining year in the L.A.–San Francisco rivalry. For years Los Angeles teams had destroyed Bay Area teams. There were exceptions, mainly in the form of an Oakland A's dynasty and great Oakland Raiders squads, but until Joe Montana and the 49ers lit up pro football, the scales were heavily weighted in favor of the south. In the 1980s, however, the Dodgers slumped a little, the Rams slumped a lot, and USC fell precipitously, at least by their lofty standards. California and Stanford were not exactly bringing back memories of Brick Muller and Frankie Albert, but they would, over the next few years, compete on a relatively even playing field with Southern California and UCLA. The old Bruin basketball dominance was a thing of the past.

The defending World Champion Dodgers struggled, and the Angels did not consistently contend. America's national pastime was a Bay Area affair, with Oakland beating San Francisco in the "earthquake" Series. Coming in confluence with the 49ers' utter dominance, it seemed to Southern Californians as if the globe was off its orbit.

While Murray loved San Francisco's skyline, bridges, bay, and mountains, he was not enamored of its people, its politics, its low rent anti-L.A. fans throwing garbage and screaming obscenities at Tommy Lasorda. Over the years Murray had found a certain amount of satisfaction in writing how divine providence seemingly smiled on the Southland while turning San Francisco into a symbolic pillar of salt.

In returning to a theme he had developed over the decades, he declared that Los Angeles had hosted major sporting events almost annually—Super Bowls, Rose Bowls, World Series, NBA Finals, basketball rivalries, collegiate football wars, two Olympics—virtually without a hitch. The weather was always perfect, the fans well behaved, the events well ordered, minus riots and disasters. But San Francisco, a place that hosted a major event only occasionally, yet seemed doomed by dame fortune in the form of a completely rare Pacific rainstorm (1962) and a 7.1 magnitude earthquake (1989).

Try as Jim Murray might to put Northern California down, to put them off and laugh them away, they were comers by 1989. John Robinson's Los Angeles Rams were no match for the 49ers. When they met in the NFC championship game, it was a joke: San Francisco 30, Los Angeles 3. Afterward Murray wrote, "I thought Joe Montana was human." He "glows in the dark." Giving him the ball was tantamount to "giving Rembrandt a brush or Hemingway a pen." For "'Joe World' . . . 'good field position' is his own three-yard line." He returned to his well-worn comparisons: Spencer Tracy acting, Jascha Heifetz fiddling, Ty Cobb at the plate, and one of his favorites, the ballet artist Vaslav Nijinsky.

After the 49ers annihilated Denver in the Super Bowl, Murray wrote a column on January 29, 1990, that was so good that picking out its best lines is impossible. First, he listed things "that shouldn't happen," such as clubbing baby seals. At the end of the list, he added "the Denver Broncos in the Super Bowl." "Where is the Humane Society when you need it?" he wrote. "Where are those organizations against cruelty to dumb animals?" The Broncos "went to their fate like guys going to the electric chair. . . . Cagney did it better. . . . It wasn't a game, it was an execution. It was the biggest mismatch since the Christians and the lions."

Murray urged Bud Grant and the Vikings to return in order to reclaim their "Super Bowl record for futility." The Broncos were "the William Jennings Bryans, the Harold Stassens, Tom Deweys of football. . . . They should have a clause in the wire agreement with the league that they don't have to play in a game under 5,000 feet. And they shouldn't play the San Francisco 49ers anywhere."

Not only were the 49ers better, "they looked better in their uniforms. . . . The outcome was as foregone as a tidal wave." Joe Montana probably could "walk on water" and bullets "probably bounce off him." Giving him tools like Jerry Rice and Roger Craig was like "giving a lion horses." Anybody who enjoyed the Niners' destruction of the Broncos probably enjoyed pictures of "the German Army going through Belgium. The 49ers aren't a team, they're a scourge. A dynasty . . . an empire."

In 1989 one of the great feel-good human interest stories in sports history played out in Los Angeles. Jim Abbott was an All-American pitcher at the University of Michigan. He had led his team to defeat the vaunted Cuban national team in international competition. He was now pitching for the California Angels, having ascended to the Major Leagues without playing in their farm system. This made him exceptional enough, but great athletes were not exactly a novelty in the City of Angels. What made Abbott so different was that he had only one arm. That one arm, his left, was the one he used to mow down opposition batsmen in short order.

"Too often, the Major League ballplayer is portrayed as a churlish, graceless individual who comes into public view brushing the little kid autograph seeker aside, refusing to pose for pictures, announcing irritatedly that all he owes his public is a .293 average or an appearance at a baseball card show for which he gets $10,000," wrote Murray. One could half-imagine the ears of the nameless many he called out getting red. "There are, to be sure, a few who fit this unflattering image. They take the $2 million and run. The fans' love is unrequited. The record books sometime identify these worthies as Most Valuable Players. The public concept of what these letters stand for is quite different. So, it gives me great pleasure today to check in with a different kind of story, the account of a Major League player who belongs to the world at large, is a citizen in good standing with the rest of the community, a man who cares."

Murray wrote about a despicable incident in which a little girl in Indiana lost her hands when somebody planted a bomb in a K-Mart store. "[The blast] didn't kill Erin," Murray wrote of the five-year-old. "It just blew off her left hand. You don't even want to think about it. . . . In all the outpouring of sympathy for little Erin, one letter came marked with the logo of the California Angels." It was a graceful, beautifully eloquent letter from Abbott encouraging the child. He wrote that while the loss of his hand was a handicap, "I figured that's what the Good Lord wanted me to work with. . . . With dedication and love of life, you'll be successful in any field you choose. I'll look forward to reading about you in the future." "Now that, you have to say, is the way to get an autograph," wrote Murray.

In an article about former Steelers star quarterback Terry Bradshaw, whom many considered "dumb," Murray wrote of the Hall of Famer, "Some dunce! With a football in his hands he was Einstein." His March 24 column, "Pete Rozelle Sold Entire Nation on His Sport," stated, "Michelangelo has his David, Da Vinci his Mona Lisa—and Rozelle has the Super Bowl." As a public relations man, "he could make Castro President of the U.S."

In a column on the Unser racing family, Murray wrote, "Victory Lane is like Buckingham Palace, the ruling family's ancestral home."

He wrote a utilitarian column about German tennis sensation Steffi Graf, mainly a question-and-answer piece. Charlton Heston afterward wrote Murray to endorse his nomination of Graf for Sportsman of the Year.

Murray wrote a wistful column about his hero, Ben Hogan. He recounted how hard Hogan had tried to break into the golf tour in the 1930s. When he played at Pasadena's Brookside Park in 1931, "Bread was only a nickel. But nobody had a nickel." The golfers played for oranges, which Hogan lived on for a week. Murray followed the Hogan piece with a paean to his favorite course: the beautiful Riviera Country Club in the Palisades, "a grande dame of American golf courses. A golf tournament at Riviera is like a World Series at Yankee Stadium, an opera at La Scala, a waltz in Vienna, a war in the Balkans. Fitting."

14

Love, Tragedy, Redemption

In a column dated March 16, 1986, called "The Sport That Time Leaves Alone," Murray wrote one of his most quoted lines: "I've never been unhappy in a ballpark."

Jim Murray came to his social pathos by virtue of his upbringing. He had a big, extended family of uncles, Runyonesque characters, little guys, underdogs. He was shaped by the misery of the Great Depression. Being an Irish poet, he saw the world through the lens of tragedy, as did such disparate men of the Isle as Dylan Thomas, C. S. Lewis, James Joyce, Oscar Wilde, William Butler Yeats, and Jim Morrison. Murray was a product of parochial schools and Christian faith. Born in the shadow of the Great War, he saw his country fight in three more major conflicts, against the evils of Nazism and communism. He knew how lucky he was to live in freedom.

But his 1986 column, in which he said he was never "unhappy in a ballpark," masked the fact that covering sports was an escape from his troubles, from the troubles of all humanity, perhaps even a respite from original sin, something innocent and pure in a world where these are rare commodities. It also masked sorrow, for Jim Murray's social pathos came not just from the priests at Trinity College or the sight of Depression bread lines. He lived it, up close and personal.

Murray dedicated his 1965 book, *The Best of Jim Murray*, "to my three sons, Ted, Tony, and Ricky, who have never read my columns and doubtless won't read this book, and my daughter, Pammy, who won't, either. To their mother, Gerry, who not only read, but, bless her, laughed at all the jokes." The dedication implies some frustration on the part of the great scribe, who, although he influenced many Americans, could not bridge the generation gap with his own children.

Chapter 18 of Murray's 1993 autobiography is titled, "The Baby of the Family." It begins, "There hangs in my bedroom a picture some 35 years old, and it is the first thing I see when I get out of bed in the morning. And it hurts to look at it." Jim and Gerry Murray had two older boys, Teddy and Tony, and a daughter, Pammy. The "baby in the family" was named Erick Patrick, but he went by Rick or Ricky. Gerry had a hysterectomy shortly after he was born. He looked like his mother, with big brown eyes, dark skin, and a generous mouth. He usually smiled. In photos, Ricky always looked like he had a cold or was stuffed up. Ricky loved and trusted his sister. He loved his mother. Murray recalled that he always called out, "Mom," when he came into the house.

In 1956, when Ricky was three, the Murrays moved to Malibu from Pacific Palisades, which Gerry and Jim decided was "too urban." They wanted a wide-open place where their children could run free. They bought an acre and a half of property in Malibu, which they later sold to Bob Dylan. It was on headlands off Point Dume, where "pirates once off-loaded their stolen gold," said Murray. It was next to a place called Paradise Cove. The beautiful sand and sea, the good life in Malibu, seemed idyllic. But too much "good life" in the form of money, parties, girls, sex, drugs, alcohol, and Hollywood immorality can turn a place from "idyllic" to tragic.

Malibu is the home to the Hollywood elite, including Barbra Streisand, Martin Sheen, and Nick Nolte. But most of these people came from someplace else. By dint of hard work, talent, and perseverance they forged success in the competitive world of movies, music, and entertainment. They pulled themselves up by the bootstraps, surviving, struggling against all odds until they reached the top.

Murray was also in the entertainment business, of a sort. He too was from someplace else and had, by hard work, perseverance, and talent, risen to the top. But these winners of the American Dream grow up and have children whom they raise in luxury. The odds alone make it unlikely any will ever come close to matching their famous parents' success.

Some of these children of privilege who grew up and hung out together in Malibu in the 1960s and '70s included the Penn brothers, Sean and Chris; the Sheen brothers, Charlie and Emilio Estevez; and Rob Lowe. Many of these children were in the headlines at one time or another for some kind of indiscretion. And these are the ones who made it big. For every success story, hundreds of kids have been frustrated by expectations, failure, and temptation.

Ricky was "totally a product of that environment," wrote Murray. "That meant surfing, guitars, the beach life, a cut-off from the frantic pace of the city. . . . It looked like paradise. So, I think, did Gomorrah." Murray said that the experience left him feeling the same way about guitars as a rabbi feels about a swastika. "I associate it [the sound of a guitar] with terror in the night, years when you picked up a ringing phone or answered a knock at the door with a pounding heart." The "paradise cove" where pirates once smuggled treasure, where bootleggers once unloaded their illegal booze, was by Murray's time where drug smugglers landed their dope. The Murrays had unwittingly moved to the West Coast distribution center of hard narcotics.

Murray became a columnist with the *Times* five years after he and his family moved to Malibu. Before that, when he worked for *Sports Illustrated*, he had been on a weekly deadline heavy on editing duties. His hours at *SI* had been Monday through Friday, nine to five. At the *Times* they were 3 p.m. to midnight, including every Friday and Saturday night. He rarely had time for church on Sundays. He had to be at Dodger Stadium, the Big A, the Coliseum. Or he was out of town, with the Lakers, at the Indy 500, the Super Bowl, March Madness.

In the meantime, the '60s snuck up on the greatest generation. *Gidget* had been replaced by The Beatles, the Stones, and hedonism. Murray had steeled himself to protect his kids from alcohol—he could speak that language as he'd known it in his youth. Yet rebellion, war protesters, free love, and drugs were an insidious, new, subversive enemy stealing his kids' souls.

Murray wrote plainly that marijuana was a gateway drug leading to harder narcotics. He saw it up close. First he saw it with his neighbors. Then it happened to his family. The generation gap was in full swing, and his words to his son fell on deaf ears. Catholic guilt, Christian temperance, family values, old-style morality—all this was one big guilt trip to the younger generation.

To cope with his home life, Murray turned to his talent as a writer. Hoping they could band together, he prepared a pamphlet to be distributed to other Malibu parents. He did not realize that many of those parents thought it "cool" to smoke dope with their kids; they believed permissiveness in child rearing was a virtue. When the cops were called, they blamed them for being "pigs" if they happened across some narcotics at a too-loud party. If they were lucky, they never got a call from the coroner. "You could get 'em marching in the streets to save the whales," Murray wrote. "It was just too hard to organize a march or committee against drug abuse."

Ted was serving in the army. Tony was good enough to play baseball at the University of California–Berkeley. Ricky was left to his own devices. He tried to follow in his mother's footsteps as a musician. He had skills on the guitar and, especially in the Malibu atmosphere, saw a future in rock 'n' roll. Keith Moon of The Who, Mick Jagger of the Rolling Stones, and many, many other stars and troubadours could be found at the local clubs, on the beach, at parties, at the grocery store. The temptations of the rock lifestyle were extraordinary.

"His idol was Jimi Hendrix," recalled Murray. "That should have told us something." The Murrays did not even know who Jimi Hendrix, one of the most famous guitarists in the world, was. He died in part from a drug overdose; incoherent, he passed out while lying on his back and choked to death on his own vomit. He was not the only rock star to leave this mortal coil in such a manner. "By the time we found out, it was too late," Murray wrote of Hendrix's "influence."

Ricky attended Santa Monica High School, known as SaMoHi, where many sons and daughters of the rich and famous went to school. Charlie Sheen once was a pretty good pitcher there. It was one of the bigger prep sports powerhouses in L.A. County in its heyday. The Vikings produced many football champions, but baseball was the school's specialty. Rick Monday matriculated there. Tim Leary was a superstar at SaMoHi. He led the Vikings' summer American Legion team to the 1976 national championship before his All-American career at UCLA and star turn with the 1988 World Champion Dodgers.

Ricky Murray did not play sports at SaMoHi. He played the guitar. One day the Murrays received a phone call from a counselor at the high school. Ricky had been caught with drugs. A genial fellow, the counselor tried to assure them that this sort of behavior was a phase, a sign of the times, but not so serious as to be life-threatening. It would pass. He had seen it before and knew what he was talking about. The counselor indicated that it would be best for him to handle the problem. Kids responded to his easygoing manner. Parents became emotional and created the wrong vibe. The counselor asked Murray to "stay out of the picture," to not impose his middle-class morality and, for God's sake, his Catholic guilt upon his son.

Murray was OK with the plan until tragedy struck. The counselor's own son was on drugs too, and one day, on an LSD trip, he killed his sister with a shotgun while she watched television. Later, unable to overcome his demons, the young man climbed up a telephone pole on Sunset Boulevard and set a match, immolating himself against the electrical current in a horrifying scene.

Jim and Gerry were on their own and had no answers. Rick was eight when Murray became a columnist. He didn't know how to live up to his father's celebrity and fame. He turned from sports, feeling he was not capable of following in such big footsteps. Murray was consumed by his work and often out of town or out of the house. His days were spent hunched over his typewriter, conjuring up witticisms about John McKay or Walt Alston. Once Murray's daughter, Pammy, came home upset because "Emperor Hull" on KMPC "ranked on" her father all morning for something he wrote in his column. Slowly Murray's children began to understand the public nature of their father's work. Murray thought he could get closer to his kids by writing about their little league or beach exploits or about Gerry in columns called "Mom Sez."

"It all went by too fast," Murray wrote in 1993. "One minute they were all in the back of the car, shiny-faced, on their way to Disneyland. In no time, they were growing moustaches, letting their hair grow, insisting on torn jeans to wear at school." Ricky started riding a motorcycle. He became defiant. Murray was bewildered. His youngest son started growing pot in their backyard. That was when it got really bad. Years of late night phone calls from police, concerned parents, and counselors followed. Murray "clung to the column like a life raft," but his poor wife was left to deal with the situation on her own.

The Murrays' neighbors tried to comfort them, saying that pot was not so bad, that everybody did drugs, that it was part of the music scene, that half the rock songs extolled its virtues. Drugs unleashed inhibitions and increased both sexual desire and creativity. Murray, who liked to pull a cork with John McKay at Julies and unwind with a dram of Scotch when he came home at night, felt like a hypocrite. Hey, all the great Irish poets were alcoholics, right? Hemingway was a famous drunk, his great writing seemingly spurred by his bouts with drink and subsequent adventures, but then again he put a shotgun to his head.

Murray's boss, Otis Chandler, had a reputation for being Hemingway-esque, but he was a health freak, a bodybuilder who neither drank nor smoked.

Regardless, Ricky was not around to observe Chandler's example and make it his own. America's youth was affected by movies like *The Graduate*, which depicted Pasadena–San Marino wealth in all its privileged hypocrisy, with the youthful Dustin Hoffman declaring he wanted to be "different"—it may as well have been written about the Chandler family.

The Murrays tried everything—screaming, yelling, recriminations; kicking Ricky out of the house; inviting him back; psychiatry. The psychiatrist told Murray his son was "just a vagabond, a nomad." Murray tried to use his contacts to promote his son's career as a musician, but his efforts were half-hearted since "I was a Beethoven man myself."

Once Gerry and Jim found their son homeless. They took him home. He planned a trip to England to work on his music. He spent a miserable year living as a bum, playing his guitar in the dirty, drafty underground. He moved to New York and lived with unscrupulous characters in the worst part of town. Gerry and Jim did not really want to know the gory details. When Jim visited, he was horrified at the squalor of his son's life.

Ricky returned to Los Angeles penniless, but by then his addiction was a morass, resulting in petty thefts, arrests, and scuffles with the law. Murray landed his son a low-level pressroom job at the *Times*. They had to let him go. He slept on the job. Ricky was arrested and sent to the county honor farm in Saugus. Would this be his wake-up call? Ricky told funny stories about the other inmates. He had his dad's gift for storytelling.

■ ■ ■

Bruce Jenkins grew up almost next door to the Murrays in Malibu. He attended Santa Monica High School and the University of California with Tony Murray and joined the *San Francisco Chronicle* in 1973. He is now a leading sports columnist and immediately understood the importance of Murray's son's story. "I'd known the Murray family since 1955, when they moved to Malibu and his son, Tony, and I were in second grade together," recalled Jenkins.

> My father, Gordon Jenkins, was a well-known composer and knew Jim well; they were often at parties together. But I wasn't at all close to Tony at the start. He had a nasty Irish temper and was a total brat through grade school. He never struck me or any of my other friends as a good

guy. But in the tenth grade, riding the bus together from Malibu to Santa Monica High School, we became close friends. I started hanging out at the Murrays' house because Tony and I turned out to have so much in common, but it didn't hurt that I'd wanted to be a sportswriter since the eighth grade. Now I've got Jim Murray, the greatest of all writers, virtually next door.

Jim never took the time to give me any particular advice about the business, and that wasn't surprising, because he gave very little time to his own kids. I was at that house two or three times a week, often for hours at a time, and I rarely saw Jim. He worked in an office that was separate from the house, so he couldn't be distracted, and he was always in there. His work ethic was so fierce, it left him with virtually no time for his family.

Linda McCoy-Murray was protective of Jim's legacy, particularly as it relates to this issue. "Maybe Jim did not spend a lot of time with his kids," she stated. "That's what that generation was like. My own mother raised us. My dad worked two, three jobs and was never home. This was not unusual, especially in those days. Jim was not unusual."

"But he'd come out of there to watch the big sporting events, and that's where he had a deep, everlasting effect on me," continued Jenkins.

We're sitting there watching Bill Russell against Wilt Chamberlain, or Johnny Unitas dueling Bart Starr, and it was priceless to listen to Jim's comments during a game. His comments were biting, often sarcastic, but he revered the great athletes and loved to write about them. I learned then that you can never write enough columns about Unitas, or Arnold Palmer, or Willie Mays, because people always want to know about the great ones. And I watched Jim's utter dismay when some complete unknown took the lead in a major golf tournament. Where's Arnie? Where's Nicklaus? Jim wasn't truly happy until the great ones took over, like Ben Hogan, the athlete he respected above all others.

The best moments of all were at the Murrays' dinner table. They never struck anyone as a particularly close family, especially with the three boys straying so far from the mainstream path, but they always gathered for dinner and, at least when Jenkins was around, had an uproariously good time. All the boys were incredibly funny, just as wickedly sarcastic as their father. So were Pammy and Gerry. They basically took turns shredding each other, in an incisive but good-humored way. Whatever issues were in place, they were forgotten at the dinner table. For that hour or so, everybody was a comedian. There were times when Jenkins was laughing so hard, he could barely see straight, and "I can't tell you enough how much that affected my own sense of humor. I developed a sense of sarcasm, and timing, that wouldn't have happened otherwise."

But a chasm developed in the family. The children had the gift of humor and sarcasm but lacked the passion to turn it into a writing career like their dad had. Ted became a nice, responsible adult, but he was a "holy terror back then," recalled Jenkins. It was almost painful to watch him mercilessly trashing kids on the school bus. Tony had more options because he was one of the best athletes in school. He focused on baseball, but he could have played any sport.

Jenkins was a basketball player who hung out with a group of guys at SaMoHi who were all pretty good athletes as well as budding intellectuals. Their whole mission at lunchtime was to find where Tony was sitting, so they could gather around him and witness his humor in action. "My God, was he funny," recalled Jenkins. He went on to theorize that Tony's humor masked a loneliness, even though he "seemed to have it all." Ricky "wanted nothing to do with good grades or even girlfriends," but Jenkins believed that Tony was talented enough to be drafted out of high school, sign a pro contract, and be on his way as a pitcher.

They went to Cal together, and one time, during a trip to San Diego, Murray set up a dinner with Tommy Lasorda and invited Jenkins to come along. "Tommy was just a minor league manager at the time, but he had a lot of influence, and if anything, we thought the Dodgers would draft Tony as a favor—even though he had the talent to be considered on merit," said Jenkins. "For some reason, that never happened. He wasn't drafted at all."

Jenkins recalled that even though Tony was a solid collegiate pitcher, Murray rarely saw him pitch. He was too busy watching Sandy Koufax, Don Drysdale, or Don Sutton. Even when Tony pitched at USC and UCLA, his father was not in the stands. "To some extent, that was a sign of the times," he said. "Fathers weren't like the kind you see today, doting on their kids, driving them to their games and helping them with homework. They were always off working, and for Jim, it was all about the column."

Jenkins believed that Tony lost direction when he was not drafted out of Cal. "He could have been anything," said Jenkins. "Maybe not a doctor or a lawyer, but a professional. He had the looks and the charisma to really go places in life, and we all envied that. The first four years at Cal, Tony and I shared apartments together. We were inseparable. But we set up our curriculums to take another year, to stay out of Vietnam, and something happened over that summer." It was Berkeley in the '60s. Jenkins and Tony Murray lost touch. Tony did not graduate. Occasionally he and Jenkins met. Jenkins was shocked to see him balloon to three hundred pounds, but he still retained his sense of humor.

In 1982 Ricky Murray came home and was clean for a while until he met a girl named Laurie. She was a valley girl and a druggie. They moved in together, but it was the beginning of the end. Jim and Gerry tried to support them, but Ricky and Laurie could not pay rent or live normally. Ricky lived wherever he crashed. Sometimes he was with Laurie; sometimes he was not.

Ricky continued to dream that his music would be discovered. His lifestyle was part and parcel of the scene. He was arrested for fighting and came home. His parents dressed him for his appearance before the city attorney. He was always amiable, easygoing, willing to go along. Murray defended his son to the city attorney, but it was obvious Ricky was getting a break, probably because of his famous father.

The night of the hearing the Murrays had their two-year-old grand-daughter with them. She enjoyed seeing her Uncle Ricky and was sad when he had to leave. They drove him to his ramshackle apartment. It was the last time they saw him alive.

Murray went to Las Vegas, to interview boxer Gerry Cooney and for the City of Hope banquet. When Gerry and Jim came home Murray noticed a card stuck in the knob of the front door. "Oh, there's a card there," he said. "Someone's been here."

The card was from a city policeman. It stated, "Please contact the L.A. County coroner at 226-8001 re.: case #82-7193." Murray wrote about this in his autobiography. "I shake as I write this," he wrote. He called the coroner. Somebody said, "We've got your son down here in the morgue." Case #82-7193 was Ricky Murray. It was June 6, 1982. He was twenty-nine.

That night he had gone to a party, filled with music, laughter, and girls. He laced his drink with codeine and an arcane chemical known in the drug world as "a load." He drank until he passed out. He never woke up.

Gerry was inconsolable. She wept uncontrollably, screaming, "My baby! Not my baby!" He was the little boy in the photo Jim Murray woke up to the rest of his life, every day blaming himself. Only time has revealed the truth about what the 1960s wrought upon America.

Rick Reilly's 1986 *Sports Illustrated* profile of Murray focused on this terrible event. "Rearing teenagers in the late '60s and early '70s was a bitch, though the Murrays seemed to have done okay," he wrote. "Tony pitched for Cal and, at one time, had scouts bird-dogging his games. Ted and Pam were good kids, and Ricky, the baby, was a delight. 'He could play the piano like an angel,' Murray says."

"I don't know what happened," Murray was quoted. "Dedication is hard on the marriage, hard on the family life. Maybe it was the column. Maybe it was the Malibu beach scene. Maybe it was all of it."

"I think about it all the time," Murray told Reilly. Jim would finger that card, "wrinkled from the years it has been in his wallet," according to the *SI* scribe. "I don't know if I should say this, but it was always easy for me, the column," continued Jim. "It's not like I spent long, long hours on it. I had plenty of time to be with my family. . . . But I don't know. You lose a son and you think, 'Was I a lousy father?'"

"I don't know if he went to church," recalled Art Spander. "I do know his kids got into drugs, Ricky and Tony in particular. Jim didn't have a lot of forgiveness. He had no understanding of that and just thought it was wrong and made no real effort to understand it. It ruined Tony. Those kids grew up in Malibu during the drug culture. When Jim died they were all at the memorial service. I know he was close to his granddaughter."

"I thought Jim had a good relationship with his kids," said his friend Bill Caplan.

His colleague Ross Newhan recalled,

All I can say about the comedic aspect of Jim, from the standpoint that a comic sometimes tells jokes to hide sorrow, is that I knew Jim from the mid-1960s and he was always the same writer, and those were years before tragedy befell him. I don't know if any of those events impacted his writing. It seems to me they did not. However, I'm sure the column may have been a terrific source of output for him, the life with Tom Lasorda, an escape from his troubles, but no, I do not see that he changed his writing due to it.

For Jim Murray, who called himself a "semi-famous father," there was in addition to Tony's troubles "another load to bear" after Ricky's death.

■ ■ ■

Gerry Murray never smiled again. After Ricky's death, she lost her zest for life. Her eyes were dead. Murray considered himself a dysfunctional father and replayed the event leading to Ricky's death over and over in self-recriminations. Gerry never blamed him, but he felt he should have been blamed. He had taken his son to rehabilitation, tried to have doctors scare him straight. Rehab counselors had blamed Murray for pursuing a successful career at the expense of his family. Now he was left with only his guilt, their words stinging him.

Six months after Ricky's death, Gerry visited her sister in Seattle. When she returned, she noticed that her handwriting trailed off. Her speech was slurred. They figured it was an inner-ear disorder. One night as they lay in bed she told Jim, "Hold my hand. I know I'm dying."

"In that moment, I knew it, too," recalled Murray.

They went to Dr. Gary Sugarman. The CAT scan showed a brain tumor. The cancer started in her colon and metastasized in the liver and brain. Gerry had a year to live. The year was a blur. She did not really have pain. She had phlebitis after colon surgery. She had little will to live after Ricky's tragedy. "It isn't as if I'm leaving nirvana," she said.

> It's been five years of hell. My baby son is dead, my other son is gone. Ricky was the only one who truly loved me.
>
> I don't want to leave my little granddaughter. What makes me sad is I'll never see our desert [condo] again.

Gerry periodically tried to play music but could not. She and Jim went to the desert for their thirty-eighth wedding anniversary. Her brother and sisters came out to celebrate. A while later Gerry slipped in the middle of the night and hit her head. She and Jim wept. The next day her head throbbed. The next day they went to the hospital. She lapsed into a three-month coma. The chemotherapy did not work. Doctors tried a device called a shunt to relieve pressure on her brain. Administering the invasive shunt was a difficult decision, as it could have left her paralyzed.

Jim Murray regularly went to work amid the laughter of the Dodger Stadium club house and the wisecracks of Tom Lasorda. His colleagues knew he was going through hell and tried to be respectful. Jim probably appreciated the levity as a sop to his own sorrows.

Gerry awoke from her coma with no real memory, but she recognized her husband. Plans were made to send her to the Thalians' Clinic for rehabilitation. Then she slipped into another coma and died. She and Jim had been married thirty-eight years.

The first X-rays had showed that the cancer had not spread. But there had been a mix-up at the radiology clinic. "Sorry," the doctor said. "The cancer has metastasized."

"The most terrible collection of syllables in the language," Murray said.

"She always came into a room like a sunrise," a neighbor said of Gerry. She was buried next to Ricky.

■ ■ ■

On April 3, 1984, Murray's column "She Took the Magic and Happy Summer with Her" appeared in the *Los Angeles Times*. "This is the column I never wanted to write, the story I never wanted to tell," it led. Murray wrote that he "lost the sunshine and roses, all right, the laughter in the other room. I lost the smile that lit up my life. . . . God loved Gerry," as did everybody else. He wrote of her "big gorgeous brown eyes" and how "she never did anything to be ashamed of."

She was

> this little girl running across a field with a swimming suit on her arm, on a summer day on the way to the gravel pit for an afternoon of swimming and laughing. . . . I don't mean to inflict my grief on you, but she deserves to be known by anyone who knows me. She has a right to this space more

than any athlete who ever lived. I would not be here if it weren't for her. I feel like half a person without Gerry. For once, I don't exaggerate. No hyperbole. If there was a Hall of Fame for people, she would be number one. She was a champion at living.

She never told a lie in her life. And she didn't think anyone else did. Deceit puzzled her. Dishonesty dismayed her. She thought people were good. Around her, surprisingly, they were. Her kindness was legendary.

She loved God. I mean, He made the trees, the flowers. He made children, didn't He? And color and song, and above all, babies. She knew He'd take care of her.

She loved babies. Anybody's. She played the piano like a dream.

Rough-hewn athletes, he continued, fell for her charms and her piano playing. She went to her death with faith. She bore the loss of her son.

Reilly's *Sports Illustrated* feature came a couple years after Gerry passed away. It was in some way Murray's cry for help, his pronouncement that his job, its settings—baseball stadiums, sports arenas—while they had taken him away from his family on many an occasion, ultimately were his refuge. His opening up to Reilly was therapeutic.

Called "King of the Sports Page," the Reilly piece was dated April 21, 1986. "The thing about Jim Murray is that he lived 'happily,' but somebody ran off with his 'ever after,'" Reilly wrote. "It's like the guy who's ahead all night at poker and then ends up bumming cab money home. Or the champ who's untouched for 14 rounds and then gets KO'd by a pool-hall left you could see coming from Toledo." Murray, "got mail from Brando," was "mentioned in a Governor's state of the state address," and "flew in Air Force One." "How big is Murray? One time he couldn't make an awards dinner so he had a sub—Bob Hope.

"Murray may be the most famous sportswriter in history. If not, he's at least in the photo," but the end is all wrong. The scripts got switched. They killed the laugh track, fired the gag writers, and spliced in one of those teary endings you see at Cannes. In this one, the guy ends up with his old typewriter and some Kodaks and not much else except a job being funny four times a week.

They say that tragedy is easy and comedy is hard.

Know what's harder?

Both at once.

"It wasn't supposed to be this way," Murray wrote.

I was supposed to die first. . . . I had my speech all ready. I was going to
look into her brown eyes and tell her something I should have long ago.
I was going to tell her: "It was a privilege just to have known you."

I never got to say it. But it was too true.

Reilly wrote that on the way to Palm Springs, Gerry, wearing a wig after
chemo treatments, had a sudden hankering for her first milkshake since high
school. It was apparently their last laugh together.

"I have sat down and attempted humor with a broken heart," Murray
wrote of the experience. "I've sat down and attempted humor with every possible facet of my life in utter chaos. . . . *Carmen* was announced. *Carmen* will
be sung." He wrote with the voice of the doctor, the accusatory people in the
rehab center, ringing in his ears, the image of Ricky and Gerry in his head.
Through it all he wrote over "those infernal voices."

"You write punch lines your whole life and then the last joke is on you,"
wrote Reilly.

Reilly attended a banquet at the Hotel Bel Air with Murray. Famed athletic figures like Red Auerbach, Bob Lanier, and Bob Uecker were in awe of
him. The American League Most Valuable Player from 1970, Boog Powell,
was too dumbstruck to even approach him. "I haven't ever met him," said
Powell, "but I've been reading his stuff for many years. And he's written about
me, I don't know, half a dozen times, but I've seen him in a locker room only
twice. He's a great man. I'm one of his biggest fans."

"This is how it is now for Murray," wrote Reilly. "He is in that the-legend-
walks-and-talks-and-eats-breakfast stage. The Last King of Sports writing, boys,
sitting right over there."

In the middle of all this tragedy, he was named the nation's best columnist
for 1984 by the Associated Press sports editors. Murray was still going strong,
his writing all he had left, more awards in his future.

"Why he has never been awarded the Pulitzer Prize is an unsolved mystery," wrote Reilly. Only Red Smith, Dave Anderson, and Arthur Daley of the *New York Times* had won it for sportswriting.

"If Murray worked for the *New York Times*," said Dan Jenkins, author of *Semi-Tough*, "he'd already have three."

"Gerry's gone," said Murray. "So what? I'll be watching TV once in a while and I'll see somebody we knew and I'll say, 'Gerry, come take a look at . . .' And then I'll catch myself."

Friends told him to move out of his home in order to forget, but he did not want to forget. The only place with life was the corner of a small downstairs bedroom where he wrote his column by the light of a lamp and a window, straining his weak eyes while staring at a portable computer. He had a magnifying monitor installed. "It is chilling to watch him with his back to the door, his shoulders hunched over an eerie green light, writing jokes for the greater Los Angeles area," observed Reilly.

Murray never missed a column. "What else would I do?" he said.

He showed the *Sports Illustrated* columnist a three-by-five photo on his piano. "This is my favorite," he said.

I don't know if she'd like it or not. But I like it. Look at those eyes. Look at them. There's just no jealousy in those eyes. The final curtain is pretty bad, isn't it? The last scene, the last act, is pretty bad.

Put it this way. It'll never sell in Dubuque.

Murray did not laugh at his own joke.

"I cried when he wrote of the passing of his lovely wife Gerry," recalled Vin Scully.

■ ■ ■

She was a "pint-sized dynamo with boundless energy and infectious laughter, whose perfect size-two physique belies her brute strength—inner and outer." Linda McCoy was about twenty years younger than Jim Murray. She first met him in 1969. At the time, she worked for the Indiana Pacers of the American Basketball Association. The team president asked her to drive Murray around the week he was planning on spending in Indianapolis for the 500. Murray's eyes were already failing. He was unable to handle a rental car on unfamiliar roads. "I thought, this is going to ruin my weekend," McCoy-Murray said. "He was old enough to be my father. He looks at me and says, 'Do you have a driver's license?'"

McCoy was a vivacious, athletic blonde. Murray immediately had a fond, paternal feeling for her. She thought he was attractive for an older man, but was just that—an older man. For McCoy, it was nice to be with a sportswriter who did not treat her condescendingly. It was long before the age of the "sports babe," the women in the clubhouse, on the sidelines, and in the booth. Sports were a fraternity. She was a pioneer in a man's world, trying to hold her own, to gain grudging respect.

Over the years, McCoy and Murray ran into each other at various sporting events. She moved to New York.

"One day in the fall of 1985, I asked a mutual what happened to Jim Murray?" she said. "Does he still write that column? Is still alive? My friend said, 'Yes, it's very sad, he lost his son to drugs and alcohol, his wife died, he had open heart surgery and lost an eye.' I said, 'I'm sorry I asked.'"

She sent him a birthday card. She did not want it to be a sympathy card. She wanted it to be something to cheer him up a little bit. She wrote something with a little "wit and sarcasm." Murray read it and smiled. Was it his first genuine smile since 1981, 1982? Something made him write her a letter.

The wit and charm of *his* letter caused her to pick up the phone and call him. She was living in New York. He was in L.A. Would he be on the East Coast anytime soon? He said he hated the East Coast, but then remembered that the U.S. Open was at Shinnecock on Long Island that year. The *Times* would probably assign him the story. So she met him at the tournament, and "the rest, as she says, was history," wrote Shelly Smith of ESPNLosAngeles.com.

Linda McCoy was Jim Murray's redemption. It is possible readers of the *Los Angeles Times* and national fans of his syndicated column were given an extra decade or so of his great talent because she came into his life when he was at his lowest point. Blindness, Ricky's death, Gerry's tragedy. He had his column, his work, his clubhouse repartee with Tommy Lasorda, but at night the poet of Brentwood returned to a big, empty house.

Friendship became romance. Romance became marriage. Marriage became partnership. Nobody was going to deny Jim's right to joy in his own life.

McCoy-Murray identified Murray as a a product of the Great Depression, a man of faith, but also as a man who was disappointed that his children seemed caught up in the zeitgeist of a new, permissive era. "He was never off a payroll," she said.

That was very important to him. His work ethic was such that it described his political identity. Jim was a Christian. I would not say that he wore it on his sleeve. He had his sorrows, but he had his Christian faith since grade school, and he had his sorrows, and his basic faith pulled him through a lot of tragedy. He said, "I only go to church so I have something to do on Sunday mornings."

He was not a regular church-goer. He was not compelled that he had to get to church. I went with him to a couple of midnight masses. In later years he did not go to church that much because he found some of the biggest hypocrites in church. He hated holidays because that's when all the problems started in his family, the drinking, but he had deep faith. He was something of an Irish stoic. He probably applied Catholic guilt with his family. He was not all about joie d'vivre. He did not reveal himself to the core.

I would agree that Jim sometimes revealed his true beliefs between the lines of his columns. Like the column when he referred to "God's writers . . . Matthew, Mark, Luke and John." So if you're asking me, did he believe in God, I'd say sure. We'd talk about it. He'd ask me, "Do you believe in God?" I would say, "Do you believe in God?" He'd say, "Sure I do," and he'd say, "I hope there's a God," and he'd chuckle like he's challenging me, and he'd talk about heaven. I had a younger view, and I was raised Lutheran, a Midwestern Protestant, so I was taught differently. Jim really believed there was a heaven, but let me tell you, Jim believed in Judgment Day, believe me.

"There's a Judgment Day and it's coming," he'd say. Jim made Old Testament references in his column, too, like writing that Lyle Alzado was a prophet railing against the sins of his fellow man. He would absolutely write about that kind of stuff.

Jim disliked hypocrisy and saw it in Malibu when he lived there. He tried to raise awareness over the use of drugs among the kids but could not generate concern even though it was their kids, but was frustrated that they'd rally to save the whales. He'd read about a mountain lion that killed two kids and there'd be a big rally to save the cubs after the mother was shot, but nobody seemed to care about the kids who died. They'd raise money to save the lion. He'd draw a line in the sand and say, "What is going on in society? I don't belong in this world." He was like a nineteenth-century man.

Murray and his new wife traveled to Super Bowls, horse races, golf tournaments, and World Series games. She was his driver. His failing eyesight was no hindrance. She loved sports, had grown up with it, chosen it as her profession. Now she had a Jim Murray column twenty-four/seven.

"I'd give him some compliment about something he did," she said.

"Oh, Linda, sweetheart, six months after I'm dead, they won't even remember my name," he would reply.

Oh, how wrong he was.

15

The Great Scribe in His Twilight Years

By the early 1990s the *Los Angeles Times* had passed the *New York Times* with the most subscribers of any daily newspaper in the world. Many readers believed that the paper was the single best on the planet. Otis Chandler's vision had come true.

"I can't say for sure we were the best in the country," said sports editor Bill Dwyre. "I guess I'd say it had to be in the 1980s and early 1990s. Maybe the London *Times*. I can't say . . . we were the equal of any paper."

But Otis had handed the keys to the kingdom to Tom Johnson, Shelby Coffey III, Bob Erberu, Mark Willes, and Kathryn Downing; and they had collectively, in short order, allowed what the Chandlers made great to become less than outstanding. Two factors contributed to this. First, after Otis Chandler relinquished and then was pushed out of power, the paper quickly allowed itself to become politically correct, even left-leaning. Second, the rise of the Internet drained readers away.

The top of the newspaper game, from the 1980s to 1991, was fraying by 1992. The *Los Angeles Times* was hemorrhaging money. At fault was not just the unimpressive leadership of editor Shelby Coffey III. Bob Erberu, a USC graduate, well placed in Los Angeles society, somehow found himself at the top of the *Times* after Chandler's departure. He was the chairman of the Times Mirror Company.

"The family should have taken Erberu out and shot him," said Dan Akst, a business columnist. The general attitude among *Times* staffers was that Erberu "wrecked that company" in a maze of big-money deals, stock options, and inside agreements between Erberu and the family. They all became rich, but they also triggered the demise of a newspaper. The national media noticed everything. *Newsweek* and *Newsday*, among others, ran stories about the *Times*'s financial problems.

On "Black Friday," July 21, 1995, 750 people were fired at Times Mirror Square, a move related to a myriad of bad business deals. CEO Mark Willes presided over the worst of them, a partnership deal with the Lakers' new basketball arena sponsor, Staples, in which Times Mirror and Staples split the advertising revenues on a special issue of the *Sunday Times Magazine*. The deal, of course, broke standard journalism practices, and Willes engendered tremendous criticism for the fiasco from all sources. Otis Chandler chimed in with public criticism. Petitions were circulated in-house protesting the deal.

Finally Chandler and old hand Bill Boyarsky, one of his leaders in the glory days, approached Michael Parks to say enough is enough. They communicated their profound distaste for Willes's wheeling and dealing to the entire staff. The result: cheers throughout the corridors. Old photos of Chandler popped up. He represented a cult of personality, a rallying cry against inferiority, political correctness, bad marketing, and all other forms of unimpressiveness. He was a champion, a winner. He was admired, an icon. He was heroic.

"Otis is Zeus," deputy managing editor John Arthur raved. Bill Dwyre was quoted in *Privileged Son* as saying, "Otis was General Patton and you want to go out and get on the tank and ride with him. If Patton comes back and says, 'Let's go! There is one more mission,' you go with him." Dennis McDougal added, "Otis was also Odysseus, home from 20 years of hard sailing and not at all happy with what the suitors had done in his absence to his palace and his Penelope—his one true mistress, his *Times*."

National attention followed, and the paper was forced to back out of the Staples Center deal. Willes, Downing, and Parks were all deposed but were not replaced by Otis Chandler or even anyone like him. Unfortunately, the final indignity to the Chandler legacy was endorsed by the Chandler family itself. On June 12, 2000, the *Los Angeles Times* was sold to the Tribune Company, parent company of the *Chicago Tribune*.

■ ■ ■

There is little evidence that Jim Murray involved himself much in the politics of the *Los Angeles Times* in the 1990s. He no doubt had an opinion. His politics probably differed from the changing view of his paper, but he was always moderate, not offensive to either side. Besides, he had gone through too much over the previous decade-plus to concern himself. Maybe the long toil of life was the reason Chandler had sidelined himself for the most part while his old charges were "Waiting for Godot," as Dennis McDougal wrote.

Chandler and Murray. Two old warhorses of the newspaper game. Now, as a strange new decade was under way, there was just Murray. Over at Dodger Stadium, Vin Scully. In an Encino condominium and on Saturdays at Pauley Pavilion, John Wooden. They were the old guard of Los Angeles. Jim Murray, the world historian, had to be fascinated by the events unfolding as the 1990s began. Born two years after the Russian Revolution, he had lived to see its aftermath murder more than a hundred million of his fellow human beings. Now the former Soviets were opening up their archives. Murray was one of many who thought he would never live to see the dissolution of the USSR.

One true indication of how outstanding a writer Murray was came in that first year of the new decade, when he was awarded the Pulitzer Prize. The punditocracy had longed bewailed the fact that after nearly thirty years at the *Times* he still did not have one. *New York Times* sports scribes had won it, but not Murray, nor any sportswriter in California, the West, or any newspaper other than the *New York Times*. As Slim Pickens said in *Blazing Saddles*, "What in the wide, wide world of sports is goin' on here?"

Murray and Linda McCoy-Murray flew to New York, where they officially accepted the Pulitzer Prize from the Columbia University School of Journalism. Murray was typically modest and funny. "I'm perfectly astonished at getting a Pulitzer," he said.

Joseph Pulitzer and Horace Greeley must be spinning in their graves. I always thought you had to bring down a government or expose major graft or give advice to prime ministers to win this. All I ever did was quote Tommy Lasorda accurately.

One of the nicest things about the Pulitzer was the elation of my friends. Frankly, that was my Pulitzer and I'm grateful to the Pulitzer Committee for making it possible to hear from so many old pals and to share the honor with them.

This is going to make it a little easier on the guy who writes my obit!

Lasorda pitched in the Major Leagues, managed the Dodgers to two World Series titles, and is in the Hall of Fame. He has said that among the things he is most proud of was the fact he came to Murray's mind when he decided how to respond to the Pulitzer.

The congratulations came in, far and wide:

"I'm old enough to have read the best of Arthur Daley, Red Smith and Dave Anderson, but the Jim Murray work is at the 'head of the class,'" opined former president Gerald Ford, an ex-football star at the University of Michigan.

"When someone has brought as much joy and enlightenment to others as you have, he sure as hell deserves something terrific in between," said actor Jack Lemmon.

"Not many guys have a Spinks and a Pulitzer and you certainly deserve both," said Jack Lang, the executive secretary of the Baseball Writers Association of America, referring to Murray's receipt of the prestigious J. G. Taylor Spink Award, the BBWAA's highest honor.

Pete Rose called Murray "one of the fairest and most knowledgeable writers around."

"Congratulations, it's about time!" said dancer Gene Kelly.

"We are thrilled but not surprised," said actor Jimmy Stewart and his wife, Gloria.

"You have a true gift for writing in a way that makes all sports fans look forward to the morning paper," wrote former president Reagan, now in retirement at his Santa Barbara ranch, where he could relax with the *L.A. Times* every morning instead of getting national security updates. "Your writing enriches our lives and I am proud to be among your many fans."

"It's about time the prize committee came to its senses and gave the prize to the one man who could retire the trophy if he wanted to," wrote political columnist George Will of the *Washington Post*. Will was a huge Cubs fan who occasionally delved into baseball writing. Jim had favorably reviewed Will's book *Men at Work*.

"If I wrote you a congratulatory letter every time I think you deserve one you'd be hearing from me every day," wrote comedian Steve Allen.

Murray's writing "has proved to be as important to me (and countless readers) as my orange juice, coffee and cereal," said TV game show host Monty Hall.

Kirk Douglas wrote, Jim "gives so much pleasure to others."

"Those two winners alone keep the Pulitzer at the front of the pack," network news anchor Tom Brokaw said of Red Smith and Jim Murray.

"It is nice to see 'them' make it official," remarked Jack Whittaker.

"Roy Riegels ran the right way," joked Tom Callahan, hearkening back to the 1929 Rose Bowl, when a California player accidentally ran the length of the field in the opposite direction of his team's goal line, giving Georgia Tech the win via the margin of a safety.

"Did you get the prize for your funniest lines—your expense accounts?" joked Bill Shirley, the *Times's* former sports editor.

"You are one of the people who has always made me proud to do this work," stated writer Mike Lupica.

"How many Indy 500 wins does it take to equal a Pulitzer?" asked driver Danny Sullivan.

The *New York Times* "monopoly was broken when you so deservedly were awarded a Pulitzer last month," stated NFL Commissioner Paul Tagliabue.

In addition to the Pulitzer, Murray received the Associated Press sports editors' recognition for best column writing.

"I came to the *Times* in 1968 and eventually worked for the Orange County edition, covering baseball and the Angels," recalled Hall of Fame baseball writer Ross Newhan.

We were working acquaintances. I saw him a lot at Dodger Stadium and Anaheim Stadium. I sat next to him at several World Series games. Like Vin Scully he was as nice and good a person as he was a great writer.

Look, Jim I'm sure would tell you he was in the entertainment business. He wasn't a sports writer, per se. No, I don't think so, he was not just a sports writer, but he intermingled sports with a tremendous talent, with a touch for entertainment.

The *L.A. Times* became great during these years. Otis Chandler deserves a tremendous amount of credit. He recognized that the *Times* could not be a great paper until it nationalized and did a better job of covering the news. Otis created worldwide bureaus and deserves the credit. This was a huge step in gaining worldwide national recognition for Jim.

We had great reporters in the bureaus and outstanding sports writers, headed by Jim. He was very much responsible for the national recognition. It got to the point where you would say, "I'm with the *L.A. Times*," and they'd say, "Oh, that's Jim Murray's paper." It still happens to me. People always bring that up.

■ ■ ■

After USC won the 1985 conference championship under Coach Stan Morrison, the Trojans felt they were in a position to wrest away the mantel of basketball greatness that had been largely unclaimed since John Wooden's departure from UCLA a decade earlier. Morrison recruited the best incoming class in the nation. Called the "four freshmen" and led by two Philadelphia wunderkinder—Hank Gathers and Bo Kimble—they were expected to lead the Trojans to the Final Four and maybe even a national championship.

Instead, Morrison left and was replaced by George Raveling. Three of the "four freshmen" departed. That was the end of USC's basketball glory. Gathers and Kimble opted to stay in Los Angeles with Loyola coach Paul Westhead, who led the Lakers to the 1980 NBA championship before being forced out in a power struggle with Magic Johnson.

The old days of excitement at Pauley Pavilion were over. Now, everybody was flocking over to Loyola, a little Catholic school near the airport, to watch Gathers. He was the most exciting player in college basketball, his team the greatest, high-flying story in the game.

Gathers died on the court of a heart attack in 1990. Murray's column began with A. E. Housman's poem, "To an Athlete Dying Young." How could a "franchise basketball player" be a "walking invalid?" he wrote. "What kind of cosmic joke is at work here" when athletes like Gathers and Lou Gehrig, "the most powerful baseball player I have ever seen," could within a short time be made so weak he could not "lift a cup of coffee"?

The Los Angeles Dodgers were pedestrian at best, but Murray noted that they remained excellent in the announcer's booth. In "His Touch Made Dodgers Special" on August 26, he wrote, "Scully without the Dodgers was Caruso without an opera." It was Murray who pronounced Vin the "most valuable Dodger."

When former Michigan legend Tom Harmon passed away, Murray either recalled (or made up) the following story. Harmon had been one of three Heisman winners on the Rams. The others were Les Horvath and Glenn Davis. Ruth Hirsch, the wife of Rams teammate Elroy "Crazy Legs" Hirsch, saw the award at all their houses on social occasions. During a party at Harmon's, Harmon's wife dusted off her husband's 1940 Heisman and announced what it was. "Oh, is that what that is?" Mrs. Hirsch blurted out. "I thought everybody had one!" In the same column, Murray repeated a great punch line by an emcee at a banquet who noted that Harmon, a World War II fighter pilot, had been involved in two plane crashes, one in China and one in South America. "I don't know how to tell you this," the emcee said to Harmon, tongue in cheek, "but we were at war with Japan and Germany. What were you, on the way to bomb Peru?"

When political columnist George Will wrote *Men at Work*, Murray joked that as soon as he saw the title, "I knew right away it wasn't about Washington, D.C." He said that if a wonk could write a book on baseball, maybe he should write one "analyzing the State Department's policy in Latin America, which, come to think of it, is not too different from the St. Louis Browns at that."

■ ■ ■

In 1991, the United States wiped out Saddam Hussein's Republican Guard and swept to victory in the Persian Gulf War. At that moment, in the aftermath of the fall of the USSR, it is possible America was the most powerful empire in world history.

The Los Angeles Lakers were at the end of the "Showtime" run. The glory days of Larry Bird and the Boston Celtics were also coming to a close. In a February column on the Celtics, Murray wrote, "Basketball needs the Celtics. It's no fun beating the Charlotte Hornets or the Miami Heat. Beating the Celtics is climbing Mt. Everest, swimming the Channel, breaking the bank at Monte Carlo." Boston was "like an old dowager. They never throw anything away." Like the Yankees, the Celtics turned journeymen from other teams into all-stars.

It was the age of Michael Jordan and the "last hurrah" of Magic Johnson. The two legends met and youth was served when Chicago ran the Lakers out of the NBA Finals in five games. "Pro basketball, like Caesar's Gaul, was divided into three parts—Michael Jordan, Magic Johnson and Larry Bird," Murray wrote in his autobiography. Of Jordan he wrote, "You needed the RAF [Royal Air Force] to stop him."

That year Murray wrote one of his best-remembered columns about a subject close to his heart, Cincinnati Reds non–Hall of Famer Pete Rose. When reflecting upon his long career and the choices he made, Murray once realized that had he not been a sportswriter, he never would have met Rose. Banned from baseball for life and not allowed in the Hall of Fame because he bet on games when managing the Reds in the 1980s, Rose was a controversial subject. People took sides. Murray was clear: Rose should be in the Hall of Fame. There was "no such person" as Pete Rose. It was as if baseball was trying to tell us to pretend he never played. "Pete Rose never played the game for 24 years with the little boy's zeal and wonder until, if you closed your eyes, you could picture him with his cap on sideways, knickers falling down to his ankles and dragging a taped ball and busted bat behind him, looking for all the world like something that fell off Norman Rockwell's easel," he wrote.

Murray argued passionately on Rose's behalf. He wrote that he was really not a "figment of our imagination." He was not a "cartoon character." He argued that all the years Babe Ruth was addicted to rye whiskey it was illegal. "I wish I could figure out why guys who kill eight nurses in five states get people holding candle vigils outside their prison cells while Pete Rose gets the book thrown at him," he wrote, adding, "I'm a law-and-order man myself." He wrote that Rose was no genius, but that should not be held against him.

Rose had met his match when he went up against Commissioner of Baseball Bart Giamatti, whom Murray compared with Inspector Javert in *Les Misérables*. "The indefatigable, relentless, implacable upholder of the law on the track of his quarry, the helpless victim of his own addiction, who only happened to be the greatest hitter in the annals of baseball, whom Giamatti was accusing of betraying the game that made him," he wrote with dramatic flourish. "[Giamatti] could quote the *Iliad*—or tell you why the Red Sox blew the 1949 pennant with equal expertise and enthusiasm. . . . He saw himself as a kind of complicated Pope." Murray added, "There never was a deadlier face-off than Giamatti vs. Rose. Nobody won. Baseball lost. . . . Like World Wars, there were no clear winners. They should set it to music and put it on Broadway. I have the name for it. 'The Miserables.'"

In March Murray wrote a column about baseball language in "Reads between the Lines When Talkin' Baseball." "Everybody wins the pennant," he wrote, while spring and baseball are "perfect for each other" because they both exuded optimism. "We can play with anybody in the game" really meant, "We can play with them. We just can't beat them." "We're as good as any team in the league" actually meant the "Carolina League." "This team doesn't know the meaning of the word choke" really meant they did not know the meaning of much of anything. Because "the only thing lower than their batting average is their IQ." When a manager was reminded of "great combinations of the past," Murray wrote, he was secretly referring to Laurel and Hardy or the Marx brothers. To have "great balance" meant nobody could catch, throw, or hit. Whether a player had a "lot of desire" could be verified by asking "any waitress in town" or adding up "paternity suits and sexual harassment charges." A manager who emphasizes fundamentals had no choice when the team was a bunch of .218 hitters. "We're going to surprise a lot of people" could mean the owner shelled out $30 million for "overpaid underachievers." "He's going to be my stopper!" meant he stopped a winning streak.

When overweight old-timer George Foreman made a comeback, fighting the powerful Evander Holyfield, Murray wrote, "One guy looks like a Greek god. The other looked like a Greek restaurant." Foreman resembled a "plate of hamburgers or a pizza with everything." (Holyfield was in great physical shape, Foreman was overweight.)

Jockey Bill Shoemaker "asked little of life. And got it." (He was never handed anything.)

In "Whatever It Was, Arnie Still Has It," Murray wrote, "Look! Mickey Mantle isn't hitting curveballs into the seats anymore. Willie Mays isn't hauling down three-base hits in center field. Rod Laver isn't blasting anybody off Centre Court at Wimbledon." But Arnold Palmer was still excelling at golf. He caught the essence of the old pro when he declared, "He never hit a safe shot."

Of driver Rick Mears, Murray wrote that the headline "Mears Wins Indy" would become as standard as "Iowa Goes Republican" or "Taxes Go Up."

After years of joy, in which it "was good to be alive and at a Laker game," Murray wrote a poignant piece about a player he had great love for, Magic Johnson. Called "Warning, HIV: No Hiding Now" (November 10), it came on the heels of Johnson's shocking admission that he had tested positive for human immunodeficiency virus (HIV). Murray predicted Johnson would not "hide" but would take on his disease aggressively and in public. He was right. If Johnson could beat HIV, Murray wrote way back then, "I want to see that smile!" Johnson remains healthy with no reason to believe he will not remain so.

■ ■ ■

Nineteen ninety-two was such a dismal year that Murray found himself writing about the Clippers. Their coach, Larry Brown, was "America's Bedouin, the Vanishing American" who moved from job to job to job. He was "just a drifter," Murray wrote.

In a column on the Indy 500, Murray returned to a theme he often visited: the comparison of race car driving and the L.A. freeways, which he contended may well have been as challenging and dangerous. He had been writing satirical columns about the Hollywood Freeway since the 1960s. Little had changed on the roads to make the articles any less relevant.

On May 17, Murray revisited ex-Lakers coach Pat Riley ("L.A.'s Showtime Becomes Crunch Time in New York"), who was now successfully handling the Knicks. It was a more standard journalistic piece, absent his colorful turn of phrase. But his December column on tennis great Bjorn Borg was incisive. First, Murray pointed out that by the time Borg was twenty-six, he had accomplished almost everything his sport could offer. Then he compared Borg to Babe Ruth, Pete Rose, Rocky Marciano, even Jack Nicklaus, none of whom had hit their full stride by that age. Borg was burned out and admitted it in a candid statement. "I remember the '81 final against McEnroe at Wimbledon," he said of his legendary rivalry with the American. "I felt as if I were just playing backyard tennis."

Murray's June 16 column on boxing champion Evander Holyfield revealed a part of Murray's personality. He wrote about Muhammad Ali screaming, "I am the greatest!" but obviously admired that Holyfield, according to promoter Lou Duva, "never raised his voice in his life." "Maybe Holyfield could get more credibility if he went around banging on bars and bragging, making noises, showing disrespect, sneering at his opponent, belittling his skills," Murray wrote, adding that he was not raised to act in such an immature manner. Holyfield had not been raised "to be a loudmouth"; he had been raised "to be a champion." Reading between the lines, one found a tacit criticism of Ali's prideful attitude.

Murray's July 26 column, "Reveling in Spotlight of World," was a letter addressed to Baron de Coubertin, who had founded the modern Olympics at Athens in 1896. It was a curious inquisition in which the columnist pointed out that in the century that followed, the Olympic Games, created "to produce a race of happy people who would never again have to go to war," unintended or not, ushered in the worst wars in human history. Murray the traditionalist was somewhat aghast at the commercialism of the Games. Nineteen ninety-two was the first year the Soviets could no longer compete as a monolith. It was also the first truly "professional" Olympics, led by America's Dream Team NBA squad. The column was filled with historical references to the Greeks, Hollywood extravagance, communism, German militarism, and Woodrow Wilson's failed vision of democracy.

In a piece about long jumpers Carl Lewis and Mike Powell of UCLA, Murray wistfully described Lewis's long pursuit of Bob Beamon's record, set in the rarefied air of Mexico City in 1968. Now in Barcelona, Lewis was making his "farewell tour," evoking comparison with Jesse Owens, Babe Ruth, and Ted Williams. Powell ultimately broke Beamon's record; the competition between him and Lewis was heated.

On September 17, Murray penned "The 'Tying Irish' Just Doesn't Make It." Notre Dame coach Lou Holtz ran the ball into the line against Michigan with a minute left in a 17-17 tie in the era before overtime. Murray thought that that action was unconscionable but also in the tradition of Ara Parseghian, who infamously "tied one for the Gipper" against Michigan State in 1966. Once upon a time, Murray had been an East Coast Catholic with a strong rooting interest in Notre Dame. Now he was firmly a Los Angeleno, less admiring of Notre Dame's great history. On September 22 Murray paid homage to Jimmy Cannon, "a pal and an idol of mine," who wrote an occasional column called "Nobody Asked Me But." Murray called reminiscing of Cannon "good fun" and a "day off." He penned his own version of the column, riffing on opinions about grown men wearing caps backward, his Uncle Frank, Lee Harvey Oswald's guilt, Roseanne Barr, student-athletes, Woody Allen movies, and other minutiae.

Murray took on a controversial subject in a piece about Karl "the Mailman" Malone of the Utah Jazz. Magic Johnson was making a comeback, but Malone was fearful of competing against a player who had HIV. Malone had cuts and scabs all over his body from diving after balls and was worried that he could be vulnerable. Murray interviewed a number of players and found that these concerns were widespread.

After Michigan beat Washington, 38-31, in the Rose Bowl, Murray lamented that the event was a shadow of its once-proud self. With USC and UCLA in down periods, the contest—once the cream of collegiate football—now was "a sandlot game," a "fight in a bar at two A.M. All offense."

After the Super Bowl, played that year at the Rose Bowl, Murray wrote "Image Problem Is Everything," returning to a time-honored theme, the winter weather and public image of Los Angeles on television. It was interesting, he observed, that it never rains in L.A. during sporting events broadcast on national television. The weathercasters thought the Super Bowl would be wet, but Murray said if anyone had asked him, he could have told them the weather would not be inclement. "I don't have to know meteorology," he wrote. "I know L.A." When the city "knows the world is going to be looking on at her, she gets out the eye shadow, lipstick, puts on her net stockings, her highest heels and shortest skirt, piles her hair up in a beehive, bats her eyes and adopts her most seductive pose." Like an old-time movie star, "she always looks her most glamorous in public." He pointed out that indeed it did rain in Los Angeles, but never on "major sporting events." Only one Rose Bowl game had ever been rained on. Murray recognized that the odds were vastly against rain only one New Years since 1902, implying that there was something magical or mystical to this phenomenon. Fog, fires, smog, wind—all were part of the L.A. landscape, but they were never televised in an international event.

■ ■ ■

In 1993 Jim Murray was in his "twilight years." He decided to write *Jim Murray: The Autobiography of the Pulitzer Prize Winning Sports Columnist*. Macmillan published it.

On April 25 Murray again addressed the notion of San Francisco, which he wrote was "not so much a city as a myth" and was "in the United States but not of it. It is so civilized it would starve to death if it didn't get a salad fork or the right wine. It fancies itself Camelot but comes off more like Cleveland. Its legacy to the world is *quiche*. People speak in whole sentences and polysyllabically. It suffers from a superiority complex."

When the City lost Joe Montana, "You would have thought they were losing the Golden Gate Bridge, Nob Hill, Coit Tower, cable cars, Fisherman's

Wharf, the Embarcadero." The superstar was "the most visible symbol of the City by the Bay since *Dirty Harry*." Once saluted as "the Paris of the West," the Parthenon of the Golden West, it was on a losing streak whereas Los Angeles, the "complicated hobo jungle to the south, has long since passed it as a center of commerce, finance, even, if Herb Caen will forgive me—culture. San Francisco has nothing but its frayed legacy left."

Its World Series got rained on or suffered an earthquake. It built a stadium that was immediately a "haunted house." Murray joked about weather reports referring to "the coldest day since July 6." Montana had "brought a new element to the City—winning," and by the early 1990s the rivalry between L.A. and San Francisco was much more even. Montana had brought something that San Francisco had never known before or that was previously relegated strictly to the east bay. By 1993 the City had even sent two women, Dianne Feinstein and Barbara Boxer, to the U.S. Senate.

The Masters might have been "the Vatican of golf," wrote Murray, but the course was so tricky it was really "Devil's Island." (A real horror show.)

In a column on Mario Andretti, Murray asked, Who won the 1981 Indianapolis 500? "Penske's lawyers," replied Andretti. (Referring to litigation clouding the event.)

Murray wrote that Wayne Gretzky had achieved his goals even if he had never won the Stanley Cup. "He put hockey on Page One and Prime Time," he wrote. "That's a hat trick all on its own." (A reference to his marriage to a glamorous movie star.)

When Don Drysdale died young, Murray wrote, "God took him out in the top of the seventh." (Not unlike Frank Sinatra's "September of my years.")

On July 4 Murray wrote of his relationship with the late Arthur Ashe. He once had lunch with Ashe, who thought that the white and black races were so far apart they would never find common ground. Ashe thought that perhaps something "glandular" separated blacks from whites, from their way of thinking. Murray gulped and said that he disagreed because so many blacks had white blood in them. He pointed out that many of Gen. William T. Sherman's Union soldiers fathered children with freed black slaves during the "march to the sea." At first Murray thought he had "overstepped our relationship." But Ashe, a "well-read man," knew about this history and agreed, pointing out he was a product of it, being light-skinned and from the South himself.

Ashe had disagreed with an NCAA law establishing certain academic requirements for athletes. Georgetown basketball coach John Thompson had called it "culturally biased," but Ashe took what can only be described as a conservative approach, stating that the real bias was to hold blacks to lower standards without expecting them to do as well. Murray quoted Ashe extensively, his highest form of compliment since he so often fell in love with his own ability to turn phrases. Ashe was a man he respected tremendously.

Murray wrote a column about the newest superstar of tennis, Pete Sampras of Palos Verdes Estates. "On court, waiting for a serve, he frequently hangs his head like a guy who is a suspect in a child murder or has just spilled soup on his hostess," he wrote. After he has slammed another service ace past opponents, he "looks apologetic." Murray compared Sampras's tennis ability to Ted Williams's talent at baseball, as big a compliment as possible. Watching him was like seeing Stan Musial with a full count or Joe Louis "with his man on the ropes."

When Reggie Jackson entered the Hall of Fame, Murray wrote that he "had the most exciting at-bats in the history of baseball. He didn't swing at a pitch, he pounced on it like a leopard coming out of a tree." "He finished his swing like a pretzel" and looked like "a corkscrew."

The crazy World Series between Philadelphia and Toronto was "one for the ages. But was it baseball? Lord, I hope you didn't let the kids stay up to watch it! . . . It wasn't a game, it was baggy pants comedy." Toronto's 15-14 win was "four-and-a-half hours of batting practice." Mitch "Wild Thing" Williams "wasn't wild." He "threw these nice straight strikes—and Toronto hit them all over the place for six runs and the victory."

Buffalo Bills coach Marv Levy "reads Dickens and Shakespeare" and "runs a football team the way Plato might." His game plan "might be likened to a symphony." Levy had coached at California, "about as far from a football factory as you can get, west of Harvard," while his upcoming opponent, Dallas coach Jimmy Johnson, coached at Miami, "about as close to being a football factory as you can get, football's version of *The Dirty Dozen*."

■ ■ ■

Nineteen ninety-four was one of the ugliest years in the history of sports. Ice skater Tonya Harding directed a thug to bash the knee of her American competitor, Nancy Kerrigan, prior to the Winter Olympics. Both the Rams and the

Raiders left Los Angeles after the season ended. Georgia Frontiere took the Rams to St. Louis. Al Davis and the Raiders departed for Oakland. The Major League Baseball Players Association went on strike.

The lack of a new pro football stadium concerned Murray, who openly asked whether Los Angeles had lost its soul. The town that built "the Coliseum, the Rose Bowl, the first freeways, the movie business," that "brought the Olympics to America," that effectively chose not to participate in the Great Depression, and then all but saved the Olympics in 1984, that always knew how to get things done, that "made pro football, saved Major League baseball, put pro golf on the map," that laughed at naysayers—"we had guys, we had drive, we had vision," he wrote. Not anymore, he said, lamenting the weak leadership in the city and the state and the recent term "political correctness." He complained that Christopher Columbus of all people was now being "dumped on—by people who would be stomping grapes or picking tarantulas off banana bunches if he didn't have the guts to sail off to the end of the world in the first place."

Under the current political class running the city and the state of California, "the Dodgers would still be in Brooklyn, the Rams in Cleveland and the Olympic Games in bankruptcy."

The loss of the Rams and Raiders was nothing compared with what the baseball players' union did to America, when the players struck in August. They never returned. The World Series was canceled. It would have been the first year of the new play-off format. Tony Gwynn of San Diego was threatening to hit .400. Barry Bonds and Matt Williams of San Francisco were in sight of Roger Maris's record of sixty-one home runs. Greg Maddux of Atlanta was having one of the best seasons in history. None of it mattered. The players left the fans twisting in the wind in an act of greed and selfishness unmatched in professional sports history.

Murray wrote, "Once upon a time in this country there was a game called baseball. You would have loved it." The "best afternoons of your life were spent in a ballpark." A poet wrote that time spent in a ballpark "didn't count against your life span," that it made you younger. Suddenly dead, the game's epitaph read, "Here Lies Baseball—Negotiated to Death."

He asked,

What's October without a World Series? Italy without a song? Paris without a spring? Canada without a sunset?

Once upon a time in this country, we had a World Series. You would have loved them. Ruth pointing. Sandy Koufax curving. Pepper Martin stealing. Kirk Gibson homering.

You should have been there.

It was all San Francisco in the fall. Led by two Hall of Famers, quarterback Steve Young and wide receiver Jerry Rice, the 49ers annihilated all opposition. Young was so good that although he did not actually make people forget Joe Montana, he forced them to acknowledge that nobody, including Joe, could have done it better.

Rice was spectacular in the Super Bowl. In "You Can't Burn Rice, but He Can Easily Burn You" (November 29), Murray wrote, "Jerry Rice, like second hand smoke, germ warfare and insider trading should be banned." He should "carry a surgeon general's warning on his helmet. . . . He's not really a player, is their view. He's a terrorist. He works undercover, so to speak. He's the NFL's Jackal." Defensive backs were not sure if he was "real." He was "the phantom of the opera." Opponents recognized him by "police composite." He "would make a world-class spy," detectable only by "radar." He has a "rap sheet longer than the Gambino family." He could "outrun you" and "outsmart you." He was "an uncontrolled substance" who should be "illegal anyway." Murray finished the column by writing that Rice "probably arrives by saucer. From outer space."

Young, leading San Francisco to a 49-26 thrashing of the San Diego Chargers, arguably had the greatest Super Bowl in history. The great linebacker Junior Seau led San Diego. What a "fine kettle of fish" Los Angeles fans found themselves in. Here they were, the home of two failed franchises, one already packed and gone, the other on its way out the door. The biggest event in sports was played in Miami between a rival team a hundred miles to the south and another archrival four hundred miles to the north. Coming on the heels of the O. J. Simpson murder, it was one of the low points of the decade for once-proud L.A.

After undergoing a complicated surgery, Murray joked that he had entered Cedars-Sinai "a bigger underdog than the San Diego Chargers. You got me and 40 points. Vegas wouldn't post a line." He wrote that he went into the hospital and, on awakening after surgery, discovered that Oregon had played in a Rose Bowl and the Rams were in St. Louis.

Murray was prescient in his column about Andre Agassi when he wrote, "Oddly enough, he didn't seem to particularly care for his line of work." The tennis star confirmed this observation years later in his autobiography.

In "Football Once Was a Sport" (March 13), Murray wrote that the college game was once a sport for the "raccoon coat" crowd. Coaches like Knute Rockne were actually "part of the faculty," whereas the press created a plethora of "Galloping Ghosts, Four Horsemen, Dream Backfields, Fighting Irish." Scholarship players were once called "ringers." Then they eliminated the middleman, that being college. The football team no longer had much in common with the school. Players no longer had their picture in *Sports Illustrated* but "in the post office." Football "went from being a sport to being a business . . . another mercantile or entertainment conglomerate."

In a column about basketball player Charles Barkley, Murray went way out of his way to argue that he was something other than the clown he acted. Taking Barkley seriously was one of the few things Murray did not get right.

In a May 15 column on pitching star Orel Hershiser, Murray repeated one of his most famous lines. Hershiser, once a pitching sensation who could not be touched, now survived on guile and guts. He was like a "swimmer crossing shark-infested waters with a nose bleed." This line was picked up by Hollywood as a metaphor for immoralities and lies.

The premise of "sharks in the water" was continued on July 7 when Murray trod familiar ground from his youth by interviewing "the great DiMaggio" (as Ernest Hemingway's character, the old Cuban fisherman, refers to him in *The Old Man and the Sea*). In the column Murray once again used the oft-repeated phrase, "DiMaggio would have been waiting for it." This was the line fans would use when complaining about one player or another. They knew Joe DiMaggio could make the plays whoever was currently on the field could not.

The Yankees of DiMaggio's era "came to the ballpark in three-piece suits and shined shoes, cut hair and clean shaven," Murray wrote. "Their image was that of a company of Swiss bankers, not terrorists. Joe DiMaggio never got in a brawl on or off the field." Murray did not mention that the baseball great used to hang out with mob boys in New York.

Fans had no empathy for DiMaggio because he made it all look so easy. When he was young, the great Ty Cobb had acted as his unofficial agent, writing letters to the Yankees demanding that the rookie be paid more. Cobb's efforts earned DiMaggio an $8,500 contract, and in return, Cobb received free meals in DiMaggio's Fisherman's Wharf restaurant in his later years.

When "Brazil won the World Cup, 0-0," Murray said that it was "like watching two woolly mammoths struggle in a tar pit all afternoon and end up gumming each other to death."

After Arnold Palmer retired, he wrote, "Palmer and golf were synonymous." Without golf, Palmer was as out of place as "John Wayne without a horse, Ruth without a bat, Carl Lewis on a bicycle. An offense against nature." Palmer "came along just as television did and it was a marriage made in golf heaven." He "didn't make golf, he just put it on page one."

■ ■ ■

"Don't Tell Him Golfers Only Drive for Show" (February 26, 1995) detailed the power-golfer John Daly. Fans love big hitters who win by big scores, Murray wrote. "The fans like movies titled *The Terminator, Rambo, Superman*." Laurence Olivier was a better act but "John Wayne sold tickets. . . . We go for Babe Ruth, Jack Dempsey, tennis players nicknamed 'The Rocket,' not 'Bitsy' or 'Bunny.' We want the 'Sultan of Swat' . . . 'the Manassa Mauler' . . . the 'Brown Bomber' . . . not guys named Evander or Ezzard." Murray mythologized Daly's penchant for long drives as opposed to "laying up" and playing the short game.

The Raiders made their return to Oakland official in June 1995. Murray wrote, "The Raiders were in Los Angeles but not of it," that they never worked their way into the city's hearts.

On June 5 in "A Little Guarantee Makes a League of Difference," Murray wrote that a New York icon, "Broadway Joe" Namath, was a legend above "many others whose careers were better. . . . Joe had an ongoing relationship with Johnnie Walker Scotch and most of the chorus girls of his day. . . . Joe never had any trouble with zone defenses, but he was intercepted regularly by curfew." Now married with kids, Namath, the "perfect passer," was waking up with his children every day at 5:30 in the morning. "I can remember when I was just getting in at that time of the morning," he recalled.

Murray wrote "You Heard It Yelled Here First" on July 19. It was his paean to St. Andrews, the legendary Scottish golf course. Despite health problems,

Murray had made the trek to "golf's shrine. It's fountainhead. Its Garden of Eden."

The 1995 big league baseball season limped along. Fans were still furious at the strike that cost them the previous year's World Series and several games at the beginning of the '95 campaign. The Angels thrilled their fans all summer long, but then joined the 1964 Phillies and the 1969 Cubs among all-time September choke artists. Randy Johnson and Seattle rallied to capture the West. Atlanta beat Cleveland in the World Series.

Baltimore's Cal Ripken began healing the rift with the fans when he broke Lou Gehrig's long-standing record for consecutive games played. Baseball fans loved the game so much they had short memories. Murray said that this fact reminded him of one of his favorite novels, Somerset Maugham's *Of Human Bondage*, featuring a character named Philip Carey. Carey falls hopelessly for a "sluttish" waitress named Mildred, who "keeps scorning him, cheating on him, abusing him, throwing things at him until you couldn't bear to look." Baseball fans were the same. On opening day in 1995, there was no drop-off in attendance. The fans just accepted the players back without recrimination. "That'll teach 'em not to mess with us!" he wrote. "We cut attendance by 38 people in Toronto."

When Ripken closed in on Gehrig's record, Pat Jordan of *The Sporting News* called it a "bore." Murray, in contrast, made his sympathies perfectly clear. "First of all, before we go on, let me tell you where I'm coming from," he wrote in "Old School Is Fine, Thank You" (August 31), one year after the strike. "To begin with, I've had it up to here with tabloid America. The glorification of the rebel, the outlaw, the guy who makes up his own rules. And lives by them. You know what I'm talking about." Athletes whose "wives plant one on the jaw of officials, basketball players who make millions and don't show up for team practices and make magazine covers, scofflaws whose very criminality gives them celebrity, the whole sorry, sick panoply of sports in the '90s." He went on about his own grandfather, who was due at work every day at seven, "so he was usually there at six." He "raised eight children. He went to church every Sunday. He worked 14 hours a day." Murray deplored the "worship of the splashy and the trashy," especially when "sneering at the accomplishments of the dependable, the reliable, the guys who show up for work every day because that is the way they were brought up, that I rise to make a point of order." Cal Ripken and Murray's grandfather "have a lot in common." On top of everything, Ripken had never broken any "barroom mirrors, gotten into a scuffle with the cops, missed the team plane." He did not even chew tobacco. As far as Murray was concerned, the Cal Ripkens of this world were "good copy."

When Mickey Mantle passed away after battling alcoholism, Murray displayed a lifetime of literature, education, and wisdom. He never cottoned to the Yankees, but in death he found humanity he could finally relate to. Opening with an F. Scott Fitzgerald quote, "Show me a hero and I will write you a tragedy," Murray wrote, "'A success' is often just the opposite." He quoted Lord Byron, who wrote of Napoleon Bonaparte, "his life would be the funniest comedy of modern times were it not caked in human blood."

Murray openly wondered what would have happened had Mantle played in Texas or California, someplace other than New York. He conjectured that Mantle was frightened by the haut monde of Manhattan, and that this led to his need to escape to alcohol.

On September 14, Murray wrote "What They've Done to Game Is a Crime." He asked, Who is number one in college football? It was Nebraska. "And how would we know? Well, for a start, one guy on the squad is charged with attempted murder and two others are charged with assaulting former girlfriends and another with carrying a weapon." Given these sordid details, the team surely "sounds like a national champion."

The year before Nebraska was number one, "Florida State was the reigning champion. Half a dozen players were illegally treated to a $20,000 clothing and shopping spree by wanna-be agents." Before that, Miami claimed number one with a team photo that should have been "hung on the post offices instead of national magazines." Colorado was number one in 1990 with a "worse arrest record than the Mafia." Murray pointed out that legendary Nebraska coach Tom Osborne was a total hypocrite. He cultivated one of the cleanest personal images in sports, living a exemplary life . . . except when it came to recruitment of players, but this certainly made him one of many.

Along with Cal Ripken, Dodgers manager Tommy Lasorda, was also "good copy." Lasorda was the last of a dying breed, and in many ways his departure from the scene—he was leaving as Dodgers manager—portended the end for the great Murray. Men like Lasorda, the colorful, the iconoclastic, the Runyonesque types who dotted the sports landscape, made Jim's job fun and a little easier. Casey Stengel, Leo Durocher, Red Auerbach, Bear Bryant—Murray knew them all. Many—a disproportionate many perhaps—had been part of Murray's Los Angeles: Red Sanders, John McKay, Tommy Prothro, Rod Dedeaux, Bill Rigney, Al Davis, and even more modern fellows like Pat Riley. Now Lasorda was leaving as the others had. Murray understood that his like would not be seen again.

"Who will speak for baseball when Tommy's gone?" he wrote in "He's Still Big Dodger in Dugout" (October 15). "One of those tight-lipped, monosyllabic bores who manage those Midwestern teams or sit glaring from the corner of the dugout as if they were watching the fall of France? Gimme a break!" Tommy was "Casey Stengel and Yogi Berra rolled into one. . . . Disney would have drawn and animated him." Murray made fun of the dingbats who said baseball was too slow. "If you're in a hurry, go to an airport," wrote the man who said he was never unhappy at a ballpark. Lasorda always said, "Where else would you rather be?" Murray and Lasorda captured baseball's ambience perfectly.

"Tommy is full of harmless hokum . . . but not when it comes to his country," Murray wrote. "Tommy will tell you the world is lucky there's a United States of America in it and if you don't think so, the conversation is over. . . . He's never said, 'No comment' or 'That's off the record' in his life."

The playing of "Conquest" was silenced by USC's resounding football loss to the Fighting Irish. Defeat at the hands of UCLA followed, but Troy still won the Pac-Ten Conference. They defeated a surprising Northwestern team in one of the liveliest Rose Bowl games ever played. "When Pittsburgh teams came out here in early years to lose, 47-14 and 35-0, the whisper was, they had spent all their time on the Sunset Strip," Murray wrote. Northwestern "even came to Planet Hollywood and sportingly joined in all the hoopla, hype and fun," but "didn't leave their game in a nightclub."

■ ■ ■

There was almost nothing to cheer about in Los Angeles sports in 1996. The lack of athletic glory mirrored the city's dismal straights. The state of California seemed to be a different world from the cutting-edge place that led the way in the 1960s, 1970s, and 1980s. L.A.'s doldrums mirrored the increasingly unimpressive *Los Angeles Times*, the paper that kicked Otis Chandler out and the one Jim Murray was now writing for in his twilight years. The only success came from San Diego, where Ken Caminiti, leading the Padres to the division championship, was voted the National League's Most Valuable Player.

It was the age of Michael Jordan and the Chicago Bulls. The Bulls' amazing 1995–96 run eclipsed Los Angeles in that they established themselves without question as the greatest single-season team in history. Previous contenders for such a lofty place in the pantheon included the 1967 76ers, 1972 Lakers, 1983 76ers, and 1987 Lakers. "You go to see Michael Jordan play basketball for the same reason you went to see Astaire dance, Olivier act or the sun set over Canada," Murray wrote of the Bulls' superstar. He was "Heifetz with a violin. Horowitz at the piano." Other players on the court never knew where he was until he yelled, "Up here!" He was as "unstoppable as tomorrow." He was 6 foot 6, "until he's airborne, that is. Then he becomes 20 feet." When Jordan faced Magic Johnson, it was "the most publicized confrontation since the second Dempsey-Tunney. It came out more like the second Louis-Schmeling." "Man, they're scary!" said Magic of the Bulls. "We should send them to Bosnia," Murray wrote of Chicago. When Jordan's team was at 41-8 (eighteen straight and counting toward the Lakers' 1972 record of thirty-three—they did not break it), Murray suggested that the league should make it "illegal for him to make a basket without one foot (or both) on the ground." Jordan was up there with Babe Ruth, Bill Tilden, John Unitas, and Wayne Gretzky.

From there Murray transitioned not just to horse racing but in his typical incongruous manner, political feminism. "I'd appreciate it if you'd keep this from Gloria Steinem, Bella Abzug or any of those fire-eating women's activists, but a female has never won the Santa Anita handicap," Murray wrote in a piece about horse racing. "I mean, talk about runaway sexism."

Murray wrote "Legend of Legends Is What Power Begat" about Jack Nicklaus. "No one ever saw him throw a club or kick a ball-washer or heard him cuss a caddie," he wrote.

"Oscar De La Hoya is too good to be true," Murray wrote on June 6 of the handsome, Los Angeles–born boxer dubbed the Golden Boy. "I mean, he's more priest than pug, more altar boy than home boy." He was "too pretty" and spoke as if in "confession." Murray compared him to Mother Teresa and St. Francis of Assisi. When De La Hoya destroyed his opponent, Murray came up with this humdinger: "It wasn't a fight, it was an execution. As one-sided as an electric chair. If you liked that, you should get a collection of Stalin's home movies."

Murray made another pitch for Pete Rose on July 18, when he wrote that while he—Murray—was in the Hall of Fame, Rose was not. "I have a lot of difficulty juxtaposing those two ideas." Murray added, "Why pick on me?" Rabbit Maranville was in Cooperstown with a .258 career average. Murray said Rose was barred from "a Valhalla he richly deserves admittance to." He offered to give Rose his spot in the Hall of Fame.

The Olympic Games were held in Atlanta in 1996. In a post-Soviet world, the United States dominated. Before the Opening Ceremony, Murray tackled the enormous question, "Who would you have to say is the greatest athlete of the century?" He mentioned Babe Ruth, Henry Aaron, Muhammad Ali, Joe Louis, Bill Tilden, Don Budge, Pele, Joe Montana, Sandy Koufax, Michael Jordan, and Jim Thorpe. Then he suggested the answer was "Carl Franklin Lewis, Esq., of the New Jersey and Houston Lewises."

On September 22, Murray wrote about an interview he conducted in Anaheim with Mark McGwire of the Oakland A's. He had more than fifty home runs, and Murray wanted to know if he could break Roger Maris's record of sixty-one. McGwire said he could not do it in 1996, "but some year? It's possible."

Nobody really understood what was happening at the time, but 1996 could easily be pinpointed as the height of the steroid era. McGwire juiced, as did José Canseco. According to reports, Barry Bonds did not start taking performance-enhancing drugs for a few more seasons, but Ken Caminiti of San Diego was built like a football linebacker. An average player out of San Jose State, he developed in a short period of time into a superstar, but it did not last. He eventually died from drug use.

The New York Yankees won the World Series. Just as the success of the 49ers and the election of Bay Area senators symbolized Los Angeles' loss of power, Orange County in bankruptcy and the rise of the Yankees, coinciding with the most glorious decade in the Big Apple's history under Mayor Rudy Giuliani, emphasized how far L.A. had fallen. There was a time when L.A. was "the place," when New York City was depicted by dreary movies like *Marathon Man* and *The French Connection*. Under Giuliani and Yankees owner George

Steinbrenner, New York was Fun City once more. It was again viewed as a town of glamour, hot nightspots, and gorgeous models on the arms of young sports heroes like dazzling rookie shortstop Derek Jeter. L.A. and the *L.A. Times* were just muddling along, battling mediocrity in all its forms. Only Jim Murray and Vin Scully, it seemed, still represented greatness, each assigned to report brilliantly on the doings of the second rate.

Of the Yankees' return to form after a long down period, Murray wrote after the 1994 strike, the team that once "almost killed the game with their ruthless excellence" now "may have saved it. . . . And that's good for business."

Greg Norman was "Golf's Job" (November 14). He played with the "boldness of a bank robber." Murray wrote of Aristotle in comparing Norman's "undeserved misfortune" with others.

When Tiger Woods made the scene, Murray saw his greatness immediately and declared, "Golf is now a five-letter word. It's spelled 'W-O-O-D-S.'" As he did with Willie Mays, Murray had to confirm that there was "such a person as Tiger Woods," that he was not made up. He was "John Wayne on horseback, as heartwarming as a Lassie movie. Beaver Cleaver with a two-iron." In an interesting and prescient prediction, Murray wrote that Woods was the perfect ethnicity for America in the coming century.

■ ■ ■

UCLA's basketball program, which seemed to be back on track under Coach Jim Harrick, took a huge hit when Harrick was fired for filing falsified expense reports. He was replaced by a young, slick unknown with almost no experience, Steve Lavin. The sound of silence from unenthused hoops fans in Westwood was deafening. This was the program John Wooden built? In 1997 UCLA basketball's decline seemed to be another metaphor for the fall of a great city, its giants replaced by unimpressives in sports, politics, and Hollywood.

With little to be enthusiastic about, Murray continued on a theme he regularly returned to: the lack of purity in collegiate sports. He reached into the ancient past by writing that the "'Four Horsemen' produced three coaches and a Federal judge"; he was referring to the famed 1924 Notre Dame backfield. By 1997 "backfields sometimes seem to produce more defendants than judges."

Penn State coach Joe Paterno, however, was a "throwback" whose teams graduated 87 percent of their seniors. "He looks more like a nuclear spy than a football coach," Murray wrote. Most coaches of great note had fields named after them. At Penn State the library was named after the former Brown literature major. Penn State's uniforms looked like "the 1908 Frank Merriwell Yales."

When boxer Mike Tyson bit the ear of opponent Evander Holyfield, Murray was compelled. "I don't know what he could do to restore his dignity and professionalism," he wrote. "Become a vegetarian, for starters." He wrote a public letter to Tyson. The Brooklyn thug seemed the very picture of what Murray had come to despise in sports: overpaid, violent, criminal, reprehensible, and dumb as a box of rocks. Still, Murray wrote that despite Tyson's atrocious acts, he was misunderstood. In fact, Murray liked Tyson and admired the former champion's understanding of boxing history. But he was disgusted with the most recent acts of the out-of-control man. "I don't want to say I defended you to many of my friends, but I did tell them I saw another side to the brute they perceived in mid-ring," Murray wrote. In later years it was revealed Tyson's behavior was the result of not being on medications that later tamed him.

The ugly thug nature of sports was on full display in 1997. Latrell Sprewell of the Golden State Warriors attacked and choked his coach, P. J. Carlesimo. Murray was appalled that San Francisco mayor Willie Brown "cheered Sprewell to the echo and said the coach had it coming. It might be the first time in history a Mayor of a city endorsed aggravated assault." Sports were now filled with dumbbells who took the slightest authority or coaching as, "You're dissing me." The reason, Murray felt, was that too many athletes lacked "a strong father figure in the home to lay down the law." Between the lines he seemed to be saying that a libertine society had failed, and now its spawn were loosed on the land.

He turned from stupidity and criminality to intelligence and grace in an obituary about former NFL commissioner Pete Rozelle. In it Murray wrote, "Pro football became an American tribal rite."

In "Divine Course for Disciple of Golf," Murray wrote, "My late wife used to say, 'If Jim ever gets to Heaven and Ben Hogan isn't there, he ain't staying.'" Larry David's *Curb Your Enthusiasm* picked this theme up a few years later when David imagined himself in heaven playing golf with Hogan (along with Dustin Hoffman as a foul-mouthed Moses).

"I hope today they have in Heaven this little 18-hole golf course with trouble on the right," Murray wrote after Hogan's passing. Paradise would look "suspiciously like Riviera in 1948." Murray did not wish to blaspheme, but imagined that if God played Hogan, the Good Lord would have to take a "five-handicap."

■ ■ ■

In 1998 President Bill Clinton was besieged by allegations of sexual harassment, intimidation, molestation, assault, and rape from women across America. In the course of answering a lawsuit about his harassment of an Arkansas woman named Paula Jones, Clinton lied under oath. The sordid affair came to a head when Clinton lied about the extent of his sexual relationship with White House intern Monica Lewinsky and was subsequently impeached. Most felt the act was disgusting but ultimately not worthy of removal from the presidency.

In the end the Republicans could not muster the votes to oust Clinton. Many thought that the punishment did not fit the crime; plus, political calculations entered the equation. Had Clinton been booted from office, Vice President Albert Gore Jr. would have become president, and he would have had the imprimatur of office while running for election on his own two years later.

At seventy-eight years old, Jim Murray was getting old in 1998. His health was failing him. His writing did not suffer a bit. Vin Scully's biographer, Curt Smith, said,

There are striking parallels between Jim Murray and Vin Scully. Scully was born eight years earlier on a November 29. Murray was born on December 29. They both became "first among equals." Both their lives were similar in that both were born in the urban East, Murray in Hartford, Scully in the Bronx. Both were Irish Catholic. Both worked their way through school. Both graduated from fine schools, Murray from Trinity, Scully from Fordham. Both knew early on what they wanted to be. Both were Republicans. Both joined institutions of great renown. In the case of Murray it would be hard to get a more distinguished journalistic enterprise than *Time* magazine under Henry Luce between 1948 and

1955. Then he joined this itty-bitty enterprise that became *Sports Illustrated.*

Scully joined the most popular baseball team in America in Brooklyn, and moved west with them at the height of their popularity, and became the most phenomenally popular broadcaster of all time. Murray also moved west to become the poster child for journalism with the *Los Angeles Times.* Both made language their marquees. Nobody in print, radio or TV ever distinguished themselves more by the pen or the voice.

Each dominated their profession. Scully made the Baseball Hall of Fame. Murray did, too. Scully was named the greatest sportscaster of all time in all sports, and I would think the same is true of Murray, the proof being his winning the Pulitzer Prize. You cannot be honored by your peers more than both of them have.

Both were very modest about their work, Murray's Lasorda quote that all he did was quote him correctly being proof of this. Scully just said it was a parade and he described it going by.

Both, Smith went on to say, could write for any era. Both were affected by World War II. Both were middle-class Roman Catholics who worked their way through school. Both led personal lives tinged by tragedy that the public knew little about. Scully, like Murray, suffered the loss of his first wife and a son.

Both are emblematic of the rise of Los Angeles. Both were pioneers, "De Soto or Cortes, choose your historical figure, who went where nobody had gone before and in so doing brought the big leagues stylistically to Los Angeles." They became role models, and to those in the East who thought of the people in the West as philistines, of L.A. as a backwater, they changed perceptions, "ignorance meeting arrogance."

If you were a writer you had to love the *Los Angeles Times* and the *Boston Globe*, where both encouraged writers to be gamblers and pioneers," Smith continued. "You can argue the influence of Hollywood, but it was not until Scully and Murray that the town was given real respect. It is irrefutable that Scully and Murray were the 'Roy Hobbs' of their profession, praised by association, both credited with making Los Angeles, as Ernest Hemingway said, *A Clean, Well-Lighted Place* in both fact and persona.

The Dodgers seemingly flipped their fans off in '98. First, News Corporation bought the team. Everything Rupert Murdoch did turned to gold, except baseball. Murray was not optimistic. The O'Malley Dodgers "didn't exactly run the business like a mom-and-pop store," he wrote.

> But it was a family business, catering to moms and pops. And grandpops. I don't know of any sport you can bring a granddaughter to more comfortably and confidently than Dodger baseball.
>
> I would hope that doesn't change. Before the Dodgers, L.A.'s hometown heroes were Charlie Chaplin, Douglas Fairbanks, Mary Pickford, John Wayne, Clark Gable, James Stewart and Bob Hope, to name a few.
>
> The Dodgers added Sandy Koufax, Don Drysdale, Jim Gilliam, Maury Wills, Fernando Valenzuela, Steve Garvey, Tommy Lasorda, Vin Scully and Mike Piazza, to name a few.
>
> That's not a bad trade.

But Peter O'Malley was forced to sell because reinstitution of the estate tax made it impossible to pass the team on to his heirs.

"Jim loved Walter O'Malley and had great respect for Peter O'Malley," recalled Linda McCoy-Murray. "He was a good friend. He'd be calling Peter right now, aghast over what has happened to the Dodgers with the divorce case of the McCourts." Murray's hope that Dodger Stadium would continue to be a place to bring granddaughters took a blow in 2011 when a fan named Brian Stow was assaulted within an inch of his life by a couple of gangbangers just for wearing Giants gear. This was the cornerstone of an HBO *Real Sports With Bryant Gumbel* episode on stadium violence.

His April 26 column on Tim Salmon of the Angels was first-class Murray. The gist of it was that Salmon was so good he earned the right to act like "the Star." Instead of acting like boor Albert Belle, Salmon acted "as unassuming as a butler. He hustles. He works out. He takes outfield. You'd think he was trying to make the team, not lead it." His great ability gave him the right to be "insufferable," but instead he was "as taken for granted as the U.S. mail," as dependable as "the tides." The "archangel" was utterly modest, a trait Murray admired.

Mark McGwire of the St. Louis Cardinals hit seventy home runs that season. He beat out Sammy Sosa of the Chicago Cubs, who finished with sixty-six.

The home run chase was credited with saving baseball after the 1994 strike. In retrospect it became tainted as the steroid era. A subsequent piece on "the Right Honorable Mark David McGwire" was laudatory, but in retrospect it reads with skepticism. Murray did not seem to suspect anything amiss at the time, but the reader today knows better.

In "How Can NFL Not Miss Us?" (August 9), Murray wrote, "The blackest day in the pro game's history was the day Carroll Rosenbloom jerked the Rams out of the Coliseum and took them south. He skewered the picture permanently. It was the main step in a series of steps that left L.A. abandoned on the doorstep with a note pinned on it."

Murray wrote of two great tennis stars of the era. "He Needs to Stay Focused" was about former hotshot Andre Agassi. "Nobody had a longer freefall in the history of sports than" the flashy fellow from Las Vegas who once said, "Image is everything." Andre was making what ultimately turned out to be a successful comeback. "If it's a question of image, it's coming back into focus better and better day by day and may soon overshadow them once again," Murray wrote.

Pete Sampras "has only one personality," he wrote. "He's the kind of guy who repairs divots, pays his taxes, is in bed by 11, he doesn't get into bar fights, throw anybody through plate-glass windows. He doesn't drink and drive, probably goes to church, takes his spoon out of his coffee before drinking it. He gets his hair cut and doesn't dye it purple. He wears white on the court. He doesn't even have an ear ring." In an age in which bad guys were good guys, Murray wrote that Sampras was "hopeless."

"The last time I spoke to [Murray] was at a press conference at the Friar's Club in Beverly Hills," recalled Murray's friend, boxing promoter Bill Caplan.

> Azumah Nelson from Ghana was the featherweight champion, a great fighter. I called up Jim and asked him to come and he said, "Okay, come pick me up and take me to the press conference." That was the last piece he ever did for me.
>
> He had the vision problem. For years he was legally blind. He had surgeries done at the Jules Stein Eye Institute and got enough of his vision back to get a driver's license again. I got in the habit of picking him up and taking him to an assignment. I walked into his house in Bel Air one

time and asked to use his restroom. I'd been in the house many times, it was a beautiful home and every wall was filled with awards. But in the garage were framed awards stacked up against the wall. I was just admiring them and for some strange reason, Jim was kind of a stiff Irishman, a wonderful man but not big on grabbing, hugging and kissing. I grabbed him and gave him a kiss on the cheek, and I said, "I just would like to thank you," and he accepted it and said, "You're welcome," but he was uncomfortable.

I've known George Foreman since he was18. I've been close to him a long time. He's an ordained minister and very spiritual, and I mentioned this to George, and he said, "You were saying good-bye to him, Bill."

Jim would say over the years, "I'm thinking of hanging it up" at least 45 times. He'd bring it up, and I'd argue and say, "No, you can't quit."

"Well, you know it's harder now, I have to think about it more," he'd say. I told him he's writing better than anybody else, "you'll get old real fast. . . . You've been doing this all your life. . . . You're the best at it."

It was the only thing that made him happy and he never did quit.

For the great Jim Murray, it was all grist for the mill. He had seen it all. He saw Ruth hit a home run. He saw O. J. run the field. He saw Jordan fly. He also saw his boss, Otis Chandler, unceremoniously dumped while the newspaper they built together changed irreparably. He stuck it out, despite illness, surgeries, heart problems, poor eyesight. He huffed and puffed his way down and then back up the long stairway at the Coliseum to get quotes after games, returning to the press box to finish his stories. He battled the traffic to Dodger Stadium and Anaheim. Supported by his wife Linda, he was able to get it done. The landscape had changed. Thousands of readers wrote letters to the *Times*, often complaining about its politics. There is no evidence that anybody wrote—or e-mailed, as they now did—complaining, "Murray's past his prime" or "C'mon, Murray's so yesterday." Just as Vin Scully was an icon, secure in the love of a city, so too was Jim Murray. Named America's Best Sportswriter by the National Association of Sportscasters and Sportswriters fourteen times and named National Sportswriter of Year for sixteen years, he was still the best of the best. He was seventy-eight.

16

Sic Transit Gloria

"Thus passes the glory from the world." At the end of *Patton*, George C. Scott in voiceover as the great general in repose says, "For over a thousand years, Roman conquerors returning from the wars were given the honor of a triumph, a tumultuous parade." As they walked the parade route amid great fanfare, "a slave stood behind the conqueror holding a golden crown and whispering in his ear a warning: that all glory is fleeting."

Jim Murray, who first began reading about the Romans when, as a sickly child he received the gift of books and history while recovering in bed, who studied the lessons of Rome, of the British Empire, of Hitler's attempt to conquer, of Stalin's thirty-year reign of terror, of the "grand experiment" that was his beautiful America—a land he loved with a passion—knew that "all glory is fleeting." His grammar school priests had warned, "Pride goeth before the fall." Man's ultimate downfall in a sinful world had given him the wisdom and discernment to understand humanity's relationship with God, which was based on this most-fleeting little adventure on earth, a mere grain of sand when measured against eternity and truth.

How they had come and gone. Ruth, larger than life, masher of the most gargantuan of shots, was felled by age and dead from cancer a few years later. Gehrig was gone in the wink of an eye. Koufax and Drysdale, princes of the city, were sore-armed and retired. Big D, handsome and articulate, was dead before his time. Tyson, the champion, was felled by his own self-destructive forces.

Murray had seen them all. His own glory was not so fleeting. He had arrived in the City of Angels forty-four years earlier, bright-eyed and happy to leave the old neighborhood, where some GI's mother might wonder why the 4-F "Murray boy" ran around healthy while her own flesh and blood was sleeveless or worse.

In 1998 he was still banging away on his typewriter, now a word processor. Unlike so many of the dinosaurs, Murray had adapted to spell check and cut-and-paste. But this glorious ride, the column, had been fleeting. There was also Gerry and her "big beautiful eyes" working the piano in a Fairfax district tavern. There were Teddy and Tony and Pammy—and the "baby in the family," Ricky, now gone.

Otis Chandler? Gone. John McKay, John Wooden? Gone. Walter O'Malley? Gone. My God, Peter O'Malley was gone and with him the Dodgers, their glory years seemingly gone for good.

On the morning of August 16, 1998, Los Angelenos woke up as usual. A hot summer day. Some coffee, a donut, cereal, some fruit. The *L.A. Times*. A routine unchanged. "You Can Teach an Old Horse New Tricks" was about the successful jockey Chris McCarron. It was typical Murray—funny, incisive. In celebration of a Free House victory at Del Mar, he wrote, "He's not a What's-His-Name anymore. He's a Who's Who. . . . The bridesmaid finally caught the bouquet. The best friend got the girl in the Warner Brothers movie for a change. The sidekick saves the fort. . . . Anyway, it's nice to know getting older has its flip side." These were the last words of the column.

Murray's wife had accompanied him to the Del Mar race track near San Diego to spend the afternoon in the hot sun. The day the column appeared, they made the laborious drive back to Los Angeles. The trip entailed heavy traffic, a checkpoint near the San Onofre nuclear plant, rush hour in Orange County, the infamous "south bay curve," and then airport congestion. They finally made it home.

"We were home and he looked at me and said, 'Linda, something's not right,'" McCoy-Murray said, "and he was gone." It was a heart attack. He had been battling poor health for the better part of six years, and at that point, he was a wreck. On August 16, 1998, he shuffled off this mortal coil. The great Jim Murray was gone. His second wife, Linda McCoy-Murray; three children, Pam Skeoch, Ted, and Tony; and two granddaughters and a stepson survived him.

"The thing that made me most unhappy was that he was no longer in the Sunday *Times*," recalled Bill Caplan. "I read his last column and that Monday I got a call and it was the bad news. Somebody from the paper called and it was like, 'Oh, my God.' He suddenly got sick, it was a shock, and I called his widow. I called Linda and cried like a baby. I said, 'I apologize, I'm trying to

SIC TRANSIT GLORIA   213

give you comfort,' and she said, 'I understand,' because she knew the effect
Jim had on people."

■ ■ ■

The writer who loved metaphors and symbols, who lived in a time and place
and for an institution filled with symbolism—American Exceptionalism,
California Dreamin' and the paper that built on those dreams, the promise and
fulfillment of L.A., the world of sports as playground of the New Rome, much
of it played in a place called the Coliseum—was dead. His passing symbolized
that of the *L.A. Times*. Otis Chandler had left in increments, each with the
promise that he was still involved, that it was still his paper. The paper changed
its structure, its corporate culture, and its politics; it lost its panache in the
1990s, but it still had Jim Murray. It was as if the Yankees still featured
DiMaggio or Mantle, even at the end.

There were other significant events. Otis had written his letter to the staff
to protest the Staples Center fiasco, which sports editor Bill Dwyre likened to
Patton rounding up his troops for a final mission. But the charge fizzled out.
Otis and the rest of the Chandlers took their money and ran. The paper was a
shell of its old self after that.

Now that Murray was gone too, the paper was left to its own devices in a
world of Tribune Companies and news groups; a world of Kathryn Downings,
John Puerners, Jeffrey Johnsons, David Hillers, and Eddy Hartensteins; a world
of journalism school graduates possessing better smarts and literary knowledge
than Otis Chandler, but not one-tenth of his common sense or vision.

"Nobody runs the *L.A. Times* anymore," said Councilman Tom LaBonge.

You can read it as fast as the *Daily News*, there's no local control, and it's
gonna be tougher in the future for newspapers. There's been a transfor-
mation of people who don't respect newspapers.

Politically they don't have as much weight as they used to. They "want
it now." I use this in speeches I make, it applies to the *Times*. It must look
like a farmer in the field getting up at four to check his crops. If someone is critical of him and his harvest at nine, then he thinks it's time to
harvest now. We want the harvest at the beginning instead of giving it
time. Without growth we'll miss those writers and leaders.

If after what Bob Erberu, Shelby Coffey III, and Mark Willes did to the *Los Angeles Times*, anybody still wanted to call it the "greatest newspaper in the world," only Jim Murray's column gave any hope to the phrase. With his death went the paper's reputation.

But life went on. Sports editor Bill Dwyre faced a daunting task. How do you replace Jim Murray? You do not. The paper had bred its fair share of talented comers: Scott Ostler, Mike Downey, Randy Harvey, Bill Plaschke, to name a few. All were perfectly good sportswriters. Ostler and Downey had the potential for greatness. The others did not. Bill Plaschke's "replacing" Murray resulted in a plethora of disdainful letters. It got so bad Plaschke joked that the column should be renamed "You're No Jim Murray."

It was not Plaschke's fault that the sports section of this once-hallowed newspaper became mundane, any more than it was Gene Bartow's fault that he was not John Wooden, or George H. W. Bush's fault that he was no Ronald Reagan. Sometimes a Mickey Mantle succeeds a Joe DiMaggio, a Steve Young takes over for a Joe Montana. Not this time.

"There was no replacing Murray at the *L.A. Times*, you can't replace a Murray, a Scully or a Chick Hearn," recalled Fred Wallin. "It's impossible to find somebody like that. Somebody else may have talent, but it's not possible to be in the class of Murray. That doesn't happen in very many lifetimes."

"I get up early in the morning," said Jerry West. "There used to be a rush for me to get the paper and read Jim Murray's column. There's no rush today. I'll tell you that."

"Kids today don't know about history, which is strange because supposedly they live in the Information Age, everybody goes to college, yet the more they learn the less they know," said Linda McCoy-Murray, who is putting together a collection of Jim's columns on women athletes over the years. "They don't know how to do research. Jim knew history and he did his research."

News of Jim Murray's passing rivaled that of any other L.A. deity or icon. He was immediately identified as a man whose influence on Los Angeles equaled that of anyone else: George Patton, William Mulholland, the Chandler family, Raymond Chandler, Dorothy Chandler, Tom Bradley, Edward Doheny, Darryl F. Zanuck, Cecil B. DeMille, Jack Warner, John Wooden, Vin Scully, or Ronald Reagan.

The letters came pouring in. Amateur Murrays wrote about "football teams that more resembled the *Wehrmacht*" and loving memories of favorite columns, Murray moments, and chance meetings with the great scribe. Colleagues and athletes all had special Murray memories.

On September 26, 2,500 fans showed up at Dodger Stadium for a final tribute to the great Murray, hosted by Bill Dwyre. It was "a star-studded funeral that would have embarrassed this most humble of men," wrote Plaschke. It was also a heartfelt tribute. In *Privileged Son: Otis Chandler and the Rise and Fall of the* Los Angeles Times, Dennis McDougal wrote that Dorothy Chandler's funeral, while well attended by a who's who of Los Angeles society, lacked great love. Not so with Jim Murray. Linda McCoy-Murray knew her husband was loved and admired, but even she was amazed at the outpouring. Every major sports personality in L.A. was there.

"You know, Shakespeare said it best, as he usually did, and when he wrote it, he might very well have been writing about Jim Murray," said Vin Scully, who of course usually did say it best. "He wrote, 'His life was gentle, and the elements so mixed in him that nature might stand up and say to all the world, 'This was a man.'"

■ ■ ■

Jim Murray was a chronicler, a herald of the twentieth century, the American Century. Not since the gladiators dazzled Rome had sports played so active a role nor been so symbolic of a society as it was when Murray was its mouthpiece, its conscience, and its booster.

In 1994, when one of his contemporaries, former president Richard Nixon, passed away, President Bill Clinton presided over the memorial service at the Nixon Birthplace and Library in Yorba Linda. "It was the age of Nixon," Clinton pronounced.

Indeed it had been. Nixon's life mirrored the growth of his hometown and his home state. Murray, who covered Nixon early in his career, before the presidency, Watergate, and his eventual rehabilitation as an "elder statesman," rode that wave. As sports became big money through television and corporate sponsorships, Murray did not merely benefit from it. He was one of the reasons its popularity grew as it did in the first place. He was certainly in the right place at the right time: post-World War II California, *Time*, *Sports Illustrated*, the *Los Angeles Times*.

Los Angeles grew like no city in history. Jim Murray was there, from the typewriter and the telegram to the computer, the word processor, and the Internet.

Murray was part of our past, not to be seen again. He is among the Mount Rushmore of our greatest writers. Legions of people who dabble not just in sports but who write screenplays, novels, report the news, and chronicle history count him as a major influence.

"Only Jim, of all the great sportswriters, always got it right and always got it funny," said Dave Kindred of *The Sporting News*.

"My, my, he was one hell of a writer, but he was even a better person, seemingly without ego, without pretension," said Jack Whittaker of ABC Sports.

While he was "one hell of a writer," perhaps more appropriately Jim Murray attained in heaven what the dustcover of his 1988 book, *The Jim Murray Collection*, said was the "Holy Grail of newspapermen—the 'column that writes itself.'" One imagines he is up there with Jesus Christ's rewrite men—Matthew, Mark, Luke, and John—doing just that, reminding them that "people read to be amused, shocked, titillated, or angered."

APPENDIX A
One-on-One with Bill Dwyre

Babe Ruth had a manager. His name was Miller Huggins. Joe McCarthy managed Joe DiMaggio. Henry Aaron played under a guy named Fred Haney. Willie Mays toiled under men named Herman Franks and Clyde King.

Jim Murray had an editor. His name was Bill Dwyre. Dwyre "managed" a team of superstars, the *Los Angeles Times* sports section of the golden age, the 1980s and 1990s. It was like Miller Huggins filling out a lineup card each day with the Murderer's Row at his disposal. Murray was his "clean-up" guy. The newspaper version of George Steinbrenner, Otis Chandler, gave Dwyre a near-unlimited budget to produce a section unequalled before or since.

A Wisconsin native, Notre Dame graduate, and former sportswriter who covered Kareem Abdul-Jabbar in Milwaukee before coming west as Murray did, he provided an exclusive interview for this book.

Q: When did you become sports editor of the *Los Angeles Times?*
A: June of 1981.

Q: Did you ever have reason to change anything Jim Murray wrote?
A: Once or twice Jim got overly sexist, old guy stuff. We talked about it, very minor stuff, maybe two or three items in fifteen or twenty years.

Q: Did any other writers ever try to imitate Murray, and who came the closest to him?
A: Every other writer of that day tried to imitate him. The most successful was Rick Reilly, who adored him, but nobody's Murray. Bad imitations of him were horrible, and there were plenty of those. Scott Ostler was clever, quick, and funny. He always was quick with the lines, but I would not say he really "imitated" Murray. There was nobody like Jim Murray.

Q: Did Murray and Otis Chandler have a good relationship?

A: Yes, Otis was in on the general hiring of Murray. It was down to Murray and Mel Durslag, then with the *Los Angeles Herald-Examiner*. He liked something about Murray. Durslag was better known as a writer. He was syndicated whereas Jim was with *Sports Illustrated*, but not featured as a "star" yet. Durslag was under contract and getting him to come over was problematic, which was a reason he was not hired, but as I recall, Otis Chandler settled on Jim Murray and got him.

Q: Did you ever discuss politics with Murray? Was he a Republican or a Democrat?

A: Never had to. His politics were the same as mine. He would not go to The Masters because of their policies toward black membership. He would not soften that stance until they came around to change. Based on his views, mainly regarding race in the civil rights era, I would say he was a "liberal Democrat" from the standpoint of social issues. He was a champion of human rights. He may well have been a conservative Republican when it came to money.

Q: Did you ever discuss Christianity with Murray, and was he open about his faith? Did you ever see Murray's religion and/or politics in his columns by reading between the lines?

A: Never. He was, like me, a basic Irish Catholic, although I'm not sure what that means. He discussed the death of his son Ricky with me, but in that respect he was a typical, stoic Irishman. He did not open up or psychoanalyze himself. I spoke to him a lot about his son's death, but these were conversations between two stoic Irish Catholic guys.

Q: Jim was a traditionalist. He moved from Malibu to Brentwood in part because of the drug scene that affected his family. Did he ever complain to you about the attitude of Malibu residents, who may have been as permissive as their own kids, who never responded to his efforts to do something about rampant drug use?

A: Yes, he did. He did make the move partly for that reason. His home was perched near where the bootleggers once unloaded Prohibition booze, and then in his day, it was where drug smugglers came to shore.

He saw it and did not like it. He sold his house to the rock star Bob Dylan. Dylan was, like Murray, viewed as a "poet," and perhaps Jim thought he was selling to a kindred spirit. He specifically told Dylan he would only sell his house if he promised to keep it as it was, it had special meaning to him, the den overlooking the ocean, you know. A while later Murray drove out there and Dylan just tore it up, changed the whole landscape. Murray despised him for that. There were only two guys Jim Murray really disliked. One was Bob Dylan, and the other was his namesake, Eddie Murray of the Dodgers. He was cantankerous and uncommunicative.

Q: Ben Hogan was his favorite subject to interview and write about. After Hogan who else was there?

A: Ben Hogan he loved, in that he came as close to having control over the game as anybody. There's the famed story where he asks his caddy a question, and the caddy says, "138 or 139 yards," and Hogan replies, "Well, which one is it, 138 or 139 yards?" Murray loved that kind of stuff.

Koufax was high on his list. He was friends with Tommy Lasorda. He loved Jerry West, who was such a figure of psyche as I wrote about as well. But he loved writing about Elgin Baylor. How cheap he was, stuff he went through on the road. Baylor was a man of hype and that sort of thing triggered his greatest writing. Murray was like any other writer in that his best work came when his subject was great.

He always provided a quality column, but if he wrote about a gymnast or rower, unless there was something excessive in excellence or stupidity, his best stuff came when he was very interested in a great athlete like Elgin Baylor, to name just one. Therein came the confluence of best writing about the best: Jim Murray in his prime writing about Willie Mays in his prime. I mean, this is the essence of his art. Tom Seaver, greatness, things that inspired him. The biggest sports, the most well-known stars, the biggest stages were where he excelled, although unquestionably he was responsible for upgrading some sports figures through his sheer talent, Al Scates being an example. "Al Scates is to volleyball what Napoleon is to artillery."

Q: Did Jim ever have bad days?

A: There were many times he'd have bad days, when I would cringe at something he wrote. You mentioned one, when he went overboard about Frank Howard. "When Howard arrives in town they call in the Army. . . . Howard wasn't born, he was founded. . . . When Howard shows up Fay Wray goes into hiding. . . . Howard's homers are not measured by tape measure but by aerial photography." So sometimes he went overboard, but Jim Murray "batted .920."

Sure, the subject matter makes or breaks the column. Writing about some gymnast might not have interested him as much as Roberto Clemente, but over the years he was on the money almost every time. His "bad" columns can be counted on one hand.

Q: In my humble opinion—and maybe it's because I wrote the book *One Night, Two Teams: Alabama vs. USC and the Game That Changed a Nation*—Jim's best column was his September 13, 1970, column on that game, in which he wrote, "We welcomed the sovereign state of Alabama into the Union yesterday . . . the Constitution was ratified . . ." that kind of thing. If I asked you to rate his top twenty columns, where would you put that, and what else comes to mind?

A: I certainly read that column and agree it's in the top twenty. His best was when his wife Gerry passed away, his second best was when he lost his eye. It would be tough for me to get there, to a top twenty. Those two were 10-plus, the rest were 9.9s.

Q: Did you know his colleague Jeff Prugh, who was with him the weekend at Birmingham?

A: I just missed Prugh, Ron Rappaport, some of those guys. I knew Jeff a bit from calling in on occasion, Dwight Chapin, some went up to the *San Francisco Chronicle*. After Otis Chandler left there were shake-ups.

Q: Prugh was a close friend of mine who played a major role in helping me get my career off the ground, and in many ways it was his reminiscences of Jim that inspired this book. He passed away too young and shockingly unexpectedly. You answered my next question, which was, What were two or three of your favorite Murray columns? To what extent did Murray separate himself from Eastern writers like Cannon, Breslin, Smith?

A: He was more of a stylist. All those guys were great and had their own style, their own distinct style, but there was nobody like Murray. We would enter his columns into contests with no headline or byline, but they'd win every time. There was no hiding him; you knew it was Jim Murray. Breslin had his style, but he was more of an "articulate reprobate" filled with iconoclasm and opinions.

Jim had opinions but he enjoyed the art and craft more than pushing his opinions down your throat. When he saw something he was passionate about, a cause, he could slice and dice more effectively than anybody in the country.

Q: A subliminal effect!

A: He didn't just have a hammer in his hand like Bill Plaschke, who writes about people like that sometimes. Jim wrote about people. He made people interesting.

Q: That reminds me of something. In the early 1960s the *Times* space writer wrote a lengthy piece about some new NASA invention that was going to give us the edge over the Soviets, but Jim just said it was boring. The space writer looked at him like he was crazy, this was an important breakthrough, but Jim learned his journalism from Henry Luce at *Time*. Luce popularized the space program by featuring his astronauts with large photo spreads of their families and the launches, photo-heavy, in *Life* magazine.

A: Well, that's exactly right. If he was pissed over an issue he'd call me and say, "You know, the fact this-or-that happened is because of this-or-that." So I knew when that happened a great column was in the works. Four or five days would pass, and all the other columnists and pundits would weigh in. Then after a big discussion he'd think about it, and always, after listening to all the turkeys, he'd think about it, and he'd write a column that was just head and shoulders in thought above all the other commentary. I'd read this and just say to myself, "I wish I'd think about things like that," or "I wish I'd have thought of that." But everybody else thought about an issue with only 10 percent of the breadth and scope of Jim Murray.

Q: If L.A. erected a "Mount Rushmore" in the Santa Monica Mountains or on Mount Wilson, what five or six people would you vote to be depicted there?

A: Tom Bradley, Jim Murray, Vin Scully, Dorothy Chandler, John Wooden.

Q: How important was the sports section in separating the *Times* from competitors?

A: The sports section separated the paper from other papers. This may sound self-serving, but it was—and still is, relatively—an incredibly good product. It's not as good as it once was. We all know that. What we did was not to be arrogant about sports. We were intelligent. The section never looked down its nose upon sports. We spent money on sports. In the heyday, the *New York Times* did not spend money comparably, but our attitude, our approach separated us from them.

This was one of the ways Otis Chandler, a former jock, saw the growth of the paper. I did the 1984 Olympics. That's why they brought me in. The *New York Times* thought our approach was excessive, but Otis didn't care. I lived during the golden age of that paper. We were not provincial, while everything about the *New York Times* sports section, ironically, was provincial. They were living in the past, thinking of New York City as the sports capital, but that was a thing of the past, and the 1984 Los Angeles Olympics symbolized that. Otis knew it and spent money to take full advantage of that. It was our finest hour.

Today, the paper worships at the altar of the Dodgers, Lakers, and USC. There is no space now to add what we used to do. We've reverted to being the opposite of what we were then. We currently do that, but in the old days we covered all that and more; we covered all sports. The '84 Olympics was our masterpiece. We set the agenda. In that era we produced a massive volume of sports information every day. Daily for years we produced the best sports stories anywhere with little regard for length or space or money constraints. Otis just said, "Keep going, kid."

Q: In your honest opinion did the *L.A. Times* ever ascend to being the "best newspaper in the world"?

A: Yes. In the world? I can say for sure we were the best in the country. I guess I'd say it had to be in the 1980s and early 1990s. Maybe the London *Times*.

I can't say because of the language barrier, who knows, maybe some of the Chinese papers were equal . . .

Q: Well, perhaps I'm just an American jingoist, but first of all I'd eliminate any Chinese papers because of total government censorship. I've read the London *Times*. It's stuffy. If it's close, the *L.A. Times* sports section makes the difference.

A: Of course, the Chinese papers are a bad example. Nobody was our equal in sports. We were the best in the country. We were doing everything right back then. The talent was astounding: Jim Murray, Mike Downey, Rick Reilly, Scott Ostler, Randy Harvey, Mike Littwin, Tom Bonk, Chris Dufresne, Bill Plaschke. The talent was so deep. Just great guys. Regarding the question, we had just as many international bureaus as any other paper. I think our coverage of a variety of subjects was as in-depth and excellent as anybody. The paper was very well produced. Over time, as the *Tribune* bought us out, that changed dramatically, but overall for a time there, yes, we were number one.

Q: Do you know three or four of Murray's favorites books or authors?

A: Wow, I do not. I would be speculating.

Q: When Murray left, did something happen to the paper that could never be replaced?

A: That's the heart of it. He was a voice. He could not be a complete voice as a sportswriter, but he was a singular voice of the paper. Later Steve Lopez came the closest to matching that voice, but it's a long gap, and we do not have that kind of voice anymore.

I've never seen a columnist as revered as Murray. His son Teddy did not have his ambition, but he was the same way as Jim. In the middle of a conversation, he'd break into an Irish story like Jim. In the latter years, after the Pulitzer, there'd be so many calls for Jim to make speeches, I tried to get Teddy to make some to sub for his father.

For Jim toward the end, it was weighing on him. After the Pulitzer there were so many calls for speeches. I'd call him and ask if he'd like to speak to the Pacoima Rotary, and eventually he just had to say no, but I gave them an excuse. I'd say it was against company policy, and they'd have to run it past the sports editor. I'd look it over, and if Jim said no, I'd tell them I'd decided no.

In some cases I changed it and made it a question-and-answer, where I would get the time to monitor the speech. I spent a lot of time bonding with Jim, driving to Orange County or wherever we went. It was like father and son, the last five or six years of his life. Today, there's nothing like it. I'd have Bill Plaschke or T. J. Simers getting on my ass. I'd listen to 'em complain and say, "How do I get ahead?"

Being with Jim was the finest time in my life. He had the strength of his convictions. He would not want to have to write about Kobe Bryant every day. He knew that if you wrote about the same thing you'd lose the truck drivers. Now we're in the wrong direction, stuck on the same themes. Jim could write about a little old lady who won the 1908 Wimbledon and it was interesting. He didn't need that day's argument or controversy to pound on over and over.

Later I'd have Simers always telling me what I'm doing wrong. I got tired of worshipping at the altar of T. J. Simers and the Lakers. The fact is that sports has great characters. Jim wrote about people. That's what attracted me to him. He was so smart. I remember at the Barcelona Olympics. My wife and I would go off somewhere with the translator. Later we would find Jim at breakfast. He'd sit down and have done the *New York Times* crossword puzzle in ten minutes.

There's one more story. It was 1986–87, the Super Bowl played at the Rose Bowl between the New York Giants and the Denver Broncos. In those days the Super Bowl was played at the Rose Bowl regularly, and we were spending money like there was no tomorrow. We wanted something different, so I was authorized to hire a prominent nonsports writer to write articles from the Super Bowl, a prominent, world-class author. I hired Leon Uris, who wrote *Exodus* about the creation of the state of Israel. I think we paid him five thousand dollars apiece for three thousand words each.

So we send him down to Newport Beach where the teams trained, and we brought in his young wife to shoot photos, and he wrote some advance pieces. Now we get to the day of the game. Uris is sitting in the press box. We've got fifteen people covering every angle. Uris is sitting next to Jack

Smith and Jim Murray, two esteemed writers. The Broncos lost big to the Giants.

I'm running around, making sure I don't have guys writing the same thing. Everything's running smooth except for Uris. I look over and I see him over there next to Murray, typing and humming away. Murray and Smith, two pros in their element. Finally, the game ends, the interviews are conducted, and it's getting toward deadline. Smith and Murray are finished and packed. I go to Uris, I ask how he's doing. He's got three or four graphs. He just looks up at me and says, "I can't do this."

This guy wrote long novels that took years, two or three years in some cases, research and contemplation, but he was too intimidated by Jim Murray. Murray had trouble seeing, the game was boring, and Uris sat next to him all game while Jim tried to come up with a column. Then all of a sudden when the heat was on Jim just pounded one out and Uris is sitting there, unbelievably intimidated. He spent two or three years to write the kind of stuff he did. I had to write the last eighteen graphs for him. Considering his normal material, and Jim's penchant for historical and biblical references, he should have written something like, "As with the parting of the Red Sea the Denver Broncos' defense opened up while the New York Giants proceeded to pass through, but when John Elway and Denver tried to advance they were swallowed up by waves of Bill Parcels' defenders."

Q: What was the general attitude at the *Times* after the Chandler admonition over the Staples deal, and especially after the sale to the *Tribune*? Was there a feeling that something was lost that could never be regained?

A: We did not think that way at the time. We were so used to success and unable to imagine the horrors ahead. Now we're living them, but at the time we had no frame of reference as to what might come up when we were purchased.

Q: Discuss Murray, the rivalry with San Francisco, and San Francisco's notion of inferiority.

A: He loved San Francisco, but it was a way of poking fun at something. San Francisco amused him. For years they came up with reasons why they lost sporting events, rationalizing that it was OK to lose because winning was somehow "too American." Later when Joe Montana came along that dynamic changed, but before that San Francisco thought themselves too sophisticated to care about winning. Well, my, you talk about a fastball down the middle for Jim Murray! He loved to write about cities, like the stuff he did with Cincinnati. I was with him at a 1994 benefit, and he trashed Cincinnati, all in good fun. Some of his best lines came in those columns.

But San Francisco! Anything that was pompous, arrogant, people who walked around with an air of superiority about them, well, these were all reasons for Jim to make fun of them. His intellect was so great, and he just sliced and diced these people down to size.

Q: **You were like the Miller Huggins or Casey Stengel of sports editors, managing superstars, the Babe Ruths and Mickey Mantles of your profession. What a ride it was for you.**

A: For a kid from Wisconsin, I could not have been more blessed. I arrived in Los Angeles and Otis Chandler just said, "Go to it, kid."

APPENDIX B
Famous Last Words

On Branch Rickey

"Rickey had always been held to be the second Great Emancipator but, like the first one, he had a double motive. The first wanted to win a war. The second wanted to win a pennant."

Rickey "could recognize a great player from the window of a moving train."

On Leo Durocher

Branch Rickey said, "Leo Durocher is a mental hoodlum with the infinite capacity for taking a bad situation and immediately making it infinitely worse."

"Leo's problem was, as Runyon said of someone else, he always saw life as eight-to-five against."

When he did not get into the Hall of Fame while alive, "Leo, inevitably, finished last himself."

On Walter O'Malley

O'Malley "followed his customers."

"O'Malley had about as high a regard for the freedom of the press as Thomas Jefferson."

Of O'Malley's handling of Dodgers players, "I always thought he regarded them as obstreperous children, fiscally irresponsible, functionally illiterate and as ineducable and temperamental as horses."

"A Dodger player, in the O'Malley view, always came out looking like a Republican candidate for the Senate. He wore a tie, took his hat off in elevators and, if possible, went to mass on Sundays."

On Sandy Koufax

Jim Davenport was asked about hitting against Sandy: "Jim, with Koufax, do you look for the fastball?" "Oh, (bleep), yeah," shot back Davenport. "The curveball you can't hit anyway!"

"But, Sandy always seemed to be running from something."

On Don Drysdale

With the hitters in the league, Drysdale "could lose an election to Castro."

Hitting him is like facing "hand grenades—with the pins out."

On Maury Wills

"Maury Wills was a trendsetter but he was, ultimately, a baseball tragedy."

"Wills was the darling of Hollywood. He was more than that to the screen actress Doris Day. . . . She was smitten with Maury and began lavishing expensive gifts on him like color TV sets. The official word was the friendship was platonic but, of course, it wasn't."

"What happened to Maury after he left baseball made you want to sob. He descended into a miasma of cocaine addiction and self-destruction that confounded belief."

"Maury Wills, the ballplayer, had always been a man in firm control of his life. In all the years I studied him, I never saw Maury do a thing without a purpose, aimlessly. He was as organized a human being as I have ever seen."

"Maury Wills the addict was a pathetic sight to behold. Gaunt, grey, in thrall to a thousand raging masters. He tried briefly to manage. He was a disaster, falling asleep on the bench, putting wrong names in a lineup."

On Steve Garvey

"The harder he tried to be liked the more hostility he inspired. I don't know why. I think the notion persisted that no one could be that good. . . . He was a superstar who acted as if he would do windows."

"I liked him because he was as available for an interview as a guy running for sheriff."

"Garvey did the honorable thing: he acknowledged paternity where it appeared. He got married. He paid child support."

Garvey succumbed to "the temptation of the road."

On Walt Alston

"Walt Alston came from the kind of people who won our wars, plowed our fields, fed our children."

He came from a part of Ohio "where the train stopped only if it hit a cow."

"Every time I looked at Walt, I saw a Union soldier."

"The only guy in the game who could look Billy Graham in the eye without blushing, who would order corn on the cob in a Paris restaurant."

On Tommy Lasorda

"Tommy never talked, he shouted."

"There were two men in my journalistic career I could always count on when I ran dry and needed a column. One was Casey Stengel. The other was Lasorda."

"Tommy was as American as a carburetor."

On Vin Scully

Scully can make watching a 13-3 game interesting because he can "take you to a time and place where you are suddenly watching Babe Ruth steal home."

On Ford Frick

"Ford Frick isn't the worst Commissioner of Baseball in history, but he's in the photo. I made him no worse than second place."

On Willie Mays

"Willie Mays is so good the other players don't even resent him. . . . The only thing he can't do on a baseball field is fix the plumbing."

On Joe DiMaggio

"Joe DiMaggio played the game at least a couple levels higher than the rest of us."

On Hank Bauer

"He has a face like a clenched fist."

On Yogi Berra

"Yogi was a catcher who was as sharp as a Bronx housewife behind the plate."

On Mickey Mantle

"Mickey Charles Mantle was born with one foot in the Hall of Fame."

On Henry Aaron

"He is to enjoy only. The way he plays it, baseball is an art, not a competition. He is grace in a grey flannel suit, a poem with a bat in its hands."

On Stan Musial and Roberto Clemente

Stan Musial "was the exact opposite of Clemente. He was happy and his face knew it."

"Roberto didn't have the grace of Henry Aaron or the dash of Willie Mays, but if you put all the skills together and you had to play one of them at the same position, it would be hard to know which to bench."

On Rickey Henderson

Rickey Henderson "has a strike zone the size of Hitler's heart."

On Baseball

"It was Hamlet. It was East Lynne. It was a morality play. It was life in a microcosm. It was religion."

Going to Ebbetts Field was "about on a social level with going to a cockfight."

"And if you don't know a newspaper isn't important to baseball, you don't know baseball."

"Seven hours at the ballpark was as close to nirvana as a kid could get. You hated to see the final out."

"I don't know when we got in such a hurry that everything had to be speeded up like one of those early jerky silent movies where the sprocket slipped."

"I like to look down on a [baseball] field of green and white, a summertime land of Oz, a place to dream."

"Baseball is a game where a curve is an optical illusion, a screwball can be a pitch or a person, stealing is legal and you can spit anywhere you like except in the umpire's eye or on the ball."

"Baseball is a game played by nine athletes on the field and 20 fast-buck artists in the front office."

"The charm of baseball is that, dull as it may be on the field, it is endlessly fascinating as a rehash."

"Baseball writers are at that awkward age. Too old for girls and too young for Lawrence Welk."

"If it isn't [a business], General Motors is a sport."

On Mike Garrett

Mike Garrett's "throat has the fingerprints of every linebacker in the league on it."

On Billy Wade

"I won't say Billy was clumsy, but on the way back from the line of scrimmage with the ball, he bumped into more people than a New York pickpocket."

On Deacon Jones

"Deacon Jones is, quite simply, 20 percent of the Rams' defense. Just to equalize him requires 2.2 players."

On Chuck Knox

After Knox arrived at a press conference announcing him as coach: "A limo pulled up, the passenger door was opened, and nobody got out."

On Al Davis

"Al Davis would have been a hit-and-run cavalry officer, maybe a general, in a previous incarnation."

"The German Army went deep. So did Davis's Raiders. Blitzkrieg football was a Davis trademark."

On Fred Biletnikoff

Biletnikoff "has a name longer than the Warsaw telephone directory and a reach even longer. He can run faster than he can walk but he's harder to keep track of than a mosquito in a dark bedroom. Sometimes, he seems to have arrived by parachute."

On Lyle Alzado

Alzado "always reminded me of an Old Testament prophet, the bearded look, the angry eyes. You could picture him on a hill in Biblical times, raging at the sins of his fellow man."

"Putting a Rutgers man alongside Alzado" was like "putting a nun in the Mafia."

On Marc Wilson

"You watch Marc Wilson play football, and you wonder how he gets himself dressed in the morning."

On the Raiders

"The Oakland Raiders are football's version of The Dirty Dozen. It's not a team, it's a gang."

"It's not the Oakland Raiders, it's Quantrill's."

On Bobby Layne

"For Bobby, life was all fast Layne."

On Bob Hayes

"The only thing that could keep up with him was trouble. Trouble runs an 8.6 hundred."

On Dick Butkus

"What makes Butkus so valuable is, he often catches a football before it is thrown. This is because, in addition to catching footballs, he also catches people who have them. He shakes them upside down till they let go."

On Terry Bradshaw

Bradshaw "always gave the impression he had just ridden into town on a wagon and two mules."

On Jack Lambert

"Lambert didn't come out of a college; he escaped from the laboratory."

On Conrad Dobler

"To say Dobler 'plays' football is like saying the Gestapo 'played' 20 Questions."

On John Elway

Elway "completed more passes than the Fifth Fleet on leave."

On Football Coaches

Paul Brown "treated his players as if he had just bought them at auction with rings in their noses and was trying not to notice they smelled bad."

Norm Van Brocklin was "a guy with the nice, even disposition of a top sergeant whose shoes are too tight."

"Vince Lombardi looks as if he should be climbing down from behind the wheel of a six-wheel semi and saying, 'Okay lady, where do you want the piano?'"

"Nothing is ever accomplished by reason—look at Woody Hayes."

"Woody was consistent. Graceless in victory and graceless in defeat."

"What the iceberg was to the Titanic, what Little Big Horn was to Custer, Waterloo to Napoleon, Tunney to Dempsey, the Rose Bowl is to Bo Schembechler."

With Bill Walsh, "You half expect his headset is playing Mozart."

"I have seen guys look happier throwing up" than Don Coryell.

Of Nebraska running back Lawrence Phillip's arrest: "Getting a four A.M. call that one of your star players has just dragged a woman down three flights of stairs by the hair is like the head of Ford Motor Company being awakened to be told the assembly line has just broken down."

Asking coaches about strategy made "me feel as if I asked Einstein to explain the expanding Universe."

"I have nightmares thinking what might have happened if Edison could catch a football in a crowd, or the Wright brothers spent their evenings inventing the single wing. What if Louis Pasteur were a place-kicker?"

On Football

"The interior line must be where guys on the lam hide out."

"If you smile when everything about you is going wrong, join the San Francisco 49ers."

"The 'Peter Principle' that everything keeps rising until it reaches its level of incompetence is best illustrated by the Minnesota Vikings in the Super Bowl."

On Jerry West

"Jerry West, with such fantastic peripheral vision it was said he could see his ears."

West "has the quickest hands and feet ever seen on a guy without a police record."

On Elgin Baylor

"Elgin Baylor was as unstoppable as a woman's tears."

On Wilt Chamberlain

Chamberlain "looked, in poor light, like an office building with kneepads."

On Magic Johnson

"Magic without a basketball is . . . an offense against nature."

On Shaquille O'Neal

"O'Neal is more than a building, he's a skyline."

On Chick Hearn

"Before Chick, basketball broadcasts were just more interesting than test patterns."

On John Wooden

Wooden was "so square he was divisible by four."

On Bob Lanier

"Rumor has it his shoes are off-loaded at the Detroit River docks by tug. It takes him 20 minutes to unlace them."

On Julius Erving

"It will be interesting to see if he can be seen by the naked eye."

On Basketball

"A spy has a better social life" than an NBA referee. "The piano player in the bordello gets more respect."

On Track and Field

Bob Mathias "was brought up in the sunshine and breezes of the San Joaquin Valley, where vegetables and men grow in size to twice the national average."

"Bob Beamon was in the air just shorter than the Wright Brothers. . . . It wasn't a jump, it was an orbital flight."

"Nothing this side of Man o' War could challenge Carl Lewis in his heyday."

On Ice Hockey

"Seeing a goal scored in hockey is like picking your mother out of a crowd shot at the Super Bowl."

"Hockey is the Bloody Mary of sports."

On Tennis

"Tennis is a game in which love counts nothing, deuces are wild, and the scoring system was invented by Lewis Carroll."

"They can take only so much of a sport where a shutout is called love."

"James Scott Connors is about as popular in the world of tennis as a double fault."

Chris Evert "looked as unattainable as Garbo, a slope of Everest."

If Martina Navratilova "were a team, there'd be cries to break her up."

Getting beat by Stefan Edberg is "like getting beat by the statue of Fred Perry they have outside Wimbledon."

Pete Sampras "plays tennis like a guy dealing blackjack. All he does is beat you."

Andre Agassi looks "as if he were 10 minutes late for an appointment or trying to catch a bus."

Steffi Graf "is as German as a glockenspiel. And fittingly, she plays this kind of Wagnerian game, full of crashing crescendos, heroic passages, lyric transitions. She attacks."

"You know Monica Seles is on her game when center court sounds like feeding time at the zoo."

"The first look you get at Martina Hingis, you don't know whether to buy her a lollipop or ask her to dance."

On Boxing

"Boxing dirties almost everybody who gets into it. It's hardly ecclesiastical."

A boxer has to "punch his way out of the ghetto."

"If you saw [Sonny Liston's] footprint in the snow in the Himalayas, four expeditions would be launched to capture him."

To "Sugar Ray" Robinson, "the world looked to him like a two-pound palooka with a glass chin."

"If Jerry Quarry's life story is ever made into a book the title will be Oops!"

"With his electric hair and long-running monologues delivered in the booming bombast of Moses addressing the children of Israel, [Don] King feels he is the apotheosis of the breed."

George Foreman "could kill anything that didn't move."

Of attending the 1974 Muhammad Ali–George Foreman fight in Africa: "Let's hope Grace Kelly and Ava Gardner get to fight over me in the jungle."

"You shouldn't fight Roberto Duran, you should hunt him."

When Mike Tyson bit Evander Holyfield's ear: "That may be the most expensive dining out in history."

On Golf

"You know, golf isn't a talent. It's a trick. Just like writing a column."

"A golfer looking for new clubs is like Joe Namath on a pickup. He'll dance with every girl at the prom."

"The [golf] club has a natural instinct for trouble. It's a born outlaw. If it were human, it'd be robbing banks."

"When it comes to golf, I root for the course."

"I have a friend who calls golf the 'pursuit of infinity.'"

"For most players, golf is about as serene as a night in Dracula's castle."

"Actually, the only time I ever took out a one-iron was to kill a tarantula. And I took a seven to do that."

On Auto Racing

"It's not so much a sporting event as death watch. They hold it, fittingly, on Memorial Day."

"I'd never drive anything you had to climb in the window to start up."

On Horse Racing

"A race track crowd comprises the greatest floating fund of misinformation this side of the pages of Pravda, the last virgin stand of optimism in our century."

"Affirmed was the Star. A golden glow of a colt. A matinee idol. If he were human, he'd be Robert Redford."

Sunday Silence was "a horse they thought so little of they did everything but leave him on a park bench with a note on him: 'Won the Kentucky Derby Saturday.'"

"Charlie Whittingham has been around horses so long he sleeps standing up."

On Los Angeles Fans and Stadiums

"When the Dodgers came West, the whole mood of the franchise changed. Laid-back L.A. was a far cry from Ebbets Field. I always noted the difference in the fans from each community could be summed up in the reactions of the two-dollar bettors in the home stretch."

"'Call yourself a pitcher, Drysdale! You couldn't get my grandmother out, ya choke artist!' In L.A., the cheering was positive. 'All right, Big D, we're with you Don, baby! Let him hit! Willie'll get it.'"

"The Coliseum had about 92,000 seats—from about 28,000 of which you could actually see the game."

"Dodger Stadium is a place you can bring your granddaughter."

On Cities

Murray was disappointed in a report from Moscow on a track meet with no imagery or color of the city: "I was never so disappointed in my life. I wanted to read about people in fur hats, queues in front of Lenin's tomb. I wanted to know what Brezhnev looked like close up. I wanted to know what the cabdrivers thought about America. I got non-winning times, splits in the 1500. I hear all about Rafer Johnson, who was meeting the Russian Kuznetsov in the decathlon. I knew all about Rafer Johnson. I wanted to know about Ivan the Terrible. I had a vision of my friend coming back from Heaven and, being asked what it was like, answering 'Johnson rapped out at 16 feet two inches.'

"I resolved never to get so afflicted with press box myopia myself that I would not comment on events surrounding an event."

"I wondered out loud how you could get there since nobody ever went to Warsaw except on the back of a tank or the front of a bayonet."

He passed on Lenin's tomb because "if I want to see dead people I would go to Kabul."

In Russia "the last group of tourists able to move freely through the country was the Wehrmacht."

When they unfrocked Stalin the cartographers could do what "Hitler couldn't do—wipe out Stalingrad." It was like "renaming Gettysburg New Peoria."

Los Angeles is "under policed and oversexed."

L.A. architecture is "Moorish Nauseous."

L.A. "has a dry river but a hundred thousand swimming pools."

Long Beach was "the sea port of Iowa . . . a city which, rumor has it, was settled by a slow leak in Des Moines."

"That day in Cincinnati, I noted the state of disrepair of the city's freeway and speculated on the possibility that, if the Russians ever attacked, they would bypass Cincinnati, as it looked as if it had already been taken and destroyed."

"They still haven't finished the freeway outside the ballpark" in Cincinnati because "it's Kentucky's turn to use the cement mixer."

"You have to think that when Dan'l Boone was fighting the Indians for this territory, he didn't have Cincinnati in mind for it. . . . If Cincinnati were human, they'd bury it."

San Francisco is "not a town, it's a no-host cocktail party. If it were human, it'd be W. C. Fields. It has a nice, even climate. It's always winter."

San Francisco was the only city "that couldn't tell the difference between an earthquake and a fire" and next time would "say it was a flood."

Candlestick was built where it was "when the Ketchikan Peninsula was available."

Oakland "is this kind of town: You have to pay 50 cents to go from Oakland to San Francisco. Coming to Oakland from San Francisco is free."

Oakland was "like a fighter who needed a knockout to win."

"New York should have a big sign on it: 'Out of Order.'"

New York is "the largest chewing gum receptacle in the world."

When visiting New York, he "carefully listed my blood type on my wrist."

In New York nobody should be allowed on the street after 10—"in the morning."

In New Jersey "if you didn't have a tattoo they knew you were a tourist."

"I said Philadelphia was closed on Sunday and should be the rest of the week as well."

"I said Philadelphia was a town that would boo a cancer cure."

"63,000 fans showed up at Veterans Stadium expecting the worst. And getting it."

"Philadelphia was founded in 1776 and has been going downhill ever since."

"Minneapolis and St. Paul don't like each other very much, and from what I could see I don't blame either of them."

Louisville "smelled like an old bar rag" and had "more broken windows than any place this side of Berlin in 1945."

"I called the Kentucky Derby 'a hard luck race in a hard luck town.'"

"When Pittsburgh and Baltimore got in the World Series, I covered it by remote control."

"There were agents in the Russian secret police who had higher visibility than the Baltimore infield."

Baltimore is "a guy just standing on a corner with no place to go and rain dripping off his hat. Baltimore's a great place if you're a crab."

Chicago was "a town where Al Capone didn't have a police record even though he kept the coroner's office on night shifts."

Birmingham was a place where "'evening dress' means a 'bed sheet with eyeholes,'" where "white, male Americans are the enemies of America here. The Constitution being torn in half by the people whose ancestors helped to write it."

St. Louis "had a bond issue recently and the local papers campaigned for it on a slogan 'Progress or Decay,' and decay won in a landslide."

"You can see where these freewheeling travel tips didn't endear me to the local Chambers of Commerce."

On Other Sports

Surfer "Margo Godfrey became as familiar as the Coast Guard."

Volleyball star Karch Kiraly is "like Lawrence of Arabia, his domain is the burning sand."

Ice skater Kristi Yamaguchi is "the closest thing to a living poem as an athlete gets."

Fisherwoman Judy Pachner is successful because "the fish think she's one of them."

"Pool players are like spies—the less conspicuous the better."

Archer Midge Dandridge "makes Lizzie Borden look like a prankster."

"Not since the Christians and the lions has there been an athletic contest quite like rodeo."

Equestrian "Anneli Drummond-Hay is the most famous, fully dressed lady rider in British history."

Eight seconds on a Brahma bull "can seem like a year in an interrogation cell in the Lubyanka."

"Bulls aren't prejudiced," said black bull rider Charles Sampson. "They hate everybody, regardless of race, creed or color."

On Sports in General

"Nothing is ever so bad it can't be made worse by firing the coach."

"You can kill all the buffalo, wipe out the cavalry, rob all the banks, sell the Statehouse, run rum, or join the Mafia—but don't mess around with America's sports idolatry."

On Free Agency, Contracts, the Media, and Money in Sports

"Never envy the big star of the show. That turkey you're eating thought he had a no-cut contract."

"Today, high school kids make more than any Rockefeller then."

"A free agent is anything but."

"You can fool all of the people all of the time—if you own the network."

On Large People

Frank Howard was "so big, he wasn't born, he was founded." He is "not actually a man, just an unreasonable facsimile."

"When the real Boog Powell makes . . . the Hall of Fame, they're going to make an umbrella stand out of his foot."

Merlin Olsen "went swimming in Loch Ness—and the monster got out."

"Once, when an official dropped a flag and penalized the Rams for having 12 men on the field . . . two of them were [Bill] Bain."

On Philosophy

"Things always get worse before they get impossible."

"Anger is always a proper substitute for logic."

"The guy with the coat slung over his shoulder without his arms in the sleeves in movies is up to no good."

On Sex

"I am not big on how-to manuals anyway; my credo is, if they taught sex the way they taught golf, the race would have died out long ago."

On Society

"Heartbreak is playing to a capacity" at the Shriners Hospital.

On Himself

After election to the Sportswriters Hall of Fame, 1978: "But, what did I do—out-adjective the next guy?"

"I like to keep people at arm's length because sooner or later I'll probably have to bite 'em in the ass. Some still have the teeth marks."

"Letter from a Rookie's Wife"

Dearest Darling:

How are you? . . . I am working now at the Bon Ton Grill. . . . All the fellows from the box works ask for you and say, 'Boy, I bet if that old husband of yours could only see you in them net stockings he'd bat a thousand . . .'

The other night was election night and the bar had to be closed; so I had the whole gang over to our house. . . . The party wasn't as noisy as the papers said. . . . I didn't see why the police came. . . .

I sure want you to meet Cesar [a new roomer]. . . . [He] feels terrible he had to take this long business trip just the time you come home. . . . He'll come back. He has to; he has the car.

Faithfully yours, Cuddles.

APPENDIX C
"If You're Expecting One-Liners, Wait, a Column"

Here is Jim Murray's July 1, 1979, column "If You're Expecting One-Liners, Wait, a Column" in its entirety:

OK, bang the drum slowly, professor. Muffle the cymbals and the laugh track. You might say that Old Blue Eye is back. But that's as funny as this is going to get.

I feel I owe my friends an explanation as to where I've been all these weeks. Believe me, I would rather have been in a press box.

I lost an old friend the other day. He was blue-eyed, impish, he cried a lot with me, saw a great many things with me. I don't know why he left me. Boredom, perhaps.

We read a lot of books together, we did a lot of crossword puzzles together, we saw films together. He had a pretty exciting life. He saw Babe Ruth hit a home run when we were both 12 years old. He saw Willie Mays steal second base, he saw Maury Wills steal his 104th base. He saw Rocky Marciano get up. I thought he led a pretty good life.

One night a long time ago he saw this pretty girl who laughed a lot, played the piano and he couldn't look away from her. Later he looked on as I married this pretty lady.

He saw her through 34 years. He loved to see her laugh, he loved to see her happy.

You see, the friend I lost was my eye. My good eye. The other eye, the right one, we've been carrying for years. We just let him tag along like Don Quixote's nag. It's been a long time since he could read the number on a halfback or tell whether a ball was fair or foul or even which fighter was down.

So, one blue eye missing and the other misses a lot.

So my best friend left me, at least temporarily, in a twi-light world where it's always eight o'clock on a summer night.

He stole away like a thief in the night and he took a lot with him. But not everything. He left a lot of memories. He couldn't take those with him. He just took the future with him and the present. He couldn't take the past.

I don't know why he had to go. I thought we were pals. I thought the things we did together we enjoyed doing together. Sure, we cried together. There were things to cry about.

But it was a long, good relationship, a happy one. It went all the way back to the days when we arranged all the marbles in a circle in the dirt in the lots in Connecticut. We played one-old-cat baseball. We saw curveballs together, trying to hit them or catch them. We looked through a catcher's mask together. We were partners in every sense of the word.

He recorded the happy moments, the miracle of children, the beauty of a Pacific sunset, snowcapped mountains, faces on Christmas morning. He allowed me to hit fly balls to young sons in uniforms two sizes too large, to see a pretty daughter march in halftime parades. He allowed me to see most of the major sports events of our time. I suppose I should be grateful that he didn't drift away when I was 12 or 15 or 29 but stuck around over 50 years until we had a vault of memories. Still, I'm only human. I'd like to see again, if possible, Rocky Marciano with his nose bleeding, behind on points and the other guy coming.

I guess I would like to see Reggie Jackson with the count three-and-two and the Series on the line, guessing fastball. I guess I'd like to see Rod Carew with men on first and second and no place to put him, and the pitcher wishing he were standing in the rain someplace, reluctant to let go of the ball.

I'd like to see Stan Musial crouched around a curveball one more time. I'd like to see Don Drysdale trying to not laugh as a young hitter came up there with both feet in the bucket.

I'd like to see Sandy Koufax just once more facing Willie Mays with a no-hitter on the line. I'd like to see Maury Wills with a big lead against a pitcher with a good move. I'd like to see Roberto Clemente with the ball and a guy trying to go from first to third. I'd like to see Pete Rose sliding into home head-first.

I'd like once more to see Henry Aaron standing there with that quiet bat, a study in deadliness. I'd like to see Bob Gibson scowling at a hitter as if he had some nerve just to pick up a bat. I'd like to see Elroy Hirsch going out for a long one from Bob Waterfield, Johnny Unitas in high-cuts picking apart a zone defense. I'd like to see Casey Stengel walking to the mound on his gnarled old legs to take a pitcher out, beckoning his gnarled old finger behind his back.

I'd like to see Sugar Ray Robinson or Muhammad Ali giving a recital, a ballet, not a fight. Also, to be sure, I'd like to see a sky full of stars, moonlight on the water, and yes, the tips of a royal flush peeking out as I fan out a poker hand, and yes, a straight two-foot putt.

Come to think of it, I'm lucky. I saw all of those things. I see them yet.

APPENDIX D
Jim Murray's Career

1965   National Headliner Award.

1966–1967   Honored by the Television Academy Awards for writing contribution for the *Andy Williams Show*, Outstanding Variety Series.

1972   Alumni Medal from Trinity College.

1977   Installed in the National Sportscasters and Sportswriters Hall of Fame.

        National Headliner Award.

1980   National Headliner Award, citation for outstanding sportswriting.

1982   Red Smith Award for extended meritorious labor in sportswriting.

        First sportswriter to win the Victor Award, conferred annually on outstanding athletes based on selections by sportswriters, editors, and broadcasters across the country.

1984   Associated Press Sports Editors Association award for best column writing.

1987   Pepperdine University, Doctor of Laws degree, honoris causa.

        J. G. Taylor Spink Award for "meritorious contributions to baseball writing"; award included induction into the Baseball Hall of Fame, Cooperstown, New York, July 1988.

1990   Pulitzer Prize for Commentary.

1991   Best Sportswriter Award from the *Washington Journalism Review*.

1994   Victor Award XXVIII Hall of Fame Award "in recognition for his remarkable contribution to sports journalism as a literary art form."

1997   Lincoln Werden Memorial Award for excellence in golf journalism from the New York Metropolitan Golf Writers Association.

1998   Times Mirror 1998 Lifetime Achievement Award (for thirty-seven years with the *Los Angeles Times*).

NSSA's Sportswriter of the Year award fourteen times (twelve of those consecutively).

Books

Best of Jim Murray. Garden City, NY: Doubleday, 1965.

The Sporting World of Jim Murray. Garden City, NY: Doubleday, 1968.

The Jim Murray Collection. Dallas: Taylor, 1988.

Jim Murray: An Autobiography. New York: Macmillan, 1993.

Jim Murray: The Last of the Best. Los Angeles: Los Angeles Times, 1998.

Jim Murray: The Great Ones. Los Angeles: Los Angeles Times, 1999.

BIBLIOGRAPHY

2006 USC Football Media Guide. Los Angeles: University of Southern California, 2006.

Acuña, Rodolfo. *A Community under Siege: A Chronicle of Chicanos East of the Los Angeles River, 1945–1975*. Los Angeles: Chicano Studies Research Center, Publications, University of California at Los Angeles, 1984.

———. *Occupied America: a History of Chicanos*. New York: Harper & Row, 1981.

Alabama Media Guide 2006. Tuscaloosa: University of Alabama Press, 2006.

Avila, Eric. *Popular Culture in the Age of White Flight: Fear and Fantasy in Suburban Los Angeles*. Berkeley: University of California Press, 2004.

Barra, Allen. *The Last Coach: A Life of Paul "Bear" Bryant*. New York: Norton, 2005.

Bisheff, Steve, and Loel Schrader. *Fight On! The Colorful Story of USC Football*. Nashville, TN: Cumberland House, 2006.

Bottles, Scott L. *Los Angeles and the Automobile: The Making of the Modern City*. Berkeley: University of California Press, 1987.

Boyles, Bob, and Paul Guido. *Fifty Years of College Football*. Wilmington, DE: Sideline Communications, 2005.

Clary, Jack. *College Football's Great Dynasties: USC*. Ann Arbor, MI: Popular Culture Ink, 1991.

Collier, Gene. "Mitchell's Tale Still Twisting." *Pittsburgh Post-Gazette*, September 2, 2004.

Daily Mirror. "Jim Murray, March 13, 1980." *Los Angeles Times*, March 13, 2010. http://www.latimesblogs.latimes.com/thedailymirror/2010/03/jim-murray-march-13-1980.html.

Dalton, Dennis. *Power over People: Classical and Modern Political Theory*. Recorded course from Barnard College at Columbia University, New York. Available at http://www.thegreatcourses.com/tgc/courses/course_detail.aspx?cid=443.

Daniels, Kevin. *Game Day: Notre Dame Football.* Edited by Rob Doster. Chicago: Triumph Books, 2006.

———. *Game Day: Southern California Football.* Edited by Rob Doster. Chicago: Triumph Books, 2006.

Davis, David. "Road-Tripping with Jim Murray." SoCalSportsObserved, September 13, 2007. http://www.laobserved.com/sports/2007/09/roadtripping_with_jim _murray.php.

Dettlinger, Chet, and Jeff Prugh. *The List.* Atlanta: Philmay Enterprises, 1984.

Diaz, David R. *Barrio Urbanism: Chicanos, Planning, and American Cities.* New York: Routledge, 2005.

Dunnavant, Keith. *Coach: The Life of Paul "Bear" Bryant.* New York: Simon & Schuster, 1996.

———. *The Missing Ring.* New York: St. Martin's, 2006.

Fighting Irish: The Might, the Magic, the Mystique of Notre Dame Football. St. Louis, MO: Sporting News, 2003.

Florence, Mal. *The Trojan Heritage: A Pictorial History of USC Football.* Virginia Beach, VA: JCP Corp, 1980.

Front Page: A Collection of Historical Headlines from the Los Angeles Times *1881– 1987.* New York: Harry N. Abrams, 1987.

Gigliotti, Jim. *Stadium Stories: USC Trojans.* Guilford, CT: Globe Pequot Press, 2005.

Gildea, William, and Christopher Jennison. *The Fighting Irish.* Englewood Cliffs, NJ: Prentice-Hall, 1976.

Gottlieb, Robert, and Irene Wolf. *Thinking Big: The Story of the* Los Angeles Times: *Its Publishers, and Their Influence on Southern California.* New York: G. P. Putnam's Sons, 1977.

Gottlieb, Robert, and others. *The Next Los Angeles: The Struggle for a Livable City.* Berkeley: University of California Press, 2005.

Groom, Winston. *The Crimson Tide: An Illustrated History of Football at the University of Alabama.* Tuscaloosa: University of Alabama Press, 2000.

Halberstam, David, ed. *The Best American Sports Writing of the Century.* Boston: Houghton Mifflin, 1999.

Halberstam, David. *The Powers That Be.* New York: Alfred A. Knopf, 1979.

Heisler, John, ed. *Echoes of Notre Dame Football.* Chicago: Triumph Books, 2006.

Hines, Thomas S. "Housing, Baseball, and Creeping Socialism: The Battle of Chavez Ravine, Los Angeles 1949–1959." *Journal of Urban History* 8, no. 2 (February 1982): 123–43.

Images of Our Times: Sixty Years of Photography from the Los Angeles Times. New York: Harry N. Abrams, 1987.

"Jim Murray." SportsJournalists.com journalism forum. http://sportsjournalists.com /forum/index.php?topic=45896.35;wap2.

"Jim Murray Archive." Brad's Big Race Analysis, 2011. http://www.alydar.com /murray.html.

Kahn, Roger. *The Boys of Summer.* New York: Perennial Library, 1987.

Katz, Fred. *The Glory of Notre Dame.* New York: Bartholomew House, 1971.

Keisser, Bob. "Bam's Impact Not Forgotten." *Long Beach Press-Telegram*, September 12, 2005.

Knee Jerks. "Linda McCoy-Murray of the Jim Murray Memorial Foundation." The Knee Jerks with Eno and Big Al, September 20, 2010. http://www.blogtalkradio .com/thekneejerks/2010/09/20/the-knee-jerks—detroit-sports-talk-with -eno-and-b.

LeBrock, Barry. *The Trojan Ten.* New York: New American Library, 2006.

López, Ronald William. "The Battle for Chavez Ravine: Public Policy and Chicano Community Resistance in Post-War Los Angeles, 1945–1962." Dissertation, University of California, Berkeley, 1999.

Lumpkin, Bill. "USC Back Wasn't the Real Key to Integration." *Birmingham Post-Herald.*

MacCambridge, Michael, ed. *ESPN College Football Encyclopedia.* New York: ESPN Books, 2005.

McCluggage, Matt. "The Construction of Dodger Stadium and the Battle for Chavez Ravine." Dissertation, Chapman University, Orange, CA, 2010.

McCoy-Murray, Linda. *Quotable Jim Murray.* Nashville, TN: TowleHouse Publishing, 2003.

McCready, Neal. "Cunningham Had Impact on 'Bama Football." *Mobile Press-Register*, August 2003.

McDougal, Dennis. *Privileged Son: Otis Chandler and the Rise and Fall of the* L.A. Times *Dynasty.* Cambridge, MA: Perseus Publishing, 2001.

McKay, John. *McKay: A Coach's Story*. With Jim Perry. New York: Atheneum, 1974.

Murray, Jim. *The Best of Jim Murray*. Garden City, NY: Doubleday, 1965.

————. "Hatred Shut Out as Alabama Finally Joins the Union." *Los Angeles Times*, September 13, 1970.

————. "If You're Expecting One-Liners, Wait, a Column." *Los Angeles Times*, July 1, 1979.

————. *Jim Murray: An Autobiography*. New York: Macmillan, 1993.

————. *Jim Murray: The Great Ones*. Los Angeles: Los Angeles Times, 1999.

————. *Jim Murray: The Last of the Best*. Los Angeles: Los Angeles Times, 1998.

————. *The Jim Murray Collection*. Dallas: Taylor, 1988.

————. *The Sporting World of Jim Murray*. Garden City, NY: Doubleday, 1968.

Negrete, White, and Charlotte Rebecca. "Power vs. the People of Chávez Ravine: A Study of Their Determination and Fortitude." Dissertation, Claremont Graduate University, Claremont, CA, 2008.

Nelson, Kevin. *The Golden Game: The Story of California Baseball*. San Francisco: California Historical Society, 2004.

"No Remorse: George Soros Worked As Nazi Collaborator Confiscating The Property of Fellow." Infidel Bloggers Alliance (blog), September 7, 2010. http://www.ibloga.blogspot.com/2010/09/no-remorse-george-soros-worked -as-nazi.html.

Nyiri, Alan. *The Heritage of USC*. Los Angeles: University of Southern California, 1999.

Parseghian, Ara. *What It Means to Be Fighting Irish*. Chicago: Triumph Books, 2004.

Parson, Donald Craig. *Making a Better World: Public Housing, the Red Scare, and the Direction of Modern Los Angeles*. Minneapolis: University of Minnesota, 2005.

Perry, Jim. "Alabama Goes Black 'n' White." *Los Angeles Herald-Examiner*, September 11, 1971.

————. "USC Loses One of Its Legends with the Death of McKay." *Trojan Tail*, 2001.

Pierson, Don. *The Trojans: Southern California Football*. Chicago: Henry Regnery, 1974.

Prince, Carl E. *Brooklyn's Dodgers: The Bums, the Borough, and the Best of Baseball, 1947–1957*. New York: Oxford University Press, 1997.

Prugh, Jeff. "Anger Boiled within Gerald Ford before This Football Game." *Marin Independent Journal*, August 12, 1999.

———. "George Wallace Was America's Merchant of Venom." *Marin Independent Journal*, September 15, 1998.

———. *The Herschel Walker Story*. Fawcett, 1983.

———. "Trojans Fall on Alabama . . ." *Los Angeles Times*, September 13, 1970.

———. "Two Black Students Had Enrolled before Wallace Showdown." *Los Angeles Times*, June 11, 1978.

Rappoport, Ken. *The Trojans: A Story of Southern California Football*. Huntsville, AL: Strode Publishers, 1974.

Reilly, Rick. "King of the Sports Page." *Sports Illustrated*, April 21, 1986. http://www.sportsillustrated.cnn.com/vault/article/magazine/MAG1064748/1/index.htm.

Robinson, John, and Joe Jares. *Conquest: A Cavalcade of USC Football*. Santa Monica, CA: A. Neff, 1981.

Sánchez, George J. *Becoming Mexican American: Ethnicity, Culture, and Identity in Chicano Los Angeles, 1900–1945*. New York: Oxford University Press, 1995.

Shapiro, Michael. *The Last Good Season: Brooklyn, the Dodgers, and Their Final Pennant Race Together*. New York: Doubleday, 2003.

Sitton, Tom. *Los Angeles Transformed: Fletcher Bowron's Urban Reform Revival, 1938–1953*. Albuquerque: University of New Mexico Press, 2005.

Smith, Curt. *Pull Up a Chair: The Vin Scully Story*. Washington, DC: Potomac Books, 2009.

Smith, Shelley. "Columnist Lives on in Words." ESPNLosAngeles.com, August 18, 2010. http://www.sports.espn.go.com/los-angeles/news/story?id=5466960.

Springer, Steve, and Michael Arkush. *60 Years of USC-UCLA Football*. Stamford, CT: Longmeadow Press, 1991.

Starr, Kevin. *Golden Dreams: California in an Age of Abundance, 1950–1963*. Oxford: Oxford University Press, 2009.

Steele, Michael R. *Knute Rockne: A Portrait of a Notre Dame Legend*. Champaign, IL: Sports Publishing, 1998.

Sullivan, Neil J. *The Dodgers Move West*. New York: Oxford University Press, 1987.

Taylor, Phil. "The Tide Gets Rolled." *Sports Illustrated*, September 27, 2004.

Travers, Steven. *Angels Essential: Everything You Need to Know to Be a Real Fan!* Chicago: Triumph Books, 2007.

———. *Barry Bonds: Baseball's Superman.* Champaign, IL: Sports Publishing, 2002.

———. *Dodgers Essential: Everything You Need to Know to Be a Real Fan!* Chicago: Triumph Books, 2007.

———. *Dodgers Past and Present.* Minneapolis: MVP Books, 2009.

———. "The Eternal Trojan." StreetZebra.com, September 2000.

———. "The Four Horsemen of Southern California." In *The USC Trojans: College Football's All-Time Greatest Dynasty.* Lanham, MD: Taylor Trade Publishing, 2006.

———. *The Good, the Bad, and the Ugly Los Angeles Lakers: Heart-Pounding, Jaw-Dropping, and Gut-Wrenching Moments from Los Angeles Lakers History.* Chicago: Triumph Books, 2007.

———. *The Good, the Bad, and the Ugly Oakland Raiders: Heart-Pounding, Jaw-Dropping, and Gut-Wrenching Moments from Oakland Raiders History.* Chicago: Triumph Books, 2008.

———. "It Wasn't a Football Game, It Was a Sighting." *StreetZebra,* November 2000.

———. *The Last Icon: Tom Seaver and His Times.* Lanham, MD: Taylor Trade Publishing, 2011.

———. "Legend: A Conversation with John McKay." StreetZebra.com, March 2000.

———. *The 1969 Miracle Mets: The Improbable Story of the World's Greatest Underdog Team.* Guilford, CT: Lyons Press, 2009.

———. *One Night, Two Teams: Alabama vs. USC and the Game That Changed a Nation.* Lanham, MD: Taylor Trade Publishing, 2007.

———. *Pigskin Warriors: 140 Years of College Football's Greatest Traditions, Games, and Stars.* Lanham, MD: Taylor Trade Publishing, 2009.

———. "Rich McKay." *StreetZebra,* April 2000.

———. *A Tale of Three Cities: The 1962 Baseball Season in New York, Los Angeles, and San Francisco.* Washington, DC: Potomac Books, 2009.

———. *Trojans Essential: Everything You Need to Know to Be a Real Fan!* Chicago: Triumph Books, 2008.

————. *The USC Trojans: College Football's All-Time Greatest Dynasty.* Lanham, MD: Taylor Trade Publishing, 2006.

————. "Villa Park Wins Rivalry Game." *Los Angeles Times,* September 25, 2000.

————. *What It Means to Be a Trojan: Southern Cal's Greatest Players Talk about Trojans Football.* Chicago: Triumph Books, 2009.

————. "When Legends Played." *StreetZebra,* September 1999.

White, Lonnie. *UCLA vs. USC. 75 Years of the Greatest Rivalry in Sports.* Los Angeles: Los Angeles Times, 2004.

Wojciechowski, Gene. "USC Setting Standard for Football Dominance." ESPN.com, December 6, 2005. http://sports.espn.go.com/espn/columns/story?columnist =wojciechowski_gene&i%20d=2249925%3E%20&id=2249925.

The Wonderful World of Sport. New York: Time Life Books, 1967.

Yaeger, Don, and Douglas S. Looney. *Under the Tarnished Dome.* New York: Simon & Schuster, 1993.

Yaeger, Don, Sam Cunningham, and John Papadakis. *Turning of the Tide.* New York: Center Street, 2006.

Zakaria, Fareed. *The Future of Freedom: Illiberal Democracy at Home and Abroad.* New York: Norton, 2003.

Websites

cstv.com

jimmurrayfoundation.com

latimesblogs.latimes.com/thedailymirror/jim-murray

rolltide.com

trojanreport.com

uscfootball.blogspot.com

usctrojans.com

wearesc.com

DVD/Documentaries

Breaking the Huddle. New York: Home Box Office, 2008.

Coach Paul "Bear" Bryant. New York: College Sports Television, 2005.

The History of USC Football. Produced and directed by Roger Springfield. Burbank, CA: Warner Home Video, 2005.

Inventing L.A.: The Chandlers and Their Times. Los Angeles: KCET/Public Broadcasting, 2009.

Songs of Our Success. Hosted by Tony McEwing, 2003.

Tackling Segregation. New York: College Sports Television, 2006.

Trojan Video Gold. Narrated by Tom Kelly. Los Angeles: University of Southern California, 1988.

INDEX

ABOUT THE AUTHOR

Steven Travers, a former professional baseball player with the St. Louis Cardinals and the Oakland A's organizations, is the author of twenty books, including the bestselling *Barry Bonds: Baseball's Superman*, nominated for a Casey Award as Best Baseball Book of 2002; and *One Night, Two Teams: Alabama vs. USC and the Game That Changed a Nation* (a 2007 PNBA nominee, subject of the CBS/CSTV documentary *Tackling Segregation*, and soon to be a major motion picture). He pitched for the Redwood High School baseball team in California that won the national championship in his senior year, before attending college on an athletic scholarship and earning all-conference honors. A graduate of the University of Southern California, Travers coached at USC, at Cal-Berkeley, and in Europe; served in the army; attended law school; was a political consultant and a sports agent. He has written for the *Los Angeles Times* and was a columnist for *StreetZebra* magazine in L.A. and the *San Francisco Examiner*. Travers has been a regular panelist at USC's Annenberg School for Communication and Journalism, home of the Murray Scholars, since 2006. He writes for the political publication/website WorldNetDaily in Washington, D.C.; *Gentry* magazine; and other publications. His screenplays include *The Lost Battalion*, *21*, and *Wicked*. He has a daughter, Elizabeth Travers Lee, and lives in California.

Travers values reader feedback and can be reached by e-mail at USCSTEVE1 @aol.com or by visiting his webpage, www.RedRoom.com/member/Steven -Robert-Travers.